PSYCHOLOGICAL RESEARCH:
HOW TO DO IT

S.95

D1476628

PSYCHOLOGICAL RESEARCH: HOW TO DO IT

THOMAS J. QUIRK, Ph.D.
Associate Professor of Psychology and Education
and
Dean of Faculty
Principia College

John Wiley & Sons, Inc., Publishers
New York • Chichester • Brisbane • Toronto

Editors: Judy Wilson and Irene Brownstone
Production Manager: Ken Burke
Editorial Supervisor: Winn Kalmon

Copyright © 1979, by John Wiley & Sons, Inc.

All rights reserved. Published simultaneously in Canada.

Reproduction or translation of any part of this work
beyond that permitted by Sections 107 or 108 of the 1976
United States Copyright Act without the permission of
the copyright owner is unlawful. Requests for permission
or further information should be addressed to the
Permissions Department, John Wiley & Sons, Inc.

Library of Congress Cataloging in Publication Data

Quirk, Thomas J., 1939–
    Psychological research.

    Bibliography: p.
    Includes index.
    1. Psychological research.   2. Psychometrics.
3. Psychology, Experimental.   I. Title
BF76.5.Q57   150′.7′2   78-16812
ISBN 0-471-03118-6

Printed in the United States of America

1978 1979 10 9 8 7 6 5 4 3 2 1

CREDITS

pages 60–65. Performance Tests for Beginning Teachers: Why All the Fuss? Reprinted from T. J. Quirk, "Performance Tests for Beginning Teachers: Why All the Fuss?," *Educational Technology*, 1973, vol. 13, pp. 14–16. Reprinted by permission of *Educational Technology*.

page 66. Rating Form is extensively adapted from H. N. Mischel, "Sex Bias in the Evaluation of Professional Achievements," *Journal of Educational Psychology*, 1974, vol. 66, pp. 157–166. Copyright 1974 by the American Psychological Association. Reprinted by permission.

page 80. Table is adapted from H. Hornstein, E. Fisch, and M. Holmes, "Influence of a Model's Feeling About His Behavior and His Relevance as a Comparison Other on Observers' Helping Behavior," *Journal of Personality and Social Psychology*, 1968, vol. 10, pp. 222–226. Copyright 1968 by the American Psychological Association. Reprinted by permission.

page 82. Table is adapted from H. Helson, R. Blake, and J. Mouton, "Petition-signing as Adjustment to Situational and Personal Factors," *Journal of Social Psychology*, 1958, vol. 48, pp. 3–10. Copyright 1958 by The Journal Press. Reprinted by permission.

page 95. Rating Scale for Advertising Study is adapted from G. H. Smith and R. Engel, "Influence of a Female Model on Perceived Characteristics of an Automobile," Proceedings of the 76th annual convention. Copyright 1968 by the American Psychological Association. Reprinted by permission.

page 156. Rating Scales for the Occupation of Accountant is adapted from J. C. Touhey, "Effects of Additional Women Professionals on Ratings of Occupational Prestige and Desirability," *Journal of Personality and Social Psychology*, 1974, vol. 29, pp. 86–89. Copyright 1974 by the American Psychological Association. Reprinted by permission.

page 164. "Extrovertive and Introvertive Description." Reprinted by permission of Yale University Press from A. S. Luchins, "Primacy-Recency in Impression Formation," *The Order of Presentation in Persuasion* by Carl I. Hovland. Copyright © 1957 by Yale University Press, Inc., pp. 34–35.

pages 165–166. Second Page of Impression Formation Booklet. Adapted by permission of Yale University Press from A. S. Luchins, "Primacy-Recency in Impression Formation," *The Order of Presentation in Persuasion* by Carl I. Hovland. Copyright © 1957 by Yale University Press, Inc., p. 41.

pages 272–275. Table of Random Digits. Reprinted from P. G. Hoel, *Elementary Statistics*, 4th edition (New York: John Wiley & Sons, Inc., 1976), pp. 343–346. Reprinted by permission.

pages 276–278. "Finding the Square Root of a Number" is extracted from N. R. Ullman, *Statistics: An Applied Approach* (New York: John Wiley & Sons, Inc., 1972), pp. 544–546. Adapted and reprinted by permission.

page 288. Table of Values of *t* for the .05 Level of Significance is adapted from the extract taken from Table III on page 46 of 6th edition 1974 of Fisher and Yates: *Statistical Tables for Biological, Agricultural and Medical Research*, published by Longman Group Ltd., London (previously published by Oliver and Boyd, Edinburgh), and by permission of the authors and publishers.

DEDICATION

This book is dedicated to my two best friends, Martha and Jennifer, who supported me with inexhaustible love and affection throughout the writing of this book. This book is also dedicated to those students who have taken my courses in introductory psychology, educational psychology, social psychology, social research methods, and principles of educational evaluation at Principia College: they have taught me a great deal about the art of teaching.

To the Reader

This book is designed for anyone who wants a better understanding of the process of psychological research. It should be especially valuable to students who are taking courses in introductory psychology, educational psychology, social psychology, educational research, experimental social psychology, social research methods, or any other courses involving the systematic study of the ways in which people think, act, and feel. The methods taught in the book apply to advertising research, education, political science, sociology, consumer psychology, and other fields that depend upon an understanding of the behavior of people singly and in groups.

This is a "how to" book. It will teach you how to perform a number of psychological experiments. All of the experiments discussed in this book can be conducted by undergraduates. This book will also teach you how to summarize the information you collect and how to do some simple statistical tests to help you to interpret the results of these research studies. This book uses small sample sizes intentionally so that you can concentrate on *how* the mathematical computations are done without getting lost in a sea of numbers based on a large sample of subjects. If you are concerned that your mathematical background is "rusty," don't worry. The only math background you need to use this book successfully is skill in simple multiplication and division. This book does not attempt to teach you the sophisticated theory behind the simple mathematical concepts it does contain; we will leave that to the statisticians for some later time. It does teach you to understand the process by which psychologists do research.

Psychological Research: How To Do It attempts to organize some major concepts in the field of psychological research for the student or general reader. It does not attempt to be a text in psychological research nor does it try to provide comprehensive coverage of all the areas of specialization within the field. You should view this book as a guide which will give you a general introduction to the field and which will enable you to better understand your textbook and lecture material if you are enrolled in a formal psychology course.

Self-Tests are included in the book to give you the opportunity to test your understanding as you are reading. If you can successfully complete these Self-Tests and the problems contained in the chapters, you can be confident that you have mastered the material in this book.

Thomas J. Quirk

April, 1978
Elsah, Illinois

To the Instructor

In recent years, more and more colleges and universities are offering various psychology courses at the undergraduate level. This book is designed to serve as a general introduction to psychological research for all students in all the social sciences. This book presents the basic research ideas which are needed in psychology, sociology, political science, education, and business. In all of these disciplines, students are frequently asked to demonstrate a knowledge of the language and methods of social science research. For this reason the exercises and examples have been selected to cover a broad range of fields so that student interest can be aroused. No math background other than simple arithmetic is a prerequisite.

Past experience with numerous psychological research texts has demonstrated that either they are too simple in their explanation and examples so that the reader is never taught how to use any statistical tests, or they are intended for graduate students who have a strong background in statistics. This book, which has evolved from classroom notes based upon several years of teaching at Principia College, is intended to strike a happy medium between these two extremes.

Since a knowledge of the process of research is so essential to an understanding of how the social sciences go about testing hypotheses about human behavior, this book has been designed to meet the needs of students who are not prepared for elaborate symbolism or complex arithmetic. The language of this book is intended to be simple and understandable so that this book will be comprehensible to students of varying backgrounds, especially those with little or no mathematical background or preparation. Words, phrases, or methods of expression which students have found difficult to comprehend have been avoided, and new terminology has been held to a minimum. This book is intended as a general introduction to the process of psychological research, so readers will be better prepared to understand technical terms in more advanced texts and courses.

Since exercises provide an extremely important and integral part of any text, they have been included in abundance. All the examples and exercises relate to situations which the student can readily identify with and which are intended to spark student interest. They have been chosen from actual research situations so that the student can see where and how the simple mathematical concepts are applied.

In writing this book, I drew upon the lessons learned in three major experiences: (1) as a graduate student at Stanford University, both as a teaching assistant and as a research assistant in educational psychology, (2) from more than six years of psychological and educational research as a research scientist at the American Institutes for Research in Palo Alto, California, and as a research psychologist at Educational Testing Service in Princeton, New Jersey, and (3) as an associate professor of psychology and education at Principia College.

I have used earlier versions of this book in my own psychology classes and have required the students to demonstrate their ability to apply these concepts by designing and carrying out their own research studies. Students have been randomly assigned to research teams, and each team was permitted one class period to present the results of their study. The class rated the quality of the presentation (as did the instructor), the team rated its performance as a team, and each team member rated each other member of his or her team on their contribution to the research project; the results of these ratings were then summarized on a three-page computer printout which was given to each member of the team. This procedure has been described in a paper presented at the annual meeting of the American Psychological Association (Quirk, 1976), and copies of this paper are available from the author upon request. A brief summary of this paper is given in Appendix C of this book.

Finally, feedback—from both students and instructors—is encouraged. It is our intention to prepare the best teaching materials we can. Any comments about your use of this book and suggestions for its improvement will be welcomed. Send your comments to:

Editor, Self-Teaching Guides
John Wiley & Sons, Inc.
605 Third Avenue
New York, New York 10016

How to Use This Book

This Self-Teaching Guide is organized somewhat differently from most books. This Guide is divided into four parts, each dealing with a specific area of interest in psychological research. Each part starts with a list of objectives outlining what you can expect to learn as you proceed through that part of the book. Each of the eight chapters is divided into numbered sections called frames, most of which require you either to answer a question or to solve a problem of some kind. The answers to the questions and the problems are given immediately following each frame. As you read this book, use an index card or note pad to cover the answer to the questions and the problems. You should slide the card or pad down the page until you come to a dashed line. Write your answer to the question or problem on a separate sheet of paper; then move the card or pad down the page to check your answer against the correct one. You should be able to answer the questions and problems correctly most of the time. If you find that you have made an error, look back through the preceding material to make sure that you understand the correct answer before you continue reading.

All of the computations required in this book can be worked out by hand with reasonable effort, but if you own, or can borrow, a pocket calculator, use of it will save you a great deal of time. While a pocket calculator is not essential, it is strongly recommended, because you'll be able to work out the problems presented in this book far more easily.

For simplicity, the numbers presented throughout this book have been rounded off to two decimal places. This rounding-off procedure has followed the rule that if the third decimal place was 5 or more, the second decimal place was increased by one. For example, 2.535 was rounded off to 2.54. Sometimes your answer may not agree exactly with the one given in this book. Whenever your answer to a problem is only slightly different from the answer proposed in the book, these small differences are very likely to be due to differences in when and how you rounded off decimals. If your answer is reasonably close to the one presented in this book, you should not be concerned about these small differences.

At the end of each chapter is a Self-Test on the major points covered in the chapter, and at the end of the book is a final exam which will help you to evaluate how much you have gained from the entire book. Answers and review references are provided for all test questions, so you can evaluate your learning and review the appropriate frames on any specific topic.

We have occasionally created some hypothetical data to give you practice in working with data once you have collected it. As you read through this book, you will learn how to analyze this data and how to interpret it; the principles that you learn will apply to any simple research studies which you do yourself. At other times we will refer to published journal articles so that you can test your understanding of psychological research against the results of these articles. Whenever we refer to a published article, it is referenced by the last name of the author(s) and the date of publication; for example, when we refer to an article which was written by Thomas Quirk, Barbara Witten, and Susan Weinberg and which was published in 1973, we cite this article as: Quirk, Witten, and Weinberg (1973). The complete reference for any article cited in the book is given in the References section near the end of the book, so that you can locate any article that interests you.

This book is written in an informal, conversational style, as if the author were your private tutor, to teach you about the process of psychological research. May you enjoy it!

Acknowledgments

The working relationship between John Wiley & Sons, Inc., and me has been a very harmonious one. The staff of the Wiley Self-Teaching Guide series formed an unusual team during the writing of this book: Joyce Campbell read an article of mine in a professional journal, and a working relationship between Wiley and me resulted; Judy Vantrease Wilson responded enthusiastically to my initial presentation of the scope of this book, and her encouragement provided the stimulus for the final shaping of the manuscript; Irene Franck Brownstone cheerfully accepted the responsibility of assisting me with the editing of this book, and her straightforwardness, sensitivity, and care for the process of rewriting the manuscript were a positive force in the development of the final product; her influence appears in important ways throughout the book, and I owe her a great debt of gratitude.

Dr. David Gibbs of Principia College read an earlier version of the manuscript, and his insightful comments were very helpful in the development of the descriptions of some of the mathematical concepts expressed in this book. The final responsibility for the book, of course, rests with me.

A special appreciation is extended to Principia College for its support of the ideas presented in Chapter Eight and Appendix C through the necessary computer programming, and to the Gertsch Fund of Principia College for sponsoring the paper I presented at the annual meeting of the American Psychological Association (Quirk, 1976).

I am grateful to the Literary Executor of the late Sir Ronald A. Fisher, F.R.S.; to Dr. Frank Yates, F.R.S., and to Longman Group Ltd., London, for permission to adapt the extract taken from Table III from their book *Statistical Tables for Biological, Agricultural and Medical Research.* (6th edition, 1974.)

Several people assisted with the typing of the drafts of this book. In particular, I would like to thank Kitsy Griest, Nancy Garner, China Miner, and Martha Quirk for their help.

Contents

PART ONE

The Use of the Chi-Square Test in Psychological Research

Part I of this book focuses on how a particular statistical test—the chi-square test—can be used to analyze the data collected in various psychological experiments. The process of psychological research is often fascinating and intriguing. To give you a sense of the excitement and anticipation involved in research, this book will take you step-by-step through a series of experiments—from data collection to analysis of the data, to interpretation of the results in terms of the experimental design and hypotheses of the study, to the writing up of the results of the study.

Chapter One focuses on how we develop an impression of another person. It serves as a general introduction to some types of experiments for which the data can be analyzed using the chi-square test. Chapter Two goes more deeply into the analysis of a single experiment; it deals with our perception of the quality of an article published in the professional literature. Chapter Three again focuses on a single experiment—an advertising study designed to assess the impact of the presence of an attractive adult model on the perceived qualities of an automobile. It stresses the mechanics of an experiment—how an experiment is actually conducted—by presenting you with an experiment that you can do on your own.

By the time you complete Part I, you should have a good sense of what it feels like to participate in a psychological experiment. In addition, you should be well on your way to developing the skill of setting up and conducting simple research studies based on the models of research studies presented in this book. By the end of this book you should be able to read simple psychological research studies from published literature, to perform statistical tests on the data presented in them, to write up the results of your data analyses, and to compare your results with the author's conclusions.

Objectives

After completing Part I, you will be able to:

- apply correctly a chi-square test to determine if there is a significant difference between the responses of two groups of people.
- interpret correctly the results of an experiment by using a chi-square table.
- test for sex differences in an experimental study by using the chi-square test.
- summarize accurately, in writing, the results of a psychological experiment.
- apply the chi-square test to actual data given in published psychological research studies to determine if your use of that statistical test produced the same conclusions and interpretations as those of the study's author.

Each chapter will include a Self-Test so that you can check your progress in terms of these objectives.

CHAPTER ONE

Impression Formation

1.   Let's suppose that you are a college undergraduate sitting in a college classroom in the middle of a group of students who are taking a psychology course. It is the second day of the term. Your professor has just walked into class and made the following announcement: "We will do something different today. We will have a guest lecturer. His name is Mr. James Irving, and he is a graduate student at the University of California at Berkeley. I have written a description of him and of his background which I would like you to read. After you have read this description, you should answer the nine questions about Mr. Irving attached to the description. For each question, please circle the letter that corresponds to your opinion of Mr. Irving. We are asking you to do this so that we can get a better idea of the type of guest lecturers which you would like to have in the class during this term. We want you to fill out the questionnaire before Mr. Irving arrives so that your opinion will not be influenced by his particular personality. We are not interested in your impression of his personality, but only in obtaining some information from you about the kind of guest lecturers that you would like to have in this course during the rest of this term."

   Your professor then hands out his description of the guest lecturer and the questionnaire. Still pretending you are a student in that class, read the description and answer the nine questions, giving your opinion of Mr. Irving.

GUEST LECTURER

Mr. James Irving
University of California at Berkeley

We will have a guest lecturer today. Mr. Irving is a graduate student in the Department of Psychology at the University of California at Berkeley. He has had three quarters of teaching experience in psychology at a college in California. He is 26 years old, a veteran, and married. People who know him consider him to be a very warm person, industrious, critical, practical, and determined.

Before we begin, I would like to have your impression of Mr. Irving. This is not a test of you and can in no way affect your grade in this course. You will not be asked to put your name on this paper, so your responses will be strictly confidential. Your response will be most valuable if you are completely honest in your evaluation of Mr. Irving. What you put down will not be shown to him or in any way discussed with him. This evaluation is a private matter within this classroom. It is not a test of Mr. Irving, but merely a study of how different classes react to different instructors.

Please *reread the description of Mr. Irving that is given in the first paragraph above, and then answer the questions on the rating scale.*

RATING SCALE

Please circle one answer to each of the following questions:

1. How would you rate Mr. Irving's knowledge of psychology?

    A. knows his stuff
    B. doesn't know his stuff
    C. no opinion

2. How would you rate his consideration of others?

    A. considerate of others
    B. self-centered
    C. no opinion

3. Would you expect him to be formal or informal?

    A. formal
    B. informal
    C. no opinion

4. How sociable would you expect Mr. Irving to be?

    A. sociable
    B. unsociable
    C. no opinion

5. Would you expect Mr. Irving to be good-natured or irritable?

    A. good-natured
    B. irritable
    C. no opinion

6. What kind of a sense of humor would you expect Mr. Irving to have?

    A. good sense of humor
    B. not much of a sense of humor
    C. no opinion

7. How popular would you expect Mr. Irving to be with other people?

   A. popular
   B. unpopular
   C. no opinion

8. How well would you expect Mr. Irving to perform as a teacher?

   A. well
   B. not so well
   C. no opinion

9. How much would you enjoy taking a course from Mr. Irving?

   A. would like it very much
   B. would not enjoy it very much
   C. no opinion

As soon as everyone in your class has finished answering these nine questions, your professor asks how many students in the class have ever participated in a psychological experiment. You look around the class. Only a handful of students are raising their hands. Your professor then says: "Well, I have some news for you. You all should have raised your hands. You were just in one!"

This remark sets off a reaction in the class—many students are talking with one another trying to find out what the professor means. To clear up this mystery, your professor turns to one of the students in the class and asks him or her to read aloud the description of Mr. Irving. The student then reads the following description:

GUEST LECTURER

Mr. James Irving
University of California at Berkeley

We will have a guest lecturer today. Mr. Irving is a graduate student in the Department of Psychology at the University of California at Berkeley. He has had three quarters of teaching experience in psychology at a college in California. He is 26 years old, a veteran, and married. People who know him consider him to be a rather cold person, industrious, critical, practical, and determined.

While the student is reading the last sentence of his description of Mr. Irving, the class erupts with excitement, and several students shout: "Hey, wait a minute. That's not what my description says!"

Have you spotted the difference yet? If you haven't, go back and compare this description with the description of Mr. Irving which you read earlier. Find the difference between these two descriptions before you read any farther in this book.

— — — — — — — — — — — — — — — —

The two descriptions of Mr. Irving are identical except for two words; half of the class read a description which described Mr. Irving as "very warm," while the other half of the class read a description which described Mr. Irving as "rather cold." These two words were the only way in which the two descriptions differed. All of the students read identical instructions. The two different descriptions of Mr. Irving were sorted so that when the professor handed them out, half of the students in the class read a "very warm" description, while the rest of the students read a "rather cold" description.

2.　Asch (1946)* found that a single trait attributed to a person can have a powerful effect on the way in which information about other traits of that person is organized and interpreted. Asch found that when a string of adjectives describing a person included the word "cold," the person tended to be rated ungenerous, unhappy, unstable, humorless, and ruthless. When the word "warm" was substituted, the person was more often rated as generous, happy, good-natured, imaginative, humorous, and humane. Thus "warm" and "cold" seemed to function as central traits which changed the meanings of other adjectives.

Your hypothetical class has just simulated a study that Kelley (1950) did with students at the Massachusetts Institute of Technology. Kelley actually did have someone lead a 20-minute discussion with the class before they filled out a rating form about that guest lecturer. We've simplified Kelley's study by having you rate an imaginary guest lecturer who isn't going to give a guest lecture at all so that we can find out whether you *expected* to see a different type of person based on whether he was described as very warm or rather cold.

In the following table, we have summarized the responses of hypothetical "very warm" and "rather cold" groups to the questionnaires. Examine the table carefully and then answer the questions that follow.

---

*Throughout this book we will use a standard format in making reference to published journal articles. The reference "Asch (1946)" tells you that you can locate the complete journal citation for this article by turning to the References, an alphabetical listing (by the last name of the first author) in a section at the end of this book; this particular reference refers to an article authored by Asch and published in 1946.

If you turn to the References, you will find the following complete citation:

Asch, S. E. Forming Impressions of Personality. *Journal of Abnormal and Social Psychology*, 1946, *41*, 258-290.

The meaning of this format is as follows:

Author:	S. E. Asch
Title of Article:	Forming Impressions of Personality
Name of Journal:	*Journal of Abnormal and Social Psychology*
Date of Publication:	1946
Volume Number:	41
Pages:	258-290

Table 1.1   Results of the Warm-Cold Experiment

Question	Responses of "Very Warm" Group			Responses of "Rather Cold" Group		
	A	B	C	A	B	C
1	18	3	3	8	15	0
2	16	3	5	6	17	0
3	12	11	1	11	12	0
4	15	8	1	5	17	1
5	19	4	1	4	18	1
6	10	11	3	13	10	0
7	18	5	1	5	17	1
8	16	8	0	7	16	0
9	12	12	0	10	13	0

How many students were in the "very warm" group?

— — — — — — — — — — — — — — — — —

24.

3.   How many students were in the "rather cold" group?

— — — — — — — — — — — — — — — — —

23.   The total number of the responses *for each question* should be 24 for the "very warm" group and 23 for the "rather cold" group. (As we analyze these data, keep in mind your own answers to these questions and remember how the data were derived.)

4.   Now what do we do? We want to determine on *which* of the nine questions significantly more subjects in one group expected Mr. Irving to be a *different* sort of person than did the subjects in the other group. You might expect that if the descriptions were identical, approximately the same number of people would feel one way about Mr. Irving as the other in each of the nine questions. How about question 1? Is that difference between the responses of the two experimental groups a significant difference?

We want to analyze the results to that one question to see how our experiment came out. To do that, let's split the data into four categories and summarize them into the following table:

Question 1

	Knows his stuff	Doesn't know his stuff *or* no opinion
Very warm		
Rather cold		

How many people in the "very warm" group expected Mr. Irving to know his stuff? According to Table 1.1, 18 people circled that choice. Let's write that in the table as follows:

Question 1

	Knows his stuff	Doesn't know his stuff *or* no opinion
Very warm	18	
Rather cold		

Now how many people in the "very warm" group either expected Mr. Irving not to know his stuff or had no opinion about his knowledge of psychology? According to Table 1.1, a total of 6 people selected either choice B or choice C (3 + 3) for question 1. Add that fact in the appropriate place in the table above; then check the answer below the line of dashes.

————————————————————

Question 1

	Knows his stuff	Doesn't know his stuff *or* no opinion
Very warm	18	6
Rather cold		

5.   Each of the squares in this table is called a *cell*. Now, can you correctly fill in the two cells of this table for the "rather cold" group? Look at the data summarized in Table 1.1 for question 1, and fill in the two remaining cells for the "rather cold" group.

————————————————————

Your table should now look like this:

Question 1

	Knows his stuff	Doesn't know his stuff *or* no opinion
Very warm	18	6
Rather cold	8	15

6. Now we need to learn how to do a simple statistical test so that we can answer the following question with confidence: "Did significantly more subjects in one group expect Mr. Irving to have a greater knowledge of psychology than did those in the other group?" We will go through the process step by step.

First, let's suppose that we can label the four cells of our table as follows:

A	*B*
C	*D*

where

A = the number of people in the "very warm" group who expected Mr. Irving to know his stuff

B = the number of people in the "very warm" group who either expected Mr. Irving not to know his stuff or had no opinion about his knowledge of psychology

C = the number of people in the "rather cold" group who expected Mr. Irving to know his stuff

D = the number of people in the "rather cold" group who either expected Mr. Irving not to know his stuff or had no opinion about his knowledge of psychology

Use the data on question 1 as you complete the following arithmetic steps in our statistical analysis. (It is important that you work through these steps on your own. Do not look at the answers below until you have completed these steps.)

N (the total number of people in *both* experimental groups) = _____

$A + B =$ _____

$C + D =$ _____

$A + C =$ _____

$B + D =$ _____

$A \times D =$ _____

$B \times C =$ _____

$(A \times D)$ minus $(B \times C) =$ _____

Square your last answer = _____ (Remember, to square a number means to multiply it by itself; so $X^2 = X$ squared $= X \times X$.)

_ _ _ _ _ _ _ _ _ _ _ _ _ _ _ _

$N = 24 + 23 = 47$
$A + B = 18 + 6 = 24$
$C + D = 8 + 15 = 23$
$A + C = 18 + 8 = 26$
$B + D = 6 + 15 = 21$
$A \times D = 18 \times 15 = 270$
$B \times C = 6 \times 8 = 48$

$(A \times D)$ minus $(B \times C) = AD - BC = 270 - 48 = 222$

$(AD - BC)^2 = 222 \times 222 = 49{,}284$

7.   Now we must take these answers and put them into a formula for a special statistical test called a *chi-square test* (pronounced kī-square).* The formula looks like this:

$$\text{chi-square} = \frac{N\,(AD - BC)^2}{(A + B)\,(C + D)\,(A + C)\,(B + D)}$$

Substitute the answers you just calculated into this formula. (If you have a calculator, use it! Don't be put off by the arithmetic.)

_ _ _ _ _ _ _ _ _ _ _ _ _ _ _

$$\text{chi-square} = \frac{47\,(270 - 48)^2}{(24)\,(23)\,(26)\,(21)}$$

$$= \frac{47\,(222)\,(222)}{(24)\,(23)\,(26)\,(21)}$$

$$= \frac{2{,}316{,}348}{301{,}392}$$

$$\text{chi-square} = 7.69$$

---

*Chi-square is also expressed with the Greek letter chi, as χ^2. You may see this occasionally in published research studies and journal articles.

8.   That's a lot of work, but it is well worth the effort, as you will soon see. Now that we know that the value of chi-square for question 1 is equal to 7.69, we must interpret this value. For now, let's follow this rule:

Rule: If the value for chi-square is larger than 3.84, then there is a significant difference between the two experimental groups. (We will discuss in frame 13* why the number 3.84 was chosen.)

The value we obtained for chi-square was 7.69, which is larger than 3.84. Therefore, applying this rule, we can say there *is* a significant difference between the two experimental groups for question 1.

To understand what this determination means, let's stop for a moment to consider an analogy. Suppose that you put two different plants, both the same height, on a windowsill, and after two months you wanted to answer two questions:
(1)   Was one plant taller than the other?
(2)   If so, which one was taller?
The purpose of the chi-square test is to help us answer these two questions:
(1)   *Were* the two experimental groups significantly different from one another?
(2)   If so, *in what way* were the two experimental groups significantly different from one another?
Strictly speaking, the chi-square test answers only the first of these questions. Since our chi-square value of 7.69 for question 1 is larger than 3.84, the answer to the first question above is: "Yes. The two experimental groups did answer question 1 in a significantly different way."

But the value of chi-square by itself does not tell us the answer to the question: "*In what way* were the two experimental groups significantly different from one another?" To answer this question we must study the table summarizing question 1 repeated below:

Question 1

	Knows his stuff	Doesn't know his stuff *or* no opinion
Very warm	18	6
Rather cold	8	15

To interpret this table correctly, let's look at the "very warm" group first: 18 of the 24 people in this group expected Mr. Irving to know his stuff. Now, let's look at the "rather cold" group: only 8 of the 23 people in this

---

*Unless a chapter is specified, references are to frames within the chapter.

group expected Mr. Irving to know his stuff. This means that more people in the "very warm" group expected Mr. Irving to know his stuff than did those people in the "rather cold" group. We can, therefore, summarize our results for question 1 in the following way:

Question: Did the "very warm" group answer question 1 significantly differently than the "rather cold" group?

Answer: Yes, since our chi-square value was 7.69.

Question: In what way were the two experimental groups significantly different from one another?

Answer: Significantly more subjects in the "very warm" group expected Mr. Irving to have a greater knowledge of psychology than did those subjects in the "rather cold" group.

In simple terms, three logical possibilities exist whenever you are trying to determine whether there is a significant difference between two groups of subjects on some dimension. Suppose, for example, that you wanted to compare the heights of two groups of subjects. The three possibilities are:

(1)   Group 1 is significantly taller than Group 2.
(2)   Group 2 is significantly taller than Group 1.
(3)   No significant difference in height exists between the two groups.

Whenever the obtained value for chi-square based on a fourfold table is *less* than 3.84, only the third possibility is accepted as correct. Whenever the obtained value for chi-square is *greater* than 3.84, the third possibility is eliminated, and you must interpret the fourfold table correctly in order to determine whether the first or the second possibility should be accepted.

Note also that, logically, the following two statements are identical:

(1)   Group 1 is significantly taller than Group 2.
(2)   Group 2 is significantly shorter than Group 1.

You should now be getting a feel for how we use the statistical tool of the chi-square test to determine whether there is a significant difference in the behavior of two experimental groups of subjects (the term we use to refer to people in a psychological experiment).* Try analyzing the data for question 2 of Table 1.1. Refer to frames 6-8 for the formula and the steps.

— — — — — — — — — — — — — — — —

_____

*In your reading of published journal articles in psychology, you may come across the symbol *Ss*. This symbol stands for the *subjects* in a psychological experiment. It is not used frequently today, but in published articles you may find sentences such as: "There were 35 *Ss* in the experimental group and 32 *Ss* in the control group." The symbol *Ss*, accompanied by a number, simply tells you how many people were in each group.

Question 2

	Considerate of others	Self-centered *or* no opinion
Very warm	16	8
Rather cold	6	17

$$\text{chi-square} = \frac{47 \ (272 - 48)^2}{24 \ (23) \ (22) \ (25)}$$

$$= \frac{47 \ (224) \ (224)}{24 \ (23) \ (22) \ (25)}$$

$$= \frac{2{,}358{,}272}{303{,}600}$$

$$\text{chi-square} = 7.77$$

Conclusion: Since 7.77 is larger than 3.84, question 2 produced a significant difference. In fact, we can interpret the above table in the following way: significantly more subjects in the "very warm" group expected Mr. Irving to be considerate of others than did subjects in the "rather cold" group.

9.   Now let's complete our analysis of the questionnaire. Take out several sheets of paper, use a pocket calculator if you can, and analyze the data given in Table 1.1 for the remaining seven questions using the chi-square test. Refer to the formula whenever you need to.* Then check your answers below.

— — — — — — — — — — — — — — —

Question 3

	Formal	Informal *or* no opinion
Very warm	12	12
Rather cold	11	12

---

*When you are solving problems which require you to use the chi-square test, you will find it helpful to use the tear-our sheet of formulas in Appendix E.

$$\text{chi-square} = \frac{47 (144 - 132)^2}{24 (23) (23) (24)}$$

$$= \frac{47 (12) (12)}{24 (23) (23) (24)}$$

$$= \frac{6{,}768}{304{,}704}$$

chi-square = 0.02

Conclusion: Since the value for chi-square is not larger than 3.84, no significant difference exists between the two experimental groups for this question.

Question 4

	Sociable	Unsociable *or* no opinion
Very warm	15	9
Rather cold	5	18

$$\text{chi-square} = \frac{47 (270 - 45)^2}{(24) (23.) (20) (27)}$$

$$= \frac{47 (225) (225)}{(24) (23) (20) (27)}.$$

$$= \frac{2{,}379{,}375}{298{,}080}$$

chi-square = 7.98

Conclusion: Since 7.98 is larger than 3.84, question 4 produced a significant difference. In fact, we can interpret the above table in the following way: significantly more subjects in the "very warm" group expected Mr. . Irving to be sociable than did those subjects in the "rather cold" group.

Question 5

	Good-natured	Irritable *or* no opinion
Very warm	19	5
Rather cold	4	19

$$\text{chi-square} = \frac{47\,(361-20)^2}{24\,(23)\,(23)\,(24)}$$

$$= \frac{47\,(341)\,(341)}{24\,(23)\,(23)\,(24)}$$

$$= \frac{5{,}465{,}207}{304{,}704}$$

$$\text{chi-square} = 17.94$$

Conclusion: Significantly more subjects in the "very warm" group expected Mr. Irving to be good-natured than did the subjects in the "rather cold" group.

Question 6

	Good sense of humor	Not much of a sense of humor *or* no opinion
Very warm	10	14
Rather cold	13	10

$$\text{chi-square} = \frac{47\,(100-182)^2}{24\,(23)\,(23)\,(24)}$$

$$= \frac{47\,(-82)\,(-82)\ ^*}{24\,(23)\,(23)\,(24)}$$

$$= \frac{316{,}028}{304{,}704}$$

$$\text{chi-square} = 1.04$$

Conclusion: Since the value for chi-square is not larger than 3.84, the two experimental groups did not differ significantly for this question.

---

*Note that whenever you multiply two negative numbers, as in the case of (−82)(−82), the result is always a positive number. You should *never* end up with a negative value as your final answer for chi-square.

Question 7

	Popular	Unpopular *or* no opinion
Very warm	18	6
Rather cold	5	18

$$\text{chi-square} = \frac{47\,(324 - 30)^2}{24\,(23)\,(23)\,(24)}$$

$$= \frac{47\,(294)\,(294)}{24\,(23)\,(23)\,(24)}$$

$$= \frac{4{,}062{,}492}{304{,}704}$$

chi-square = 13.33

Conclusion: Significantly more subjects in the "very warm" group expected Mr. Irving to be popular than did subjects in the "rather cold" group.

Question 8

	Well	Not so well *or* no opinion
Very warm	16	8
Rather cold	7	16

$$\text{chi-square} = \frac{47\,(256 - 56)^2}{24\,(23)\,(23)\,(24)}$$

$$= \frac{47\,(200)\,(200)}{24\,(23)\,(23)\,(24)}$$

$$= \frac{1{,}880{,}000}{304{,}704}$$

chi-square = 6.17

Conclusion: Significantly more subjects in the "very warm" group expected Mr. Irving to perform better as a teacher than did subjects in the "rather cold" group.

Question 9

	Would like it very much	Would not enjoy it very much *or* no opinion
Very warm	12	12
Rather cold	10	13

$$\text{chi-square} = \frac{47\,(156-120)^2}{24\,(23)\,(22)\,(25)}$$

$$= \frac{47\,(36)\,(36)}{24\,(23)\,(22)\,(25)}$$

$$= \frac{60{,}912}{303{,}600}$$

$$\text{chi-square} = 0.20$$

Conclusion: Since the value for chi-square is not larger than 3.84, the two experimental groups did not differ significantly for this question.

If your answers and conclusions for these problems
differ from those given,
be sure you understand the correct answers
before you go on.

10. Let's write up the results of this research study. Take some time to write out a summary of the results of this experiment. Then check your written summary against ours to see how close you came to it.

— — — — — — — — — — — — — — — —

Significantly more subjects who read a description of Mr. Irving as "very warm" expected him to have a greater knowledge of psychology and to be considerate of others, sociable, good-natured, popular, and a better teacher than did subjects who read a description of him in which he was described as "rather cold." The two experimental groups did not differ significantly in their expectation of Mr. Irving's formality, in their opinion of his sense of humor, or in how much they would enjoy taking a course from him.

11. If you have followed the explanations so far, you already have learned a great deal about the process of psychological research—and this is only the first chapter of this book! Let's summarize what happened in our research study. We simulated a study done by Harold Kelley with students at the Massachusetts Institute of Technology. In that study, Kelley handed out two different descriptions of a guest lecturer to a class of psychology students. The two descriptions were identical except for two words: half the students read a description in which the guest lecturer was described as "very warm," while the other half read a description in which he was described as "rather cold." Kelley was interested in determining what other qualities people would use to describe a person when that person had been described in terms of a key personality trait—such as "warm" or "cold." The process by which we assume that, because a person has one certain *characteristic* in his or her personality, he or she must therefore also have a certain set of other characteristics is called *implicit personality theory.*

In Kelley's study, the guest lecturer actually led the class in a 20-minute discussion before the students rated him on a variety of personality traits. Even though the students in Kelley's study heard and saw the identical discussion, significantly more subjects in the "warm" group saw the lecturer as considerate of others, sociable, popular, informal, good-natured, humorous, and humane than did those in the "cold" group.

We can dig into the Kelley study a little deeper and expand your understanding of the chi-square test by using some of his original data. During the 20-minute discussion which was led by the guest lecturer, Kelley kept a record of which students participated in the discussion. He wanted to find out if those subjects who expected to meet a very warm lecturer would interact with this person more often during the discussion than those who expected to meet a rather cold lecturer. Kelley recorded the identity of those students who initiated a verbal interaction with the instructor, and his data produced the following results: 15 of the 27 subjects in the "very warm" group initiated a verbal interaction with the instructor, while 9 of the 28 subjects in the "rather cold" group initiated a verbal interaction with the instructor. Kelley summarized that finding in his study as follows (1950, p. 437):

"Fifty-six percent of the 'warm' subjects entered the discussion, whereas only 32 percent of the 'cold' subjects did so. Thus the expectation of warmth not only produced more favorable early perceptions of the stimulus person but led to greater initiation of interaction with him."

Are you ready to test out your statistical skills? Before you start, let me add a word of caution with regard to the use of the chi-square test. The formula which you have been using to compute a value for chi-square requires that you use *numbers*, or *counts*, to represent the people in the two experimental groups. This means that you need to be alert to the following rule:

Rule: Always use *numbers* (never percentages) to represent the number of subjects in each of the four cells of the chi-square table.

Now try out your understanding of the chi-square test by answering the following question: Was there a significant difference between the two experimental groups in Kelley's original study in terms of whether or not the subjects initiated a verbal interaction with the instructor?

––––––––––––––––––––

	Initiated interaction	Did not initiate interaction
Very warm	15	12
Rather cold	9	19

$$\text{chi-square} = \frac{55 \ (285 - 108)^2}{27 \ (28) \ (24) \ (31)}$$

$$= \frac{55 \ (177) \ (177)}{27 \ (28) \ (24) \ (31)}$$

$$= \frac{1,723,095}{562,464}$$

chi-square = 3.06

Conclusion: Since the chi-square value of 3.06 is less than 3.84, there was *no significant difference* in the number of subjects who initiated a verbal interaction with the instructor in the two experimental groups. This example makes clear the caution that you should use in *reading* a research study, so that you do not assume a significant difference where none exists. Kelley did not say that this difference was a significant difference. But if you did not read his statement carefully, you might jump to the conclusion that 15 of 27 subjects in one group compared to 9 of 28 subjects in the other group was a significant difference. In fact, it was not a significant difference at all, as this chi-square example clearly indicates when we use the cutoff value of 3.84 for chi-square.

An important point to remember when you write up the results of your own research studies is that you need to be careful not to mislead the reader into believing that you obtained a significant difference when, in fact, you did not do so.

12. Some questions may have occurred to you as you read the first chapter. We'll try to answer some of those questions here.

Question: We grouped our answers to question 4 into two categories: (1) sociable, and (2) unsociable or no opinion. Did we have to group our answers in that way?

Answer: No. If we wanted to summarize our data without collapsing responses into categories, our summary of the data in Table 1.1 would have looked like the following for question 4.

	Sociable	Unsociable	No opinion
Very warm	15	8	1
Rather cold	5	17	1

This type of summary would have produced six cells in the table. There is a formula for the chi-square test, different from the formula we have used, which we could use to obtain a value for chi-square for the six-cell table given above, but we will merely discuss the formula for six cells in frame 34 without using it to solve problems. In solving the problems presented in this book, we will use only the chi-square formula which you have already learned to use. This will require that whenever we want to use a chi-square test, we will need to collapse our categories so that we always are working with a four-cell table (technically known as the *fourfold table*).

> *Question:*   How do we know how to collapse our data to fit into a four-cell table? Which categories should we group together?
>
> *Answer:*   That's a somewhat difficult question. If you look back to question 4 in frame 1, you will see three possible ways to collapse the data for that question into a four-cell table. The first way, which we used in our analysis, is repeated below.

(1)

	Sociable	Unsociable *or* no opinion
Very warm		
Rather cold		

In what other two ways might the data be collapsed into a four-cell table?

————————————————

(2)

	Sociable *or* no opinion	Unsociable
Very warm		
Rather cold		

(3)

	Sociable *or* Unsociable	No opinion
Very warm		
Rather cold		

When we analyzed our data in class, we chose the first method of collapsing our data. We expected, based on Kelley's earlier findings, to find that subjects in the "very warm" group would perceive Mr. Irving as sociable, while subjects in the "rather cold" group would not perceive him in this way, and the first method of collapsing our data allows us to test our expectation directly. We could just as easily have selected the second method or even the third method. In Chapter Two, frame 3, we'll discuss how to decide which of the three methods to use in collapsing the data.

13. You may wonder why we chose 3.84, instead of some other number, as the cutoff point in the decision for the chi-square test to determine if there is a significant difference between the two experimental groups.

Without getting into a short course in statistics, let's briefly note that the formula for the chi-square test we are using is derived from a mathematical equation that fits a particular curve exactly. In simplest terms, the curve describes a set of possibilities for the differences between the two experimental groups under study.

The chi-square test allows us to estimate the likelihood that the results might occur by chance alone—that is, if the phrase "very warm" actually made no real difference in the students' perception of Mr. Irving. We would still not expect the two groups to have *identical* answer patterns; the two groups would probably respond to each question at least a little differently from one another. What we are trying to find out is this: How likely is it that the distribution of our results could depart as much as it does from a random (or chance) distribution? How different do the responses of the two experimental groups have to be in order for us to say with some confidence that this difference represents a *significant* difference in their responses for a specific question?

We need some way to decide when we are willing to say that an obtained difference between two groups is a real difference and not one that could be produced by chance. Current research practice requires that this question be answered in terms of the probability of an observed difference being a chance difference; this probability is referred to as a *significance level.* Throughout this book we will be using the .05 significance level. When we say that there is a significant difference at the .05 level, we mean that a difference this large could have occurred by chance less than five times in 100 trials; it could happen more often or less often, but it probably would happen about five times in 100. This means that we will accept as a "real" difference any difference that is so large that it could have occurred by chance less than five times in 100.

The following convention has been accepted among psychologists and other social scientists: If the difference between the two experimental groups is so large that we would expect to find it less than five times out of a hundred occurrences, we will assume that such a difference represents a *significant* difference between the two experimental groups. In the mathematical tables which describe the curve, the value for the chi-square equation which represents that point where there are less than five chances in a hundred for getting a difference that large between the two experimental groups *is* 3.84.*

Can you explain in your own words what it means if we have a chi-square value greater than 3.84? Try to do that now, and then check your answer against the one given below.

— — — — — — — — — — — — — — —

If we were to take several thousand random samples of subjects and compute chi-square for each sample, we would expect a chi-square value larger than 3.84 to occur in less than 5 percent of these samples. Values of chi-square larger than 3.84 would be so unusual that we would call these values *significant*. So throughout this book, whenever you find a value for chi-square larger than 3.84, even if it is only 3.85, you should regard that as a significant difference between the two groups being compared.**

14.   We have mentioned that we should never use percentages in the cells of the fourfold table because the chi-square formula requires that we use *numbers* and not percentages to represent the people in the two experimental groups. Another pitfall we need to be alert to in our use of the chi-square test is called *inflated N*. This mistake in the use of the chi-square test occurs whenever the total of the numbers in the four cells of the chi-square table is greater than the number of subjects in your sample.

For example, let's suppose that you gave a reading test to a group of 50 third-grade students in the fall of 1977, and then you gave that same reading test to these same students eight months later in the spring of 1978. You want to know: "Did the students improve significantly in their reading ability

---

*The mathematical tables are not included in this book, but you can find them in any statistics book. If you are interested, you might refer to another Self-Teaching Guide, *Statistics*, by Donald Koosis (2nd edition).

**Another convention agreed upon among psychologists is that if the value for chi-square is so large that we would expect to find that value less than one chance in a hundred, they would say that there is a significant difference between the two experimental groups at the .01 level; the value for chi-square (using the formula which you have learned to use) for which this is true is 6.64. Whenever a psychologist finds a value of chi-square (for a four-cell table) which is greater than 6.64, he is willing to say that there is a *highly significant* difference between the two experimental groups on that particular question. In this book, however, we will use only the .05 level, and, therefore, the number for chi-square that we will be looking for will always be 3.84.

during this eight-month period?" You might decide to answer this question by finding the "average reading score" for all of the students when the fall and spring scores are grouped together, and then setting up the following chi-square table:

	Above average	Below average
Fall reading scores		
Spring reading scores		

You might then count up the number of students who were either above or below this average score for both the fall and the spring testing periods and fill in the table, compute the value for chi-square, and hope to obtain a value for chi-square greater than 3.84 to signify a significant difference between these two reading scores for this group of subjects.

But if you did all of this work, your results would be incorrect. The reason is quite simple. You started out with a group of 50 third-grade subjects, and you tested them in the fall *and* in the spring of the same school year. But when you include the results of *both* testing periods in your chi-square table, you end up with a total of 100 students in your chi-square table, since every one of the 50 subjects was tested twice: in the fall *and* in the spring. The resulting table makes it appear as if you had a sample of 100 subjects when, in fact, you had only 50 children in your sample. *You can't invent imaginary subjects in your use of the chi-square test.* We can summarize this pitfall in the following rule:

> *Rule:* The sum of the numbers in the four cells of a chi-square table must equal the number of subjects (N) in the two groups being compared; whenever you have a larger sum than N, you have "inflated N" in your use of the chi-square test, and this procedure is improper.

Another way to state this decision rule is to say that the scores of the two groups being compared must be *independent*, in the sense that the scores of any one subject do not influence the scores of any other subject.

Other statistical tests exist which could be used to analyze the data resulting from two separate testings of the same group of subjects, but such tests are beyond the scope of this book. (We will have more to say in Chapter Four, frame 31 about analyzing the data for this type of problem.)

Let's check to see if you can determine whether the scores of two groups of subjects are independent.

Suppose that you gave a questionnaire to 80 college freshmen (50 males and 30 females), and one of the questions asked them to report their high school grade-point average (GPA). You want to see if there is a significant relationship between the sex of these students and their high school GPA, so you set up the following fourfold table.

	Above average GPA	Below average GPA
Males	30	20
Females	10	20

Are the values in this fourfold table independent?

— — — — — — — — — — — — — — —

Yes, they are. Each student's high school GPA will appear in only one of the four cells. And since the total number of subjects in these four cells is 80—the total number of subjects in the sample—you have not inflated N, and so this fourfold table is valid.

15. Let's try another example. Suppose that you used the same questionnaire with these same 80 students, but that you wanted to see if there was a significant relationship between the high school GPA of the 30 *female* students and their rank in class while in high school. You develop the following fourfold table:

Females	Above average GPA	Below average GPA
Above average rank in class	10	5
Below average rank in class	3	12

Are the values in this fourfold table independent?

— — — — — — — — — — — — — — —

Yes, they are. Each student's scores will be summarized in only one of the four cells, and since the total number of subjects in the four cells is 30—the exact number of females in your sample—you have not inflated N, and this fourfold table is valid.

16. Now for a final example. Suppose that you wanted to see if there was a relationship between the grade-point average (GPA) of college freshmen and their GPA as college sophomores. You mail out a questionnaire and obtain responses from 60 freshmen from two years ago at your college or university for whom you have their GPA both as freshmen and as sophomores from last year. You develop the following fourfold table:

	Above average	Below average
Freshman GPA	40	20
Sophomore GPA	20	40

Are the values in this fourfold table independent?

————————————————————

No, they are not. You have inflated N. Only 60 subjects are included in your sample, but the numbers in the cells of the fourfold table add up to 120 subjects. You have counted each subject twice: (1) the subject's freshman GPA, and (2) the subject's sophomore GPA. Each subject must appear in only one cell of the fourfold table. Whenever the same subject appears in more than one cell, you have inflated N, and you cannot use the chi-square test on these data.

17.   Another fallacy in the reading scores problem discussed in frame 14 deserves comment. The type of experimental design used in this problem has the technical name *one-group pretest-posttest design.* This design can be depicted graphically in this way:

Time 1	Time 2	Time 3
O_1	X	O_2

where

O_1 refers to some pretest given to the subjects before the treatment is administered to the subjects.

X refers to some special type of treatment administered to the subjects (for example, a film, a reading program, or a lecture).

O_2 refers to some posttest administered to the subjects after the treatment has been administered to the subjects.

The main difficulty with this type of experimental design is that several different explanations can be given for any changes detected between the pretest and the posttest. Campbell and Stanley, in their classic article on experimental design, had this to say about the one-group pretest-posttest design (1963, p. 177):

While this design is still widely used in educational research, . . . it is introduced here as a "bad example" to illustrate several of the confounded extraneous variables that can jeopardize *internal* validity. These variables offer plausible hypotheses explaining an $O_1 - O_2$ difference, rival to the hypothesis that X caused the difference. . . .

Two of these important, plausible rival hypotheses are *history* and *testing.* History is a plausible rival hypothesis because other events besides the experimental treatment X may have caused the change in scores from

O_1 to O_2. For example, if the treatment X is a film about the People's Republic of China which is intended to improve the attitude of students toward the People's Republic of China, and if the United States and China sign an important peace treaty between O_1 and O_2, and if the students' attitudes toward China show a marked improvement between O_1 and O_2, was this improvement caused by the film, by the publicity given to the treaty, or by a combination of both of these events? Since we have no comparison group of students who did not see the film, we cannot separate out these two rival hypotheses for the O_1-O_2 changes in attitude.

Similarly, the use of the pretest itself might have caused a change in attitude in the students between O_1 and O_2. Still using the example of the film on the People's Republic of China, answering the questions on the pretest may have caused the students to think deeply about their attitudes toward China to the point where they became conscious of their own prejudices toward China. If these students then made a conscious effort to become less biased in their attitude toward China, and if the students showed a marked improvement in attitude toward China between O_1 and O_2, was the improvement caused by the film, by the effects of pretesting, or by a combination of both of these things? Once again, without a comparison group of subjects who were not pretested but who were exposed to the film on China, it is impossible to separate out the effects of the experimental treatment X from the possible effects of pretesting.

The possible confounding effects of history can be reduced by shortening the time interval between O_1 and O_2. And, to the extent that the use of O_1 is not likely to influence O_2, the threat of testing as a possible confounding explanation can be discounted.

18.   We mentioned that the chi-square test can be used whenever the data can be grouped into categories. Let's explore further what we mean by categories and look at some more examples. A category is a division of a group of people or of a set of responses into some logical scheme. The chi-square test is especially useful whenever the data from a research study are collected in the form of categories. Some examples of such categories are "pass–fail," "male–female," "in favor of–opposed to," and the like. Actually, the pass–fail categories are part of the larger *characteristic* of "final course grade," and the male–female categories are part of the larger *characteristic* of "sex," and so on. Whenever data are grouped into categories, the researcher is frequently interested in asking the question: Are the numbers in the cells of the fourfold table significantly different from the numbers that would be expected to occur in each cell if the two characteristics being compared are not related to one another? For example, look at the following fourfold table:

		(Sex)	
		Male	Female
(Age)	Over 25		
	25 or under 25		

In this table, sex and age are the two characteristics being compared, and "male–female" and "over 25–25 or under 25" are the categories that apply to these characteristics. We are, therefore, asking this question in applying the chi-square test to the above table: Are the observed numbers in the cells of the fourfold table significantly different from the numbers that would be expected to occur in each cell if sex and age are not related to each other?

Let's take a moment to check to see if you understand the difference between a *characteristic* and a *category*. What is the characteristic in the following fourfold table?

(Grade-point average)	Above average		
	Below Average		

— — — — — — — — — — — — — — —

Grade-point average.

19.   What are the categories in the fourfold table above?

— — — — — — — — — — — — — — —

Above average and below average.

20.   Let's try one more example. (a) What is the characteristic in the following fourfold table? (b) What are the categories?

(Height)

Above 6′	Below 6′

— — — — — — — — — — — — — — —

(a) Height.
(b) Above 6′ and below 6′.

21.   You may wonder why we simulated Kelley's experiment with a class instead of merely telling you the results of Kelley's original research study. We did so for two major reasons. First, if we had merely told you the results of Kelley's study without having you "participate" in a similar study, you might well have dismissed the findings and not believed that they would hold true today, since Kelley's original study took place more than 25 years ago. When we actually do a variation of Kelley's study in class, we typically find that students answer the questions (in the rating scale in frame 1) in such a way that five or six of the nine questions produce a significant difference between the "warm" and "cold" groups. Once students see this type of dramatic result, they are more likely to believe that Kelley's results may still hold true today—more than 25 years later.

The second reason for doing this research study in class is that it allows us to illustrate an important technical research concept: replication of a research study. When one researcher becomes interested in the research results of another (whether he or she believes or disbelieves these results), this researcher can set up an exact replica of the earlier experiment to check on the results. This exact replica of another experiment is called the *replication* of that experiment. In your reading in psychological journals, you will notice statements like: "This experiment is a replication of an earlier study by . . .", or "Our experiment failed to replicate the results of an earlier study by . . . ."

Replication of a major research study is a very important procedure in psychological research. If different experimenters using different subjects in different parts of the country obtain the same research results, then psychologists all over the country will have more confidence in the research findings and are more likely to believe the findings as "true" about human behavior.

Let's check your understanding of the concept of replication. Strictly speaking, the experiment which we conducted in this chapter with our hypothetical class of subjects was *not* a replication of Kelley's original study. In what important way did the study discussed in this chapter differ from Kelley's original study?

— — — — — — — — — — — — — — —

Kelley actually had someone conduct a discussion with the class and then had the subjects fill out the rating scale questions afterward, while we merely asked the subjects to answer the rating-scale questions before they ever saw "Mr. Irving." This difference between these two research studies is important.

22. If you've read any published research studies in psychological journals, you have surely seen tables of the results. Let's look at how the results of our research study would appear in table form. This will illustrate how you could summarize the results of this research study if you were writing a final report for a project or if you were preparing an article for publication in a psychological journal. The results of the first three questions of our study could be summarized in the following table:

Question	Chi-square	Significance level
1	7.69	$p < .05$
2	7.77	$p < .05$
3	0.02	n.s.

When you include a table such as the above in your summary of your research study, you provide the reader with several advantages: (1) The table provides a summary of the chi-square values for each of the questions (note that the reader could compute his or her own value for chi-square and compare the result to yours to see if the computations agree with yours; occasionally an author has made an error in computing the value for chi-square, and when the value for chi-square is reported, the reader can check the accuracy of the author's computations). (2) The reader can tell at a glance at the "significance level" column exactly *which* questions resulted in a significant difference between the two experimental groups. The letters "n.s." mean that no significant difference was apparent between the two experimental groups for that question; for a fourfold table, you would use "n.s." whenever you obtained a value for chi-square less than 3.84. The letter "p" stands for probability. The expression "$p < .05$" means that the value you obtained for chi-square was greater than the value required for the difference between the two experimental groups to be significant at the .05 level (see frame 13 if you need to review the meaning of significance level); for a fourfold table, you would use "$p < .05$" whenever you obtained a value for chi-square greater than 3.84.

Another way authors of published journal articles indicate when they have obtained significant differences is to include the value for chi-square and the significance level as part of their written summary of the results of their study. Using question 2 above as an example, we could summarize the results of that question in this way;

> Significantly more subjects in the "very warm" group expected the guest speaker to be considerate of others than did subjects in the "rather cold" group ($\chi^2 = 7.77, p < .05$).

The symbols in parentheses serve the same function as the table which summarized the results for question 2. The symbol "χ^2" is the Greek letter "chi" with a "squared" symbol above it ("chi-squared"), and the symbol "$p < .05$" tells the reader that the value for chi-square of 7.77 was greater than 3.84, the value necessary for the difference between the two experimental groups to be significant at the .05 level whenever a fourfold table is used to summarize the data. You will need to keep these two ways of summarizing the results of a research study in mind when you are attempting to understand published journal articles that you read in your library.

The skills of reading a researcher's table correctly and of creating a table to summarize your own research results are both important. Let's take some time now to check your skill in this area. We've already filled in a chi-square table for the results of the first three questions of this chapter. Fill in the results for the remaining six questions in this chapter, and then check your answers against the correct ones given below the table.

Question	Chi-square	Significance level
1	7.69	$p < .05$
2	7.77	$p < .05$
3	0.02	n.s.
4	————	————
5	————	————
6	————	————
7	————	————
8	————	————
9	————	————

Question	Chi-square	Significance level
1	7.69	$p < .05$
2	7.77	$p < .05$
3	0.02	n.s.
4	7.98	$p < .05$
5	17.94	$p < .05$
6	1.04	n.s.
7	13.33	$p < .05$
8	6.17	$p < .05$
9	0.20	n.s.

If you are going to stop reading soon,
this is a good breaking point.

23. Let's check out your understanding of the chi-square test by having you work a special problem that deals with a chapel green. This problem relates to a Mr. Wizard who has made an extravagant claim. Your job is to determine by the use of the chi-square test whether his claim is justified.

Before you read the problem, let me make a suggestion about how to summarize the data. In this problem, half of the subjects will be in the experimental group, while the other half will be in the control group. These words "experimental group" and "control group" are terms with which you should become familiar. In simplest terms, the *experimental group* experiences some special set of circumstances which you are interested in studying, while the *control group* goes through an experience identical except for the specific characteristic that you are studying in the experimental group.

In the data we summarized earlier, we arbitrarily grouped the responses of the subjects into two categories for each question; for example, for question 4 we compared those subjects who answered "sociable" with those who answered *either* unsociable *or* had no opinion. In the data for the chapel green problem, we cannot do this. The data are reported in terms of the subjects' height on a scale from 1 to 28.

How can we split the subjects' height into two categories so that we can use a chi-square test on the data? The answer is quite simple. Find the average height for *all* of the students in the experiment (in both Group 1 and Group 2 combined) by putting the heights of all of the subjects in rank order from the tallest to the smallest, and then find the middle score in this set of scores. We will then have two groups: (1) subjects who are above average in height, and (2) subjects who are below average in height.

Now read your problem:

THE CHAPEL GREEN PROBLEM

Mr. Wizard, a vice-president of Stretch, Inc., is promoting a sure-fire solution to having people increase in stature. In short, he is claiming that his method is guaranteed to show that individuals who follow his suggestion will be taller than individuals who do not. And his formula is very simple: he claims that people who run around the chapel green twice without stopping will be taller than those who do not.

Is Mr. Wizard for real? Does he have any data to back up his wild claim?

In response to these reasonable questions, Mr. Wizard has supplied the following data which he obtained from a class of general psychology students at a private liberal arts college located on the bluffs of a large river in a Midwestern state. Mr. Wizard used a table of random numbers (see Appendix A for an explanation of this procedure) to assign these students to two groups:

Group 1 (the experimental group)   This group ran around the chapel green twice without stopping.

Group 2 (the control group)   This group ran the same distance as Group 1 *except* that they ran around the gym.*

---

*In establishing a control group, you should apply a procedure which is identical to the one you apply to the experimental group in all respects *except* that aspect which you desire to test in your experiment. For example, in the chapel green problem, the control group ran the same distance as the experimental group except that it ran around the gym instead of around the chapel green. This experimental design thus made it possible to isolate the effect of running around the chapel green. If we had had the control group merely sit and watch the experimental group run around the chapel green, there would have been *two* differences between the experimental group and the control group: (1) the given distance run, and (2) the *location* of the running. Either of these differences could explain any different results between the experimental group and the control group; we cannot separate them out since they both appear in the experimental group.

Immediately upon finishing their marathon, both groups were measured in height, and the following data were produced. To simplify the arithmetic, each person's height was transformed to a scale in which 5 foot tall (or less) was scored as a "1," 5 foot 1 inch was scored as a "2," and so on.

Group 1:   1, 3, 5, 7, 9, 10, 12, 13, 14, 15, 16, 17
Group 2:   7, 12, 14, 15, 18, 19, 21, 23, 25, 27, 28

Is Mr. Wizard's claim supported by the data? We'll work out the answer to this problem, step by step, using the chi-square test.
What is the first step?

— — — — — — — — — — — — — — — — —

We must find some way to categorize the data. As we noted earlier, we will categorize the subjects' heights as either above or below average. The average height for all of the subjects in the experiment is found by: (1) putting all of the heights in rank order from the tallest down to the smallest, and (2) locating the middle score in this set of rank-ordered scores.

24.   The middle score of a set of scores arranged in rank-order is a special type of "average score" called the *median.* It is a point on the scale of scores above which lie half of the scores and below which lie the other half of the scores.
Let's try a simple example. What is the median of the following set of scores:

18, 12, 5, 13, 16

— — — — — — — — — — — — — — — — —

The answer is found by arranging the scores in rank-order (18, 16, 13, 12, 5) and then selecting the middle score. Thus, the median for these scores is 13.

25.   The median score is the score in the rank-order distribution of scores which results from the following formula:

Median = the $\dfrac{N + 1}{2}$ score in the rank-order set of scores

where

N = the total number of scores in the rank-order distribution of scores.

Thus, if there are five scores, the median score is the $\frac{5+1}{2}$ = third score in the rank-order set of scores. If there are eight scores, the median score is the $\frac{8+1}{2}$ = 4.5th score, which would be halfway between the fourth and fifth score in the rank-order set of scores. For example, suppose you had these eight rank-ordered scores:

25, 23, 21, 20, 19, 18, 15, 12.

The median score in this set of eight scores is halfway between the fourth and the fifth scores in this rank-order set of scores, giving us a median of 19.5.

Whenever you are trying to split a set of scores into those scores which are "above average" versus those scores which are "below average," the question arises: What should you do with a score that is exactly *at* the median, as can occur whenever you have an odd-numbered set of scores (for example, five scores, seven scores)? Should the median score in this case be grouped into the "above average" category or the "below average" category? Throughout this book, whenever we use the chi-square test, we will always follow this rule:

> *Rule:*   Whenever a score falls exactly *at* the median score, put this score into the "below average" category.

This rule allows us to follow a convention agreed upon by psychologists (see, for example, McNemar, 1969) which says to split the scores into the groups of scores which exceed the median and the scores which do not exceed the median.*

Let's return to the hypothetical data provided for Group 1 and Group 2 in the chapel green problem. What is the median height of these two groups of subjects?

— — — — — — — — — — — — — — — — —

Did you determine that the median height for both groups of subjects combined was equal to 14? If you didn't, review frames 24-25 dealing with median scores until you do understand why 14 is the median height of the scores given in the chapel green problem. Note that the rank-order of all the scores ranges from 28, 27, 25, . . . , 7, 7, 5, 3, 1. There are 23 scores, and so the median score is the $\frac{23+1}{2}$ = twelfth score in the rank-order of scores. Whether you count down from the largest score of 28 to the twelfth score in the rank-ordered scores or count up from the smallest score of 1 to the twelfth score in the rank-ordered scores, you should arrive at the score of 14 as the median score.

---

*The reader will find different opinions on the manner in which scores should be treated when they fall exactly *at* the median score. Some authors (see, for example, Noether, 1976) suggest grouping the scores into those above the median versus those which are at or below the median; others (see, for example, Harshbarger, 1977) suggest that it is proper to place those scores which fall at the median score *either* with those scores above the median *or* with those below the median; still others (including Freund, 1976) suggest excluding from the data analysis those scores which fall exactly at the median. Throughout this book we will follow the convention suggested by McNemar (1969) and group scores into those which are above the median versus those which are at or below the median score.

26. This median height allows us to set up our chi-square table as follows:

(Height)

	Above average	At or below average
Group 1		
Group 2		

How many subjects in Group 1 have a height which is above the median height of 14?

— — — — — — — — — — — — — — — —

3

27. How many subjects in Group 1 have a height which is at or below the median height of 14?

— — — — — — — — — — — — — — — —

9

28. Now can you continue this reasoning and fill in the correct numbers in the four cells of the table given above?

— — — — — — — — — — — — — — — —

You should now have the following table:

(Height)

	Above average	At or below average
Group 1	3	9
Group 2	8	3

29. Now find the value for chi-square for the table in frame 28.

— — — — — — — — — — — — —

$$\text{chi-square} = \frac{23\,(9-72)^2}{12\,(11)\,(11)\,(12)}$$

$$= \frac{23\,(-63)\,(-63)}{12\,(11)\,(11)\,(12)}$$

$$= \frac{91{,}287}{17{,}424}$$

$$\text{chi-square} = 5.24$$

Conclusion: Since this value for chi-square is larger than 3.84, there is a significant difference in the heights of the two groups.

30. Now let's test your writing skill. Write out the results of the research study for the chapel green problem.

— — — — — — — — — — — — — — — —

Which of the following came closest to your answer?

A. Significantly more subjects in the control group who ran around the gym were above average in height than the subjects in the experimental group who ran around the chapel green.

B. Significantly more subjects in the experimental group who ran around the chapel green twice without stopping were above average in height than the subjects in the control group who ran around the gym.

A is the more correct answer. If you chose B, you probably misinterpreted the table. If you chose B, go back and study the table in frame 28 again. Do you see where you made your mistake? Be sure you understand why A is correct, before you go on. (You probably had some other questions about this experiment—read on!)

31. Look again at the table in frame 28. Note that in Group 1, the experimental group, only three of the subjects in this group were above average in height while nine of the subjects in this group were at or below average in height; note also that eight of the subjects in Group 2, the control group, were above average in height, while three of the subjects in this group were at or below average in height. This means that more subjects in Group 2, the control group, were above average in height than were the subjects in Group 1! This finding is exactly the *opposite* of Mr. Wizard's claim, and since we found a chi-square value of 5.24, this is a significant difference between these two groups. In other words, the summary of the table in frame 28 is really this: Significantly more subjects in the control group (which ran around the gym) were above average in height than were those subjects in the experimental group.

Actually, *neither* running around the chapel green *nor* running around the gym will change your height. We picked this problem merely to illustrate a point: In order to answer the question "*In what way* were the two experimental groups significantly different from one another?" we need to interpret the chi-square table carefully, or else we might interpret the result exactly the opposite from the way the study actually turned out. This can be a little embarrassing, to put it mildly!

But if we stop to think about this result for a moment, it really doesn't sound sensible. We wouldn't be likely to believe this result to be true even if we discovered it in our research findings, and we are likely to ask ourselves questions such as these: Were the subjects randomly assigned to the two groups in the proper way? Did the two groups differ in height *before* they began to run? Did we measure the heights of the subjects accurately? Is there some other factor other than running which might explain *why* we obtained a significant difference between these two groups? What else could have *caused* these two groups to be different in height (the cause–effect relationship question)? Even if we answered all of these questions to our satisfaction and decided that none of the factors seemed adequate to explain the difference in heights between the two groups, we still would be unlikely to accept the results as reasonable until we obtained the identical results with several different groups of people; that is why the process of *replication* is so important.

The main point that we are trying to make with this problem is that you need to think carefully while you are designing a study, collecting the data, analyzing the data, and interpreting the results. The blind application of statistical procedures without thinking through the problem you are trying to solve is not likely to produce fruitful research results.

32.   Some other questions may have occurred to you now that we have spent some time trying to understand the chi-square test.

You may wonder where we got the chi-square formula that we used for a fourfold table and whether we can use that same formula on other tables. In fact, the chi-square formula which we have been using throughout Chapter One can be used *only* with fourfold tables, and not with any other type of table.

This formula for chi-square we have been using is a special case of the general formula for chi-square. The *general formula* for the chi-square test is the following:

$$\text{chi-square} = \Sigma \, \frac{(O - E)^2}{E}$$

where

O = the observed frequency of occurrence in each category

E = the expected frequency of occurrence in each category

Σ = the sum of the defined variables in the formula.

Let's illustrate the use of this formula with an example. Suppose that a marketing vice-president wanted to test people's preferences for four different tastes of grape jelly. Let's suppose that she collected her data on the first Saturday in May of 1978 for 36 shoppers in a local supermarket and recorded the number of times a shopper chose each of the four tastes. In this case, her hypothesis was that there would be no difference in the proportion of selection of each taste, and since there were four tastes, each taste should have been chosen as the best taste by one-fourth of the total of 36 shoppers; thus, the expected frequency of occurrence for each taste would be nine times. Let's suppose that the following hypothetical table resulted:

Number of Times That Each of Four Tastes Was Selected as the Best Taste by Shoppers

O and E	Taste 1	Taste 2	Taste 3	Taste 4
Observed number of first choices	6	12	9	9
Expected number of first choices	9	9	9	9

$$\text{chi-square} = \Sigma \; \frac{(O - E)^2}{E}$$

$$= \frac{(6 - 9)^2}{9} + \frac{(12 - 9)^2}{9} + \frac{(9 - 9)^2}{9} + \frac{(9 - 9)^2}{9}$$

$$= \frac{(-3)^2}{9} + \frac{(3)^2}{9} + 0 + 0$$

$$= 1 + 1$$

$$\text{chi-square} = 2.0$$

In this case, for us to say that there is a significant difference between these four tastes, the chi-square value must be greater than 7.82.* Since the value for chi-square of 2.0 is less than 7.82, there was no significant difference in the number of times each taste was selected as the best taste by the shoppers.**

Let's give you a chance to test your understanding of the general formula for chi-square with a second example. Suppose that you have been hired as a research assistant by a track coach who is curious about the effect of the lane in which a sprinter runs on his performance in the 220-yard dash when this race is run "around a curve" (that is, it is not run entirely on a straight-away, but part of it requires the runner to sprint around a curve like the one which occurs at the end of a football field).

---

*The reason for this is beyond the scope of this book. The interested reader can find an explanation for this point in McNemar (1969) in the chapter dealing with the chi-square test.

**In an actual experiment, the researcher would also need to be careful about the order in which each of these four tastes was presented to the subjects. For example, if all of the subjects were presented with Taste 1 as the *first* sample that they tasted, that first taste would always influence the subsequent tastes they were asked to judge.

Suppose that you have checked the track records of all meets held on a given Saturday and you have found the following results:

Number of Times the Runner Finished First in the Race

		Track lane			
1	2	3	4	5	6
26	25	23	24	22	24

How many times did the runner finish first when he ran in lane 5?

— — — — — — — — — — — — — — — —

22

33. Let's see if you can use the general formula for chi-square to determine if there was a significant difference between these six track lanes in the number of times the runner in that lane finished first in the race.

Your first step is to determine the expected number of times a sprinter *should* finish first in the race if a sprinter was equally likely to finish first in each of these six lanes. What is the expected number of times that a sprinter should finish first in each lane?

— — — — — — — — — — — — — — — —

24

When you add up the number of times a runner finished first in the race for all six lanes combined, you should find that a total of 144 races were run (26 + 25 + 23 + 24 + 22 + 24 = 144). If there were no difference between the six lanes in the number of times a runner in the lane finished first, each lane would be expected to have the winning sprinter in it for one-sixth of the races ($\frac{1}{6}$ × 144 races = 24 races). Therefore, the expected number of times that each lane should have had the winning sprinter running in that lane was 24.

34. Now use the general formula for chi-square to determine the answer for chi-square for this problem. When six lanes are involved, you need a chi-square value greater than 11.07 to have a significant difference between the lanes.*

— — — — — — — — — — — — — — — —

————————

*The reason for this is beyond the scope of this book. If you would like to know why 11.07 is the value for chi-square at the .05 level, see McNemar (1969), and read the chapter dealing with the chi-square test.

$$\text{chi-square} = \Sigma \; \frac{(O-E)^2}{E}$$

$$= \frac{(26-24)^2}{24} + \frac{(25-24)^2}{24} + \frac{(23-24)^2}{24}$$

$$+ \frac{(24-24)^2}{24} + \frac{(22-24)^2}{24} + \frac{(24-24)^2}{24}$$

$$= \frac{(2)^2}{24} + \frac{(1)^2}{24} + \frac{(-1)^2}{24} + 0 + \frac{(-2)^2}{24} + 0$$

$$= \frac{4}{24} + \frac{1}{24} + \frac{1}{24} + \frac{4}{24}$$

$$= \frac{10}{24}$$

$$\text{chi-square} = 0.42$$

Since this value for chi-square of 0.42 is less than the value of 11.07 which we would need, there was not a significant difference between the lanes in the number of times that a sprinter finished first in the race for these 144 races.

35. Now let's see how to calculate the expected frequency for the four cells in a fourfold table. When the data from a research study are grouped into a fourfold table, a special procedure must be used to compute the expected frequency for each cell of the fourfold table. We will illustrate this procedure by the following example: Suppose that a rater has categorized each member in a group of people as either "leaders" or "followers," and you want to test the relationship between the height of the group members and their leadership ratings using the following hypothetical observed frequencies:

		(Height)	
		Tall	Short
(Leadership Ratings)	Leader	10	13
	Follower	8	11

To determine the expected frequency for each of the four cells of this fourfold table, we need to compute the "marginal total" for each of the two rows, and for each of the two columns, of the fourfold table. The marginal total is found by adding together the numbers in the two cells in each row (and in each column) as follows:

		(Height)		
		Tall	Short	Marginal Total
(Leadership ratings)	Leader	10	13	23
	Follower	8	11	19
	Marginal Total	18	24	

To obtain the expected frequency for each cell, we must multiply together the two marginal totals *which are common to a given cell* and divide the result by the total number of subjects in our study (N). The expected values are the values we would expect if height is independent of leadership (that is, there is no relationship between height and leadership). The further away the observed values are from these expected values, the more apt we are to conclude that these categories are not independent but are, in fact, *related.* Continuing this example, the expected frequency for the "Leader–Tall" cell would be:

$$\text{Expected frequency of Leader–Tall cell} = \frac{(23)\,(18)}{42} = 9.86$$

In this case, the marginal totals which are common to the Leader–Tall cell are 23 and 18, and the total number of subjects in the study is 42 (this is merely the total of the numbers in the four cells). Thus, the expected frequency of the Leader–Tall cell is 9.86.

Now you try it. What is the expected frequency of the Leader–Short cell?

13.14

$$\text{Expected frequency of Leader–Short cell} = \frac{(23)\,(24)}{42} = 13.14$$

36.   What is the expected frequency of the Follower–Tall cell?

8.14

$$\text{Expected frequency of Follower–Tall cell} = \frac{(19)\,(18)}{42} = 8.14$$

37.   What is the expected frequency of the Follower–Short cell?

10.86

$$\text{Expected frequency of Follower–Short cell} = \frac{(19)\,(24)}{42} = 10.86$$

38. Now that you have computed the expected frequencies for each of the four cells of the fourfold table, use the general formula for chi-square to compute the value for chi-square for this fourfold table, and then check your answer below.

———————————————

$$\text{chi-square} = \Sigma\ \frac{(O-E)^2}{E}$$

$$= \frac{(10-9.86)^2}{9.86} + \frac{(13-13.14)^2}{13.14} + \frac{(8-8.14)^2}{8.14} + \frac{(11-10.86)^2}{10.86}$$

$$= \frac{(0.14)^2}{9.86} + \frac{(-0.14)^2}{13.14} + \frac{(-0.14)^2}{8.14} + \frac{(0.14)^2}{10.86}$$

$$= \frac{0.02}{9.86} + \frac{0.02}{13.14} + \frac{0.02}{8.14} + \frac{0.02}{10.86}$$

$$= .002 + .002 + .002 + .002$$

$$= .008$$

$$\text{chi-square} = .01 \text{ (rounded off to two decimal places)}$$

39. How large would this value for chi-square have to be in order for there to be a significant difference at the .05 level?

———————————————

3.84

40. Why?

———————————————

Because chi-square needs to be greater than 3.84 for there to be a significant difference at the .05 level for a fourfold table.

41. Is there a significant difference between the leadership ratings and the height of the people in the group? If not, why not?

———————————————

No. Because the obtained value of chi-square of .01 is less than 3.84, and therefore there is not a significant difference between the leadership ratings and height for this group of people.

42.   Throughout this book, all of the problems deal with the special case of chi-square for a fourfold table, and the general formula for chi-square becomes equal to the special formula for chi-square that we have used throughout Chapter One of this book whenever a fourfold table is used. As you know very well by now, the special formula for chi-square for a fourfold table is:

$$\text{chi-square} = \frac{N\,(AD - BC)^2}{(A + B)\,(C + D)\,(A + C)\,(B + D)}$$

Now that you can use the general formula for chi-square for a fourfold table, do you get the same answer for chi-square when you use the special formula for chi-square for a fourfold table? Try this special formula now on the Leader–Follower problem (frames 35 to 41) and see if you get the same result for chi-square. Then check your answer below.

_ _ _ _ _ _ _ _ _ _ _ _ _ _ _ _

$$\text{chi-square} = \frac{N\,(AD - BC)^2}{(A + B)\,(C + D)\,(A + C)\,(B + D)}$$

$$= \frac{42\,(110 - 104)^2}{(23)\,(19)\,(18)\,(24)}$$

$$= \frac{42\,(6)\,(6)}{(23)\,(19)\,(18)\,(24)}$$

$$= \frac{1{,}512}{188{,}784}$$

$$= .008$$

chi-square = .01 (rounded off to two decimal places)

This is the same value that we obtained for chi-square with the general formula (we should hope so!). Whenever you are working with a fourfold table, you can compute the value for chi-square either by using the general formula for chi-square or by using the special formula for chi-square that applies only to the fourfold table, which you have been using throughout Chapter One. Both formulas produce the same answer for chi-square. Since the computations are simpler when you use the special formula, our recommendation is that you use the special formula instead of the general formula whenever you compute chi-square.

43. Since we will not be using the general formula for computing chi-square in this book, perhaps you wonder why we took the trouble to teach you how to compute expected frequencies. Actually these expected frequencies can be put to another important use. Sometimes the special formula for the chi-square test should not be used for a fourfold table. Whenever small samples of subjects are used in a research study, special problems are created for the chi-square test. To use some rule-of-thumb procedures for deciding when you should use the special formula, you need to be familiar with the expected frequencies for chi-square.

When doing research, you need to keep in mind three decision rules for a fourfold table. Each of these decision rules is based on the *smallest* expected frequency for a fourfold table. To obtain the smallest expected frequency for a fourfold table, you should multiply the *smaller* of the two row-marginal totals by the *smaller* of the two column-marginal totals and divide the result by the total number of subjects in your sample (N).

Let's practice this procedure for finding the smallest expected frequency for a fourfold table. Go back to frame 35 and compute the smallest expected frequency for the fourfold table which dealt with the relationship between Height and Leadership ratings. Then check your answer against the one given below.

— — — — — — — — — — — — — — — — —

8.14. The smaller of the two row-marginal totals is 19. The smaller of the two column-marginal totals is 18. The total number of subjects in the sample is 42 (10 + 13 + 8 + 11). Therefore, the smallest expected frequency is:

$$\text{Smallest expected frequency} = \frac{(19)(18)}{42} = 8.14$$

44. This answer of 8.14 is supposed to be the smallest expected frequency for that fourfold table. Is it the smallest expected frequency compared to the other three expected frequencies which you computed for that fourfold table? (Look at frames 35-37 again to answer this question.)

— — — — — — — — — — — — — — — — —

Yes, 8.14 is the smallest expected frequency. The other three expected frequencies were 9.86, 13.14, and 10.86.

45. Let's try one more example. What is the smallest expected frequency for the following fourfold table?

10	20
30	40

— — — — — — — — — — — — — — — — —

12.

		Marginal total
10	20	30
30	40	70

Marginal total   40   60

The smaller of the two row-marginal totals is 30. The smaller of the two column-marginal totals is 40. The total number of subjects in the sample is 100 (10 + 20 + 30 + 40 = 100). Therefore, the smallest expected frequency is:

$$\text{Smallest expected frequency} = \frac{(30)\,(40)}{100} = 12$$

46. You need to know how to find the smallest expected frequency for a fourfold table in order to use it in the following three decision rules which tell you when to use the chi-square test and which chi-square test to use.

Decision rule 1: Whenever the *smallest* expected frequency is greater than 10, use the special formula for chi-square:

$$\text{chi-square} = \frac{N\,(AD - BC)^2}{(A + B)\,(C + D)\,(A + C)\,(B + D)}$$

Decision rule 2: Whenever the *smallest* expected frequency is between 5 and 10, use Yates' correction for continuity which is included in the following formula:

$$\text{chi-square} = \frac{N\,(|AD - BC| - \frac{N}{2})^2}{(A + B)\,(C + D)\,(A + C)\,(B + D)}$$

where
$|AD - BC|$ is the "absolute value" of $(AD - BC)$ which is found by taking the difference between $(A \times D)$ and $(B \times C)$ and always considering this difference to be a *positive* difference. For example, if $A = 8$, $B = 7$, $C = 10$, and $D = 5$, then

$$AD = 40$$

$$BC = 70$$

$$AD - BC = 40 - 70 = -30$$

$$|AD - BC| = +30$$

For the formula in decision rule 1 and in decision rule 2, whenever the resulting chi-square is greater than 3.84, there is considered to be a significant difference between the two groups being compared.

Decision rule 3:   Whenever the *smallest* expected frequency is less than 5, do not use the chi-square test but use instead the Fisher Exact Test. The computation of the Fisher Exact Test is beyond the scope of this book, but the interested reader can learn how to use that test by referring to Siegel (1956, pp. 96-104).

These three decision rules are based on reasoning given in McNemar (1969, p. 262).

Let's see if you can apply these three decision rules to fourfold tables. We will give you three fourfold tables and ask you for each whether it is most appropriate to use the special formula for chi-square (used throughout Chapter One), the Yates' correction for continuity for chi-square, or the Fisher Exact Test. Remember that your first step is to compute the smallest expected frequency for the table, and then to apply the three decision rules to the resulting smallest expected frequency in order to determine which test to apply to the fourfold table.

Which of the three tests is most appropriate for the following fourfold table?

10	20
30	40

- - - - - - - - - - - - - - - - - -

The special formula for chi-square used throughout Chapter One.

The smallest expected frequency $= \dfrac{(30)\,(40)}{100} = 12$

This value of 12 for the smallest expected frequency is greater than 10, so decision rule 1 applies to the fourfold table.

47.   Which test is most appropriate for the following fourfold table?

5	6
7	8

- - - - - - - - - - - - - - - -

Yates' correction for continuity.

$$\text{The smallest expected frequency} = \frac{(11)\,(12)}{26} = 5.08$$

This value of 5.08 for the smallest expected frequency is between 5 and 10, so decision rule 2 applies to this fourfold table.

48. Which test is most appropriate for the following fourfold table?

3	6
2	4

- - - - - - - - - - - - - - - - - -

The Fisher Exact Test.

$$\text{The smallest expected frequency} = \frac{(6)\,(5)}{15} = 2.0$$

This value of 2.0 for the smallest expected frequency is less than 5, so decision rule 3 applies to the fourfold table.

Throughout this book we have used only the formula for the chi-square test that applies to decision rule 1, even though there were times when either the chi-square formula based on Yates' correction for continuity or the Fisher Exact Test would have been more appropriate. This was done to simplify the instructional objectives and the computations required to analyze the data from the problems presented in this book. Now that you are aware of the three decision rules for the use of the chi-square test, you can apply them in your own research studies.

If you would like to learn more about
how to use the Yates' correction for continuity, read on.
Otherwise, skip to the Self-Test at the end of Chapter One.

49. In frame 47, we determined that Yates' correction for continuity needed to be used in the following fourfold table:

5	6
7	8

Yates' correction for
continuity for chi-square $= \dfrac{N\,(|AD - BC| - \frac{N}{2})^2}{(A + B)\,(C + D)\,(A + C)\,(B + D)}$

$$= \frac{26\,(|40 - 42| - 13)^2}{(11)\,(15)\,(12)\,(14)}$$

$$= \frac{26\,(|{-2}| - 13)^2}{(11)\,(15)\,(12)\,(14)}$$

$$= \frac{26\,(2 - 13)^2}{(11)\,(15)\,(12)\,(14)}$$

$$= \frac{26\,(-11)\,(-11)}{(11)\,(15)\,(12)\,(14)}$$

$$= \frac{3{,}146}{27{,}720}$$

chi-square $= 0.11$

Note that the absolute value of $|40 - 42|$ is +2. You need to be careful when working with this part of the formula so that you do not make a computational error.

Now you try it. What is the smallest expected frequency in the following fourfold table?

8	4
3	8

5.26.

The smallest expected frequency $= \dfrac{(11)\,(11)}{23} = 5.26$

50.   Which test is the most appropriate one to use for this fourfold table? Why?

Yates' correction for continuity for chi-square, because the smallest expected frequency of 5.26 is between 5 and 10. (See decision rule 2 in frame 46 if you need to review.)

51. Now try computing the value for chi-square for this fourfold table using Yates' correction for continuity. Then check your answer against the one given below.

— — — — — — — — — — — — — — — — — —

2.17

$$\text{Yates' correction for continuity for chi-square} = \frac{N\left(|AD - BC| - \frac{N}{2}\right)^2}{(A + B)(C + D)(A + C)(B + D)}$$

$$= \frac{23\left(|64 - 12| - 11.5\right)^2}{(12)(11)(11)(12)}$$

$$= \frac{23(52 - 11.5)^2}{(12)(11)(11)(12)}$$

$$= \frac{23(40.5)(40.5)}{(12)(11)(11)(12)}$$

$$= \frac{37,725.75}{17,424}$$

$$\text{chi-square} = 2.17$$

52. Let's check to see how much of a difference the Yates' correction for continuity makes for chi-square for this fourfold table compared to the special formula for chi-square that you have been using throughout Chapter One.

Use the special formula for chi-square. What value do you get for chi-square when you use that formula on this fourfold table?

— — — — — — — — — — — — — — — — — —

3.57

$$\text{chi-square} = \frac{N(AD - BC)^2}{(A + B)(C + D)(A + C)(B + D)}$$

$$= \frac{23(64 - 12)^2}{(12)(11)(11)(12)}$$

$$= \frac{23(52)(52)}{(12)(11)(11)(12)}$$

$$= \frac{62,192}{17,424}$$

$$\text{chi-square} = 3.57$$

Note that when the special formula for chi-square is used the value for chi-square of 3.57 is quite different from the value for chi-square of 2.17 when Yates' correction for continuity is used. This difference becomes very important when you obtain a value for chi-square greater than 3.84 when using the special formula but less than 3.84 when using Yates' correction on the same fourfold table. In the one case you would assume there was a significant difference at the .05 level, while in the other case you would assume that there was not a significant difference at the .05 level. You need to be alert in your own research studies to apply Yates' correction whenever the decision rule calls for it.

SELF-TEST FOR CHAPTER ONE

This Self-Test is designed to show you whether you have mastered the key concepts and skills in Chapter One. Answer each question to the best of your ability. Correct answers and review instructions are given at the end of the test.

When working on these problems, you might find it helpful to use the tear-out sheet for the chi-square test in Appendix E. It will save you the time of memorizing the formula or trying to find it within this book.

Some of the problems in this Self-Test are based on real data, and some are based on hypothetical data. Whenever an article is cited in a problem, you will be working with the actual data of that published article. For example, in problem 1 you will be working with the actual data collected by Latane and Darley (1968) in their research study, and you can check your answer against their results by referring to the answer for problem 1 at the end of this Self-Test.

Whenever an article is not cited in a problem in this Self-Test, we have created some hypothetical data to allow you to practice the skills you have learned. The specific responses of individual subjects in research studies do not appear in the published articles, but it is important for you to be able to use the responses of subjects, even hypothetical ones, in order to obtain experimental results based on the chi-square test.

1.   Latane and Darley (1968) conducted an interesting study in bystander intervention in which naive subjects were exposed to a room filling up with smoke. The subjects were either alone in the room or were in the room with two of the researchers' confederates, who ignored the smoke. The authors were interested in studying the effect of the presence or absence of others on whether or not the subject reported the smoke. They found that 18 of the 24 subjects who observed the smoke while alone in the room reported it, compared to only one of the 10 subjects in the condition involving the two passive confederates. Was this a significant difference? (Note that you do not need to have the same number of subjects in the two groups in order to use the chi-square test.)

2.   Bem and Bem (1973) did an interesting study with high school seniors to assess their interest in applying for various jobs in the telephone company. The authors copied advertisements verbatim from ads and brochures used by the telephone company to recruit applicants; the authors called these ads "sex-biased" because they appeared to recruit members of only one sex for certain jobs. The authors added two other experimental conditions: (1) sex-unbiased ads which were written to attract both men and women to these same jobs, and (2) sex-reversed ads which were written to attract members of the sex opposite

to the sex of the person who was normally recruited for these same jobs. There were 20 males and 20 females in each experimental condition.

The authors summarized part of their findings (pages 13-14 of their article) as follows:

> Consider first the results for women. When the jobs of lineman and frameman were advertised in a sex-biased format, no more than 5 percent of the women were interested. . . . And when the ads for lineman and frameman were specifically written to appeal to women, nearly half (45 percent) of the women in our sample were interested in applying for one or the other of these two jobs.

(a) Was this a significant difference?

> . . . the results clearly indicate that sex-biased job advertisements still tend to discourage men from applying for jobs as operator and service representative. . . . For when the sex bias is removed, the percentage of men interested in applying for one or the other of these jobs jumps from 30 percent to 75 percent.

(b) Was this a significant difference?*

3.   Suppose that the following table summarizes, for a group of business managers, the relationship between their leadership ratings and height and that the chi-square for this design is equal to 12.86 (a value

---

*When you are given a percentage, you must divide it by 100 before you can use it in your computations.

Example 1.   If a total of 60 subjects are included in the research study, and 20 percent of them are in Group 1, how many subjects are in Group 1?

$$\frac{20}{100} = .20$$

therefore   60 (.20) = 12 subjects in Group 1

Example 2.   Eighty subjects are included in the experiment. Forty percent are in Group 1, 30 percent are in Group 2, and 30 percent are in Group 3. How many subjects are in each group?

$$\frac{40}{100} = .40$$

$$\frac{30}{100} = .30$$

therefore   80 (.40) = 32 subjects in Group 1
80 (.30) = 24 subjects in Group 2
80 (.30) = 24 subjects in Group 3
total: = 80 subjects

significant at the .05 level). How would you interpret the results? Write your conclusion and then decide whether your answer is closest to A, B, or C below.

		(Height)	
		Below average	Above average
(Leadership ratings)	Above average	25	10
	Below average	10	25

A. Significantly more managers who were below average in height had above average leadership ratings than did managers who were above average in height.
B. Significantly more managers who were above average in height had above average leadership ratings than did managers who were below average in height.
C. Neither of the above.

4. McClelland (1965) at Harvard has done research on need for achievement (nAch) for over 25 years. *Need for achievement theory* predicts that young men with high need for achievement will seek out entrepreneurial positions which will enable them to satisfy their achievement needs. He collected some data on college sophomore men at Wesleyan University in 1947 to determine their need for achievement scores and was able to gather occupational information on these students fourteen years later in 1961. He studied those men who were in business occupations in 1961 and categorized their jobs as either entrepreneurial (those requiring the individual to initiate decisions, accept individual responsibility for these decisions, receive objective feedback data about the success of his decisions, and take risks in making decisions) or nonentrepreneurial. He obtained the following result:

	Above average nAch scores	Below average nAch scores
Business entrepreneurs	10	2
Business nonentrepreneurs	3	11

chi-square = 9.90

McClelland summarized this result as follows (p. 390): "The results of this follow-up study were striking: 83 percent of the entrepreneurs had been high in nAch 14 years earlier versus only 21 percent of the non-entrepreneurs." McClelland was concerned that this result could have been due to the special type of sample he used which contained many men who were World War II veterans. He went on to say (p. 390): "It was therefore decided that cross-validation of the findings was imperative." To do a *cross-validation study* (that is, a study using a different group of subjects to see if the findings of the original study are repeated), he combined the data for the 1950 and 1951 graduating classes at Wesleyan to obtain the following table:

	Above average nAch scores	Below average nAch scores
Business entrepreneurs	18	12
Business nonentrepreneurs	12	17

McClelland summarized this table (p. 390) as follows: "The cross-validation data on the younger men are not nearly so striking but they are definitely in the same direction: 60 percent of the entrepreneurs had been high in nAch as college freshmen versus 41 percent of the non-entrepreneurs." But did the cross-validation data produce a significant difference between the entrepreneurs and the nonentrepreneurs in their nAch scores?

5. Berger *et al.* (1969) studied the relationship between promotional effort and consumer behavior in a natural environment. They placed menus on selected seats in a train and unobtrusively recorded the number of passengers who made a purchase in the train's diner. They studied the behavior of passengers over a three-week experimental period and found the following results:

Week 1

	Used diner	Did not use diner
Menu on seat	8	19
No menu	5	24

Week 2

	Used diner	Did not use diner
Menu on seat	14	14
No menu	5	20

Week 3

	Used diner	Did not use diner
Menu on seat	12	15
No menu	9	33

Did the use of a menu produce a significant difference in the passengers' use of the train's diner during:

(a) week 1?
(b) week 2?
(c) week 3?

6. Hamm *et al.* (1969) studied the effect of a free sample of hair spray on the attitudes of unmarried males at Oklahoma State University. They mailed a questionnaire to the subjects and asked them to classify the product as masculine, feminine, or neither and to indicate their intention to buy on a seven-point scale. The subjects were then mailed a free sample of hair spray and were later mailed a second questionnaire. The researchers found that 11 of the 52 subjects who were mailed the original questionnaire classified hair spray as masculine, while 41 subjects classified it as either feminine or neither. On the second questionnaire, which was filled out by these same subjects after they had received the free sample of hair spray, 19 subjects classified the product as masculine, while 33 subjects classified it as either feminine or neither. Was this a significant difference?

Answers for Self-Test for Chapter One

Compare your answers to the questions on the Self-Test with the answers given below. If all of your answers are correct, you are ready to go on to Chapter Two. If you missed any questions, review the frames indicated in parentheses following the answer. If you missed several questions, you should probably reread carefully the entire Chapter One.

1.

	Reported the smoke	Did not report the smoke
Subjects who were alone	18	6
Subjects who were with two passive confederates	1	9

$$\text{chi-square} = \frac{34\ (162 - 6)^2}{24\ (10)\ (19)\ (15)}$$

$$= \frac{34\ (156)\ (156)}{24\ (10)\ (19)\ (15)}$$

$$= \frac{827{,}424}{68{,}400}$$

$$\text{chi-square} = 12.1$$

Since this value for chi-square is greater than 3.84, there is a significant difference. Significantly more subjects reported the smoke when they were alone than when they were with two passive confederates. (frames 5-8)

2. (a) For women, 5 percent of the 20 females in the sex-biased condition
    is equal to one female; thus only one of the 20 females was interested in
    the jobs in the sex-biased condition. In the sex-reversed condition, 45
    percent of the 20 females in this condition equals 9 women who were
    interested in the job. This gives us the following chi-square table:

	Interested in the jobs	Not interested in the jobs
Sex-biased ads	1	19
Sex-reversed ads	9	11

$$\text{chi-square} = \frac{40\,(11 - 171)^2}{20\,(20)\,(10)\,(30)}$$

$$= \frac{40\,(-160)\,(-160)}{20\,(20)\,(10)\,(30)}$$

$$= \frac{1{,}024{,}000}{120{,}000}$$

$$\text{chi-square} = 8.53$$

Since this value for chi-square is greater than 3.84, significantly more
women were interested in the jobs in the sex-reversed condition than in
the sex-biased condition.

(b) For men, 30 percent of the 20 males in the sex-biased condition is
equal to 6 males; thus 6 of the 20 males were interested in the jobs in
the sex-biased condition. In the sex-unbiased condition, 75 percent of
the 20 males in this condition equals 15 males who were interested in
the job. This gives us the following chi-square table:

	Interested in the jobs	Not interested in the jobs
Sex-biased ads	6	14
Sex-unbiased ads	15	5

$$\text{chi-square} = \frac{40\,(30 - 210)^2}{20\,(20)\,(21)\,(19)}$$

$$= \frac{40\,(-180)\,(-180)}{20\,(20)\,(21)\,(19)}$$

$$= \frac{1{,}296{,}000}{159{,}600}$$

$$\text{chi-square} = 8.12$$

Since this value for chi-square is greater than 3.84, significantly more men were interested in the jobs in the sex-unbiased condition than in the sex-biased condition.   (frames 5-8)

3.   Answer: A   (frame 8)

4.

	Above average nAch scores	Below average nAch scores
Business entrepreneurs	18	12
Business nonentrepreneurs	12	17

$$\text{chi-square} = \frac{59\,(306 - 144)^2}{30\,(29)\,(30)\,(29)}$$

$$= \frac{59\,(162)\,(162)}{30\,(29)\,(30)\,(29)}$$

$$= \frac{1{,}548{,}396}{756{,}900}$$

chi-square = 2.05

Since this value for chi-square is less than 3.84, there was no significant difference between the entrepreneurs and the nonentrepreneurs in the nAch scores in the cross-validation study.   (frames 5-8)

5.   (a) Week 1

$$\text{chi-square} = \frac{56\,(192 - 95)^2}{27\,(29)\,(13)\,(43)}$$

$$= \frac{56\,(97)\,(97)}{27\,(29)\,(13)\,(43)}$$

$$= \frac{526{,}904}{437{,}697}$$

chi-square = 1.2

Since this value for chi-square is less than 3.84, the use of the menu did not significantly change the use of the train's diner during the first week of the experiment.

(b) Week 2

$$\text{chi-square} = \frac{53\,(280 - 70)^2}{28\,(25)\,(19)\,(34)}$$

$$= \frac{53\,(210)\,(210)}{28\,(25)\,(19)\,(34)}$$

$$= \frac{2{,}337{,}300}{452{,}200}$$

$$\text{chi-square} = 5.17$$

Since this value for chi-square is larger than 3.84, there was a significant difference between the two experimental groups. Significantly more subjects who had a menu placed on their seat used the train's diner during the second week of the experiment than subjects who did not have a menu placed on their seat. (Note that of the subjects who had a menu placed on their seat, 14 used the diner while 14 did not use the diner; this means that 50 percent of the subjects who had a menu placed on their seat used the diner. In contrast, only 20 percent of the subjects— 5 of the 25 subjects—who did not have a menu placed on their seat used the diner. This 30 percent difference in the use of the diner is a significant difference since chi-square is larger than 3.84.)

(c) Week 3

$$\text{chi-square} = \frac{69 \, (396 - 135)^2}{27 \, (42) \, (21) \, (48)}$$

$$= \frac{69 \, (261) \, (261)}{27 \, (42) \, (21) \, (48)}$$

$$= \frac{4{,}700{,}349}{1{,}143{,}072}$$

$$\text{chi-square} = 4.11$$

Since this value for chi-square is larger than 3.84, there is a significant difference between the two experimental groups. Significantly more subjects who had a menu placed on their seat used the train's diner during the third week of the experiment than subjects who did not have a menu placed on their seat (44 percent versus 21 percent).

Note that if the researchers had stopped the experiment at the end of the first week they would have been unaware that the menus were capable of producing an increase in the use of the train's diner, since this increase did not occur until the second and third weeks of the study. Advertising studies frequently include a time lag between the time the advertisement is first presented and when it produces a change in buying behavior, a finding which is illustrated nicely by this study. (frames 5-8)

6. If you computed a value for chi-square, you need to review the part of Chapter One which discussed inflating N in chi-square. If you refused to compute a value for chi-square, congratulate yourself on an intelligent decision.

You were probably tempted to set up the following chi-square table:

	Before the free sample	After the free sample
Classified hair spray as masculine	11	19
Classified hair spray as feminine or neither	41	33

The problem with this table is that it includes a total sample of 104 subjects, and there were only 52 subjects in the sample. This is because each subject filled out the questionnaire twice. In short, you can't solve this problem using the chi-square test!   (frames 14-15)

CHAPTER TWO

Quality of a Journal Article

1. Now let's look at a different type of experiment. Imagine that you are sitting in that same hypothetical psychology class. Your professor has just made a couple of administrative announcements at the beginning of class, and he then turns to the class and says:

> I've just handed each of you an article that was published in a journal called *Educational Technology*. The article deals with the topic of performance tests for beginning teachers. I would like you to take time now during class to read that article carefully. After you have done that, I would like you to answer the six questions that you have been asked on the last page of the article. Please read the article carefully and then circle your answer to each of the six questions at the end of the article.

He then passes out the article, and you find a paragraph of further instructions:

> In this booklet you will find an article written by an author in a professional field. At the end of the article you will find several questions relating to this article. It is not assumed that you are sophisticated or knowledgeable in this field. We are interested in the ability of college students to make critical evaluations of professional literature. We are not interested in identifying your answers, so please do not write your name on this booklet.

Now read the article by Joan R. Simpson on pages 60–65 and follow the instructions with regard to the questions which follow it.

Performance Tests for Beginning Teachers: Why All the Fuss?*
by
Joan R. Simpson

One might ask, Why all the fuss—aren't paper-and-pencil tests good enough? But how would you answer this question if you were told that the pilot flying you to San Francisco had passed only a multiple choice test? Or if you were told that the plumber or TV repairman had passed only a paper-and-pencil test about plumbing or TV repair?

When properly administered, tests of information or knowledge can be neither ignored nor discredited. They are efficient, relatively inexpensive and can tell a great deal about (in terms of this article) the prospective teacher's grasp of important concepts and principles in the subject areas in which he would like to teach. But although knowledge of subject area content is necessary for good teaching, it may or may not be sufficient. Advocates of performance tests for beginning teachers argue that the paper-and-pencil test does not sufficiently approximate the actual conditions of the classroom. They are concerned with its fidelity, that is, its degree of realism compared with the criterion situation; and its comprehensiveness, i.e., the range of different aspects or dimensions it actually measures.

Figure 1 presents a diagram of some types of tests according to their fidelity and comprehensiveness. The fidelity of a test for beginning teachers can range from the more abstract aspects of certain types of paper-and-pencil tests through film, in-basket and microteaching tests, to on-the-job performance in the public or private schools. The degree of comprehensiveness of each test varies with the number of different aspects of the criterion situation actually tested, i.e., the number of different activities representing the responsibilities and actions of a full-time teacher.

Performance Tests

A performance test simulates the criterion situation, requiring the respondent to perform a particular task rather than to respond to a question that either asks him what he would do in a particular situation or to select the one best answer from a list of alternatives. Performance tests are not new to educational research (Cruickshank, 1969). Perhaps the best way to comment on their development for teachers would be to quote what Ryans and Frederiksen (1951) wrote:

From the standpoint of validity one of the most serious errors committed in the field of human measurement has been that which assumes

*Adapted for teaching purposes from *Educational Technology*, May 1973, pp. 14–16. Reprinted by permission of *Educational Technology*.

Figure 1.   Fidelity and Comprehensiveness of Different Types of Tests

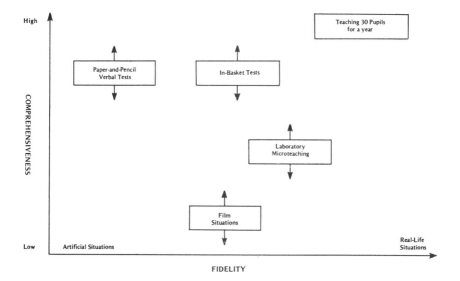

the high correlation of knowledge of facts and principles on the one hand and performance on the other. Nevertheless, examinations for admission to the bar, for medical practice, for teaching and even tests of ability to cook and sew, are predominantly verbal tests of fact and principle in the respective fields. Relatively little attention has been paid to the testing of performance as such.

The types of performance tests that can be created are limited only by the ingenuity and imagination of the test developer. Ryans and Frederiksen's classification of these tests into three types—recognition, simulated condition and work-sample—will be continued in this article.

1. *Recognition tests* require the examinee to recognize the essential characteristics of a performance or of an object; for example, a lab technician could be asked to move from one microscope to another in a laboratory in fixed-time intervals so that he could write down the identification of specimens presented on mounted slides at each microscope.

2. *Simulated condition tests* require the examinee to perform an activity designed to represent an essential task within a criterion performance. This type of test usually calls for special stimuli in the form of test instructions, audio- or videotapes, as well as special test conditions such as a laboratory or teaching classroom, pupils and furniture or equipment that represent the real-life criterion conditions. The examinee may be asked for paper-and-pencil answers as would be the case if he had to select the action he would take to a problem-vignette of a classroom scene presented on 16 mm film, or he may be required to perform a larger task, such as an extended interaction with a group of pupils.

Three good examples of simulated condition tests in education would be:

- *In-basket tests* which have been used in education primarily to assess the skills of school administrators, contain background information, memos, letters and records that an administrator could reasonably be expected to deal with in the course of the performance of his job. The examinee is asked to respond to these stimuli as if he were an administrator.

- *Tab tests* contain either perforated tabs that can be torn off the page or chemical coatings that can be erased with a pencil eraser. They can be scored by recording both the total number of tabs selected and by assigning penalties for incorrect choices. For example, the National Board of Medical Examiners has used the tab principle to require the examinee to select diagnostic tests, procedures or therapy for a patient on whom background information is provided.

- *Microteaching tests* are a new addition to educational research. Although microteaching is not real teaching in the sense that it requires live interaction between a teacher and pupils such as is provided in student teaching or an internship, it nevertheless possesses a higher degree of fidelity in terms of simulating the teacher-pupil interaction process than is possible by written tests or film tests. Although not essential to the concept, videotape equipment can be included in microteaching sessions. In order to have test conditions that would allow the performance of prospective teachers to be compared, it would be essential to control the content of the lesson, the amount of content preparation by the teacher, the directions to the teacher and to the pupils, the number of pupils of each sex, the grade level of the pupils, the length of the discussion, the training program for the observers, the observation schedule used by the observers, the amount of practice of the pupils in the test situation, and the scoring system.

Once the verbal behavior of the teacher is recorded, the next problem is to figure out how to score it. There is no shortage of categories available. Simon and Boyer (1970) listed over 2,400 categories for both teacher and pupil behavior, spread across 79 different observation systems. The creative problem, from a research point of view, involves the selection of the particular scoring categories that will be most useful in either describing an individual's performance during the testing session or predicting his future on-the-job performance. Once the scoring categories are selected, audiotapes can be used to train observers to code the pupil and teacher behavior reliably by checking the trainee's coding score against an answer key established by the research team. Figure 2 presents a sample profile of the teaching performance of a candidate that could result from a fixed-time sampling of his verbal behavior.

The category system used for scoring might differ for elementary and secondary teaching levels and for different subject areas, depending on the type of prospective teacher participating in the microteaching tests; the weighting of the components could also differ for different types of prospective teachers. Once the scoring system is established, it then becomes possible to do systematic research to study the relationship between teacher performance and pupil outcome.

Figure 2.   Contrived Profile of the
Teaching Performance of an Individual Candidate

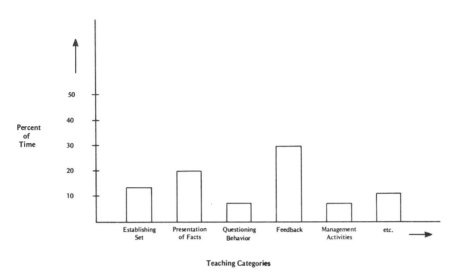

3. *Work-sample tests* provide the examinee with a controlled tryout of the task under the actual work conditions. A good example of a paper-and-pencil, work-sample test is the National Architectural Registration Board Examination, in which the examinee is given a topographical map of a building lot and asked to develop a site plan for a specified type of building (Boyd and Shimberg, 1971). Additional examples are the Seashore-Bennett Stenographic Proficiency Test (1948) and those described by Fitzpatrick and Morrison (1971) as performance tests in art, music, industrial arts, sports and physical fitness.

Construction and Use of Performance Tests

The development of a performance test for beginning teachers, a much more complicated procedure than the development of the typical standardized, paper-and-pencil achievement test, requires the following steps:

1. Specify the objectives of instruction in terms of long-term goals, specific behaviors, sample instructional items, test items and instructional materials. In industrial research this task is referred to as a formal job-analysis.
2. Select the critical aspects of the teacher's performance; for example, the critical incident technique of Flanagan (1954) might be a useful way to rank these aspects in terms of their importance.
3. Specify in detail the aspects of the critical criterion performances that you want to measure.
4. Write the specifications for the test.

5. Devise a test situation that specifies the conditions under which the performance is to be demonstrated.
6. Conduct extensive pilot tests of the performance test, using both experienced and beginning teachers, so that you can debug the test manual, verify that the schedule and tasks are performable, that the directions describe the test situation adequately, that adequate equipment and materials are provided and that time limits are reasonable. Develop a scoring system and revise the test using the information provided by the pilot tests.
7. Write a detailed test manual providing a checklist for each critical aspect in the test operation.
8. Train the test supervisors, using written materials and audio- or video-tapes, and provide criterion tests to insure that they have been properly trained.
9. Collect data on the population to be studied by the test.
10. Score the resulting data and develop norms or cut-off scores for acceptable performance levels.

Once developed, a performance test can be studied to see whether it can be used to predict success in subsequent on-the-job teaching performance, to diagnose training deficiencies in prospective teachers so that they can receive additional training on specific teaching skills and to establish a criterion measure against which other modes of testing procedures can be validated. The fact that certain types of performance tests provide a closer simulation of the teaching process than written tests does not remove them from the same scrutiny in terms of reliability and validity that is required for standardized paper-and-pencil tests. This is an important point, and one that we should not lose sight of.

Any discussion of performance tests should describe some of their disadvantages. Compared with the more popular paper-and-pencil, multiple choice tests, they are much more complicated to administer, usually test only one individual at a time, require special training for the observers who do the scoring, are more difficult to score reliably and cost more in terms of personnel time, equipment and facilities. Nevertheless, in spite of all these limitations of performance tests, we may one day, in the words of Eliza Doolittle, say to prospective teachers, "Show me!"

References and Suggested Readings

Allen, D. W., and K. Ryan. *Microteaching.* Reading, Mass.: Addison-Wesley, 1969.

Baker, E. L. Relationship Between Learner Achievement and Instructional Principles Stressed During Teacher Preparation. *Journal of Educational Research, 63,* 99–102, November 1969.

Borg, W. R., M. L. Kelley, and P. Langer. *Minicourse: Effective Questioning Elementary Level Teachers Handbook.* Beverly Hills, Calif.: Macmillan, 1970.

Borg, W. R., M. L. Kelley, P. Langer, and M. Gall. *The Minicourse: A Microteaching Approach to Teacher Education.* Beverly Hills, Calif.: Macmillan, 1970.

Boyd, J. L., Jr., and B. Shimberg. *Handbook of Performance Testing: A Practical Guide for Test Makers.* Princeton, N.J.: Educational Testing Service, 1971.

Cronbach, L. J., and G. C. Gleser. *Psychological Tests and Personnel Decisions* (Second Edition). Urbana: University of Illinois Press, 1965.

Crooks, L. A. Issues in the Development and Validation of In-basket Exercises for Specific Objectives. Paper presented at the meeting of the American Psychological Association, San Francisco, September 1968.

Cruickshank, D. R. The Use of Simulation in Teacher Education: A Developing Phenomenon. *The Journal of Teacher Education, 20,* 23-26, Spring 1969.

Fitzpatrick, R. and E. J. Morrison. Performance and Product Evaluation. In R. L. Thorndike (Ed.). *Educational Measurement* (Second Edition). Washington, D.C.: American Council on Education, 1971, 237-70.

Flanagan, J. C. The Critical Incident Technique. *Psychological Bulletin, 51,* 327-58, 1954.

Frederiksen, N. Validation of a Simulation Technique. *Organizational Behavior and Human Performance, 1,* 87-109, 1966.

Hemphill, J. F., D. E. Griffiths, and N. Frederiksen. *Administrative Performance and Personality: A Study of the Principal in a Simulated Elementary School.* New York: Teachers College Press, 1962.

Krathwohl, D. R., and D. A. Payne. Defining and Assessing Educational Objectives. In R. L. Thorndike (Ed.) *Educational Measurement* (Second Edition). Washington, D.C.: American Council on Education, 1971, 17-45.

Mager, Robert F. *Preparing Instructional Objectives.* Palo Alto, Calif.: Fearon, 1962.

McDonald, F. J., and D. W. Allen. Training Effects of Feedback and Modeling Procedures on Teaching Performance. Palo Alto, Calif.: Stanford University School of Education, 1967.

Olivero, James L. *Micro-Teaching: Medium for Improving Instruction.* Columbus, Ohio: Merrill, 1970.

Popham, W. James. The Performance Test: A New Approach to the Assessment of Teaching Proficiency. *The Journal of Teacher Education, 19,* 216-22, Summer 1968.

Rosenshine, B., and N. Furst. Research on Teacher Performance Criteria. In B. O. Smith (Ed.). *Research on Teacher Education: A Symposium.* Englewood Cliffs, N.J.: Prentice-Hall, 1971, 37-72.

Ryans, D. G., and N. Frederiksen. Performance Tests of Educational Achievement. In E. F. Lindquist (Ed.). *Educational Measurement.* Washington, D.C.: American Council on Education, 1951, 455-94.

Seashore, H. G., and G. K. Bennett. A Test of Stenography: Some Preliminary Results. *Personnel Psychology, 1,* 197-209, 1948.

Simon, A., and E. G. Boyer. *Mirrors for Behavior II: An Anthology of Observation Instruments.* Philadelphia: Research for Better Schools, 1970.

RATING FORM*

Directions: Please circle the letter corresponding to your choice.

1. Based on this article, what would you judge Joan R. Simpson's professional competence to be?

     A.   superior competence
     B.   above-average competence
     C.   average competence
     D.   below-average competence
     E.   incompetence

2. If you were to assign a grade to Joan R. Simpson's article, what would it be?

     A.   A
     B.   B
     C.   C
     D.   D
     E.   F

3. In her appeal, Joan R. Simpson was:

     A.   very rational
     B.   rational
     C.   emotional
     D.   extremely emotional
     E.   alarmist

4. Based on this article, what would you estimate Joan R. Simpson's professional status to be in terms of the perception of her colleagues?

     A.   extremely high status
     B.   above-average status
     C.   average status
     D.   below-average status
     E.   extremely low status

5. How effective would you rate Joan R. Simpson's writing style?

     A.   superior effectiveness
     B.   above-average effectiveness
     C.   average effectiveness
     D.   below-average effectiveness
     E.   minimal effectiveness

---

*This rating form is extensively adapted from H. N. Mischel, "Sex Bias in the Evaluation of Professional Achievements," *Journal of Educational Psychology*, 1974, vol. 66, pp. 157-166. Copyright 1974 by the American Psychological Association. Reprinted by permission.

6. To what extent were your opinions on the issues discussed swayed by
    Joan R. Simpson's article?

    A.   very much swayed
    B.   considerably swayed
    C.   slightly swayed
    D.   relatively unswayed
    E.   unaffected

Have you circled your answer to each of these six questions in this book? If
you haven't, take time now to do that before you read further.

———————————————————

There are no "correct" answers to these questions. Read on!

2.   After everyone in your class has answered the six questions at the end
of the article, your professor says: "Now that you have finished reading the
article, let me explain what we are doing. We have just done a psychological
experiment. How many of you read an article that was supposedly written
by Joan R. Simpson?" You look around the classroom and half of the students in the class are raising their hands. Your professor then says: "Okay.
How many of you read an article that was supposedly written by John R.
Simpson?" All the other students raise their hands in response to this
question. In this experiment, half of the class read an article which was supposedly written by Joan R. Simpson, while the other half read an article
supposedly written by John R. Simpson.
      In the nineteenth century, quite a few female authors including George
Sand (Madame Amandine Dudevant) and George Eliot (Mary Ann Evans)
decided that their literary works would be well received only if they were
published under a male pen name.
      Goldberg (1967) asked undergraduate women to read six articles from
the fields of law, city planning, elementary education, dietetics, linguistics,
and art history. Each student read a booklet of six articles, half of which had
a fictitious author with a male first name and half of which had a fictitious
author with a female first name. At the end of each article, each subject rated
the article on nine questions. Goldberg analyzed the data using a "summary
score" for each article based on the scores of all nine questions for that
article added together and found only one statistically significant difference:
for the field of city planning, the male-authored article was rated significantly more favorably than the female-authored article. When the data were
analyzed separately for each of the nine questions, based on a summed score
for all of the male-authored articles compared to all of the female-authored
articles for all subjects combined, subjects rated the authors of male-authored
articles as significantly higher in professional competence; the subjects agreed
significantly more with the male author's point of view; and the subjects felt
that the male authors had significantly higher status in their fields than did
the authors of the female-authored articles. When the data were analyzed

using all questions on all articles combined, the male-authored articles were rated significantly more favorably than the female-authored articles.

Feather and Simon (1975) tested Australian female students and found that when these students were asked to explain the academic success of post-graduate students who were identified by name only in the occupations of nursing, medicine, and teaching, the male students' success was explained as due to superior ability while the females' success was due to easy courses (in medicine only) and cheating on examinations.

Our experiment based on the article by Joan R. Simpson that you read, simulates in part a research study by Mischel of Stanford University which was published in the *Journal of Educational Psychology* in 1974. Mischel asked male and female high school seniors and college undergraduates to read a booklet containing four articles, one from each of the following occupational fields: law, city planning, primary education, and dietetics. In each booklet, two articles contained the name of a fictitious male author, while the other two articles contained the name of a fictitious female author (only the first name of the authors differed). At the end of each article, each subject rated the article on nine questions. For each subject for each article, the ratings on the nine questions were added together to form a total score for that article. There were no significant differences between males and females in their overall ratings of the articles.

Mischel found that male-authored articles were rated significantly more favorably in the traditionally predominantly male occupations of law (by high school students) and city planning (by college students) and also in the predominantly female occupation of primary education (by high school students). Female-authored articles were rated significantly more favorably in the predominantly female occupation of dietetics by both high school and college students.

Now let's find out how our hypothetical class felt about the article you read. Remember that everyone read the same article. The only difference was that the first name of the author was Joan for half of the class and John for the other half. And the six questions at the end of the article were identical except for the use of Joan or John in each of the questions to remind you of the name of the person who supposedly wrote the article you had read while you were answering those six questions. (A copy of the rating form for John Simpson is given on page 70.)

We want to analyze the data from this experiment. Our first problem is to decide just how we plan to analyze the data.

Note how you might begin to analyze the data.

— — — — — — — — — — — — — — — —

Read on below to see if your plan agrees with ours.

3.   We could analyze the data for each question separately using a four-cell table. For example, for question 1, we could split the data into four cells as follows:

Question 1

(Author of article)		Superior competence, Above-average competence, *or* average competence	Below-average competence *or* incompetence
	Joan		
	John		

The difficulty with this method of analysis is that we don't have a good rule-of-thumb yet for deciding *where* to split the responses into two categories. For example, in question 1, should we group choice C—"average competence"—with choices A and B, as above, or with choices D and E in the chi-square table? What do you think? Think about this question carefully, and then write your answer below before checking it against our answer.

— — — — — — — — — — — — — — — —

The main problem with this question is that it really doesn't have one logical answer. Putting choice C with A and B is as arbitrary as putting it with D and E. Either choice is purely arbitrary.

4.   So what do we do now? Fortunately, there is a good way to find the average score, and once we know the median score we can create two categories: above average and below average. Let's work out a rule-of-thumb now.

We want to create two categories for the responses: *above average* and *below average.* One way to do this is to assign a number to each response to each question. For example, for question 1, we could assign five points to each student who answered "superior competence," four points to each student who answered "above-average competence," three points to each student who answered "average competence," two points to each student who answered "below-average competence," and one point to each student who answered "incompetence." If we did that, we could simply find the median score of all of the students for question 1. That procedure would give us an average score for question 1, and then we could arrange our data in the following way:

Question 1

(Author of article)		Number of students whose score is above the total group average	Number of students whose score is at or below the total group average
	Joan		
	John		

RATING FORM

Directions: Please circle the letter corresponding to your choice.

1. Based on this article, what would you judge John R. Simpson's professional competence to be?

    A.   superior competence
    B.   above-average competence
    C.   average competence
    D.   below-average competence
    E.   incompetence

2. If you were to assign a grade to John R. Simpson's article, what would it be?

    A.   A
    B.   B
    C.   C
    D.   D
    E.   F

3. In his appeal, John R. Simpson was:

    A.   very rational
    B.   rational
    C.   emotional
    D.   extremely emotional
    E.   alarmist

4. Based on this article, what would you estimate John R. Simpson's professional status to be in terms of the perception of his colleagues?

    A.   extremely high status
    B.   above-average status
    C.   average status
    D.   below-average status
    E.   extremely low status

5. How effective would you rate John R. Simpson's writing style?

    A.   superior effectiveness
    B.   above-average effectiveness
    C.   average effectiveness
    D.   below-average effectiveness
    E.   minimal effectiveness

6. To what extent were your opinions on the issues discussed swayed by John R. Simpson's article?

    A.   very much swayed
    B.   considerably swayed
    C.   slightly swayed
    D.   relatively unswayed
    E.   unaffected

Let's make sure you understand this procedure. Suppose that you gave the article and rating form to a sample of 20 subjects, and their rating on question 4 was as follows:

Experimental group	Rating									
"Joan" group ($N = 10$)	A	B	A	C	B	B	A	B	C	A
"John" group ($N = 10$)	C	D	E	D	D	C	E	D	E	C

Assign from one to five points to each of these 20 ratings by filling in the table below. Then check your scoring against our answers below.

Experimental group	Score of rating									
"Joan" group ($N = 10$)	—	—	—	—	—	—	—	—	—	—
"John" group ($N = 10$)	—	—	—	—	—	—	—	—	—	—

— — — — — — — — — — — — — — — —

Experimental group	Score of rating									
"Joan" group ($N = 10$)	5	4	5	3	4	4	5	4	3	5
"John" group ($N = 10$)	3	2	1	2	2	3	1	2	1	3

5.   Now what is the median score for the 20 scores of question 4?

— — — — — — — — — — — — — — —

3. Three is the median score because four people had a score of 5, four people had a score of 4, five people had a score of 3, four people had a score of 2, and three people had a score of 1. The median score would be between the tenth and the eleventh score in this rank order of 20 scores, and therefore the median is a score of 3.

6.   Now using this median score of 3 as the average score for question 4, fill in the following fourfold table by writing in each of the four cells the number of people whose score fits into each of the four cells.

Question 4

(Author of article)		Above average in status (scores of 4, 5)	At or below average in status (scores of 1, 2, 3)
	"Joan" group		
	"John" group		

- - - - - - - - - - - - - -

Question 4

(Author of article)		Above average in status (scores of 4, 5)	At or below average in status (scores of 1, 2, 3)
	"Joan" group	8	2
	"John" group	0	10

7. We could then use this same procedure for *each* of the six questions. *Each question would have a different average score*, but by using that average score, we could compute a value of chi-square for each question and then decide which of the six questions produced a significant difference between our two experimental groups. Any question that had a chi-square value larger than 3.84 would represent a significant difference between the two experimental groups.

We could also analyze these data another way. Instead of analyzing our data separately to find out which of the six questions produced a significant difference between the two experimental groups, we can do just one chi-square test based on a *total score* for all six questions combined. How can we do that? The answer is simple. We can get a total score for each student in the class in the following way: For *each* of the six questions, give five points if choice A is circled, four points if choice B is circled, three points for choice C, two points for choice D, and one point for choice E. Then add up the scores for each question to get a *total score* for the six responses.

Try the following example to check your understanding of this scoring procedure. Suppose someone answered these six questions by circling the following choices:

Question	Choice Circled	Assigned Score
1	D	_____
2	C	_____
3	E	_____
4	C	_____
5	D	_____
6	E	_____

Assign a score value to each of these six questions by filling in the blanks above in the "Assigned Score" column. Then add up these six scores to obtain a total score. What total score did you get?

————————————————————

The total score is 12. Check your computations below if you obtained a different answer for this total score.

Question	Choice Circled	Assigned Score
1	D	2
2	C	3
3	E	1
4	C	3
5	D	2
6	E	1
	Total score:	12

8. We used the scoring procedure described in frame 7 to get the hypothetical data in Table 2.1 below.

Table 2.1. *Quality of a Journal Article Total Scores*

"Joan" group	"John" group
27	24
26	9
23	16
10	13
28	19
14	13
7	6
18	15
18	22
15	28
12	25
13	

You now have a chance to check out your statistical skills. Use these total scores to set up a chi-square table to answer the following question: Was there a significant difference between the two experimental groups in their opinion of the overall quality of the journal article?

Work out the value of chi-square for Table 2.1 to answer this question.

————————————————

Did you obtain a chi-square value equal to 0.05? If you did, you can skip the computation of chi-square given below and begin to read at frame 12.

If your answer for chi-square was not correct, or if you would like to review the problem, read on, and let's work through the solution step by step.

9.   First of all, let's check your arithmetic. Your first problem is to make sure that you have the correct average score. What did you get for the median score?

————————————————

When you arranged the scores of all of the subjects in this hypothetical research study in rank-order, you should have obtained the following set of scores:

28, 28, 27, . . . , 10, 9, 7, 6.

Since there are 23 scores, the median score is the $\frac{23 + 1}{2}$ = twelfth score in the rank-order of scores. Thus, the median score is equal to 16. If your average score was incorrect, rework your value before you go on.

10.   Now that we know the average score for our research study, fill in the cells of our chi-square table below:

(Total scores)

		Above average	At or below average
(Author of article)	Joan		
	John		

————————————————

You should have obtained the following numbers in your chi-square table:

(Total scores)

		Above average	At or below average
(Author of article)	Joan	6	6
	John	5	6

Be sure you understand how these numbers were obtained before you read any further in this book.

11. Now compute the value for chi-square for this table, and decide if there is a significant difference between the two experimental groups in their total scores.

$$\text{chi-square} = \frac{N\,(AD - BC)^2}{(A + B)\,(C + D)\,(A + C)\,(B + D)}$$

$$= \frac{23\,(36 - 30)^2}{12\,(11)\,(11)\,(12)}$$

$$= \frac{23\,(6)\,(6)}{12\,(11)\,(11)\,(12)}$$

$$= \frac{828}{17{,}424}$$

$$\text{chi-square} = 0.05$$

12. Since this value of 0.05 for chi-square is smaller than 3.84, this means that our two experimental groups did not significantly differ in their total scores representing their opinion of the quality of the journal article. We'll never become famous if all of our research studies come out this way! Even though a finding of no significant difference *is* a gain in knowledge about something, journal editors frown on publishing studies with no significant differences. (No one publishes a *Journal of Nonsignificant Differences!*)

But let's look at the data a different way. Suppose that we had a good rationale for expecting to find sex differences in the way the men and women in this class would perceive the quality of the journal article. Let's analyze our data to see if we find such a sex difference. First of all, we'll put an "F" (for female) beside the score of each woman in this hypothetical class in Table 2.1. The result is shown in the table below.

"Joan" group	"John" group
27 F	24
26 F	9 F
23 F	16 F
10	13
28	19
14	13
7	6 F
18 F	15 F
18 F	22
15	28 F
12 F	25
13	

Now we will take this data and analyze the scores for the men and women separately. Let's analyze the data for the men in this class first. Look at the table above for all those scores that do *not* have an F written beside them, and fill in the chi-square table below.

(Total scores)

Men students only		Above average	At or below average
(Author of article)	Joan		
	John		

Then compute the value for chi-square, and find out if the men significantly differ in their perception of the quality of the journal article depending on whether the author was identified as a man or as a woman.

— — — — — — — — — — — — — — — — — —

When you arranged the scores of all of the male students in rank-order, you should have obtained the following set of scores:

28, 25, 24, 22, 19, 15, 14, 13, 13, 13, 10, 7.

Since there are 12 scores, the median score is the $\frac{12 + 1}{2} = 6.5$th score, which is halfway between 14 and 15, or the median is 14.5.

(Total scores)

Men students only		Above average	At or below average
(Author of article)	Joan	2	4
	John	4	2

$$\text{chi-square} = \frac{12 \, (4 - 16)^2}{(6) \, (6) \, (6) \, (6)}$$

$$= \frac{12 \, (-12) \, (-12)}{(6) \, (6) \, (6) \, (6)}$$

$$= \frac{1728}{1296}$$

$$\text{chi-square} = 1.33$$

Since this value for chi-square is less than 3.84, the men students do not significantly differ in their perception of the quality of the journal article depending on whether it was supposedly written by a man or a woman.

13. Now analyze the data for the women students in this class. Using data from the table given in frame 12, set up a chi-square table for just the women students, compute the value for chi-square, and answer the following question: Did women students significantly differ in the way they perceived the quality of the journal article depending on whether it was supposedly written by a man or a woman?

— — — — — — — — — — — — — — — —

When you arranged the scores of all of the female students in rank-order, you should have obtained the following set of scores:

   28, 27, 26, 23, 18, 18, 16, 15, 12, 9, 6.

Since there are 11 scores, the median score is the $\frac{11 + 1}{2}$ = sixth score of 18. You should have obtained the following chi-square table.

(Total scores)

Women students only		Above average	At or below average
(Author of article)	Joan	3	3
	John	1	4

$$\text{chi-square} = \frac{11 \, (12 - 3)^2}{(6) \, (5) \, (4) \, (7)}$$

$$= \frac{11 \, (9) \, (9)}{(6) \, (5) \, (4) \, (7)}$$

$$= \frac{891}{840}$$

$$\text{chi-square} = 1.06$$

Since this value for chi-square is less than 3.84, the female students did not significantly differ in their perception of the quality of the journal article depending on whether it was supposedly written by a man or a woman.

14. Now write out the results of the entire experiment in terms of all of the students—men and women—in this experiment. Then check your summary with ours below.

— — — — — — — — — — — — — — — —

You should have written out a summary similar to the following:
     When the data were combined for men and women students in the class, the two experimental groups did not significantly differ in their total scores

in their perception of the quality of a journal article, depending on whether it was supposedly written by a man or a woman. When the data were analyzed separately by sex, there was no significant difference either for the men students or for the women students in their perception of the quality of the journal article.

15. The results of that hypothetical study were very interesting, especially since it gave us an opportunity to dig into the data to do some additional analyses. This is known as getting "more mileage" out of the data. But there is one loose end which we need to tie up. We haven't told you yet who actually did write the article you read. We told you only that it was not written by either John or Joan Simpson. Look back at the article again. Do you think that it was written by a male or a female? Circle your choice below.

   Male   Female

———————————————————

The article (Quirk, 1973) was written by a man—Thomas J. Quirk, the author of this book.

16. When you plan your own research studies, you should be alert to a potential measurement problem in studies like the one we have just examined. That problem has to do with the use of a "total score" of several questions as the basic unit of analysis of the data. Technically speaking, a composite total score should represent only one dimension of measurement; another way to say this is that the composite score should be *unidimensional* if its meaning is to be easily interpretable. The six questions at the end of the article in this chapter ask the subject to rate the author's professional competence, appeal, professional status, and writing style; to assign a grade to the article; and to indicate to what extent his or her opinions on the issues were swayed by the article. These six questions represent six very different concepts.

   Whether or not adding the scores together to form a total score that has a definite, unidimensional meaning is an acceptable procedure is a debatable question; and the answer is a matter of opinion.

   You will undoubtedly find some psychologists who will argue in favor of using a total score for these questions and others who will argue against using a total score for these questions. In any case, you should be prepared to defend your decisions about the ways in which you analyze the data in *your* research studies; the experiment described in this chapter provides a good illustration of the problem.

SELF-TEST FOR CHAPTER TWO

This Self-Test is designed to show you whether you have mastered the key concepts and skills in Chapter Two. Answer each question to the best of your ability. Correct answers and review instructions are given at the end of the test. When working on these problems you might find it helpful to use the tear-out sheet for Appendix E, where the formula for the chi-square test is included.

Whenever an article is cited in a problem, you will be working with the actual data of that published article, and you can check your answer against the actual results of that article.

1. Suppose that you conducted your own research study using a sample of college women and the materials given in this chapter to determine how the women in your sample would respond to an article which was supposedly written by a man or by a woman. (Let's keep the sample size small in order to simplify the arithmetic.) Suppose that you computed a single total score for the six questions for each subject and then found the median total score for your sample. If five of the six subjects who read the "Joan" article had scores above the median, while one of the five subjects who read the "John" article had scores above the median, was there a significant difference between your two experimental groups in their overall perception of the quality of the article? (And, if so, in what way did the two groups differ?)

2. Dember (1964) studied the effect of birth order and the need for affiliation. A frequent finding in birth-order studies is that firstborns have a higher need for affiliation (nAff) than later-borns. He had subjects write stories based on Thematic Apperception Test (TAT) pictures and scored these stories according to the need for affiliation which they expressed. He then analyzed the data separately by sex and found the following tables:

Males	High nAff	Low nAff
Firstborn	6	2
Later born	2	6

Females	High nAff	Low nAff
Firstborn	12	2
Later born	2	12

Was there a significant difference in nAff scores in relation to birth order for males? For females?

3.   Piliavin *et al.* (1969) conducted a field experiment using captive audiences on the express trains of the New York subways to see if bystanders were more likely to help victims who pretended either to be ill and collapsed during the subway ride or those who pretended to be drunk and collapsed. The authors found that the supposedly ill victim received spontaneous help on 62 of the 65 trials, while the supposedly drunk victim received spontaneous help on 19 of the 38 trials. Was this a significant difference?

4.   Hornstein *et al.* (1968) studied the effect of a person's feelings about doing a kind act on whether subjects would return a lost wallet. The experimenters "dropped" on a New York City sidewalk an envelope which contained a wallet and a letter to the wallet's owner. The envelope was addressed to the owner of the wallet, and the subjects were supposed to believe that someone had found a wallet and was on the way to the post office to return the wallet to its owner when the envelope was accidentally lost. The letter in the wallet was written either in ordinary English (the similar model condition) or in the broken English of a foreigner (the dissimilar model condition). In addition, one of three types of letters was placed in the envelopes: a neutral letter (which stated matter-of-factly that the wallet was being returned just as it had been found), a positive letter (which added that the finder enjoyed helping out the owner of the wallet), and a negative letter (which added that the finder was annoyed at the great inconvenience caused by having to return the wallet). The experimenters tested a total of 105 subjects and found the following results:*

Condition	Returned the wallet	Did not return the wallet
Similar model		
Neutral	12	8
Positive	14	6
Negative	2	18
Dissimilar model		
Neutral	4	11
Positive	5	10
Negative	6	9
Total	43	62

*This table is adapted from H. Hornstein, E. Fisch, and M. Holmes, "Influence of a Model's Feeling About His Behavior and His Relevance as a Comparison Other on Observers' Helping Behavior," *Journal of Personality and Social Psychology*, 1968, vol. 10, pp. 222-226. Copyright 1968 by the American Psychological Association. Reprinted by permission.

These data are summarized in terms of percents in Figure 2.1. Answer the following two questions:

(a)   For those subjects in the similar model condition, was there a significant difference in the number of subjects who returned the wallet when the negative condition is compared to the neutral and positive conditions combined?

(b)   For those subjects in the dissimilar model condition, was there a significant difference in the number of subjects who returned the wallet when the negative condition is compared to the neutral and positive conditions combined?

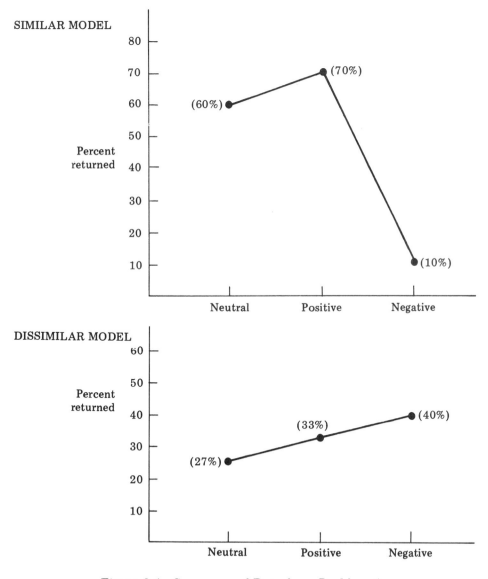

Figure 2.1. Summary of Data from Problem 4.

5.   Helson *et al.* (1958) studied the conditions under which subjects would
     either agree to sign or would refuse to sign: (1) a petition to add flood-
     lights to a fountain at the University of Texas, or (2) a petition to re-
     move all soft-drink dispensing machines from buildings of the University
     of Texas. The authors found that 96 percent of subjects in a control
     group (that is, subjects who were asked to sign the petition but who did
     not see anyone else either sign, or refuse to sign, the petition) agreed to
     sign the first type of petition, while only 14 percent of subjects in a
     control group agreed to sign the second type of petition.
          The subjects in the actual experiment were asked to sign one of these
     petitions under one of two experimental conditions: (1) immediately
     after a background person (actually a confederate of the researchers who
     was asked to sign the petition in view of the subject immediately before
     the subjects were asked to sign the petition) had agreed to sign the
     petition, or (2) immediately after a background person had refused to
     sign the petition. The authors obtained the following results:*

Condition	Agreed to sign the petition	Refused to sign the petition
Floodlights petition		
Background person signs	14	1
Background person refuses to sign	9	21
Control group	28	1
Soft-drink machines petition		
Background person signs	10	20
Background person refuses to sign	0	15
Control group	4	25

These data are also summarized in Figure 2.2.

(a)   For the floodlights petition, did significantly more subjects sign
      the petition when the background person agreed to sign it than
      when he refused to sign it?
(b)   For the soft-drink machines petition, did significantly more sub-
      jects sign the petition when the background person agreed to sign
      it than when he refused to sign it?
(c)   For the floodlights petition, was there a significant difference
      between the control group and the background person signs
      condition?

*This table is adapted from H. Helson, R. Blake, and J. Mouton, "Petition-signing
as Adjustment to Situational and Personal Factors," *Journal of Social Psychology*,
1958, vol. 48, pp. 3-10. Copyright 1958 by The Journal Press. Reprinted by
permission.

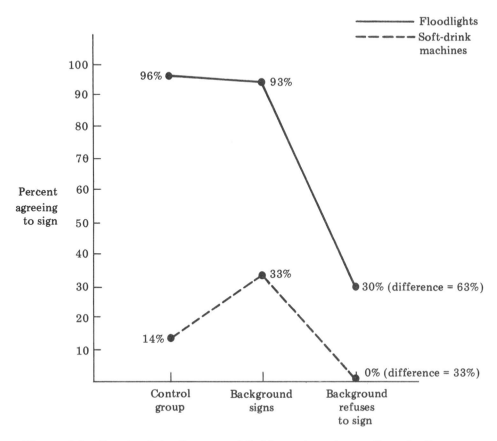

Figure 2.2. Graph of the Percent of Subjects Agreeing to Sign the Petition.

(d)   For the soft-drinks petition, was there a significant difference between the control group and the background person signs condition?

(e)   For the floodlights petition, was there a significant difference between the control group and the background person refuses to sign condition?

(f)   For the soft-drinks petition, was there a significant difference between the control group and the background person refuses to sign condition?

6.   Gewirtz and Baer (1958) studied the social initiations of children during a game after a deprivation condition in which the subjects were socially isolated from verbal approval by an adult for 20 minutes and a non-deprivation condition in which the subjects played the game immediately without waiting. The experimenters recorded the frequency with which the subjects sought social reinforcers (such as attention) from the adult during the game. They summarized their data as follows (p. 169): ". . . 20 out of the 34 subjects exhibited high scale scores after Deprivation, while only 12 of the 34 subjects exhibited such high scale scores after Nondeprivation. . . ."

Was this a significant difference?

Answers for Self-Test for Chapter Two

Compare your answers to the questions on the Self-Test with the answers given below. If all of your answers are correct, you are ready to go on to Chapter Three. If you missed any questions, review the frames indicated in parentheses following the answer. If you missed several questions, you should probably carefully reread the entire Chapter Two.

1.
                                    (Total scores)

		Above average	At or below average
(Author of article)	Joan	5	1
	John	1	4

$$\text{chi-square} = \frac{11 \, (20 - 1)^2}{(6) \, (5) \, (6) \, (5)}$$

$$= \frac{11 \, (19) \, (19)}{(30) \, (30)}$$

$$= \frac{3,971}{900}$$

$$\text{chi-square} = 4.41$$

Since the value for chi-square is larger than 3.84, there is a significant difference between the two groups. Now you have the problem of deciding *in what way* the two groups differed. To determine that, you must interpret the "above average" category correctly. Think back to the way in which each question was scored. If a student selected choice A for each of the six questions, she would have received a total score of 30 points as follows:

Question	Choice A	Number of points
1	Superior competence	5
2	A	5
3	Very rational	5
4	Extremely high status	5
5	Superior effectiveness	5
6	Very much swayed	5

Total score = 30

In contrast, if a student had selected choice E for each of the six questions, each of these questions would have received a score of one point, and her total score would have been 6. Thus, the total scores of the students would have to range between 6 and 30. Scores which were above the median were called "above average" scores. Using this scoring procedure, an above average score would be a "more favorable" judgment of the quality of the journal article than a below average score.

We, therefore, obtained the following result in this study: significantly more women students felt that the article was of higher quality when it was supposedly written by a woman than when it was supposedly written by a man.   (frames 10-11)

2.   For males:

$$\text{chi-square} = \frac{16 \, (36 - 4)^2}{8 \, (8) \, (8) \, (8)}$$

$$= \frac{16 \, (32) \, (32)}{8 \, (8) \, (8) \, (8)}$$

$$= \frac{16,384}{4,096}$$

$$\text{chi-square} = 4.0$$

For females:

$$\text{chi-square} = \frac{28 \, (144 - 4)^2}{14 \, (14) \, (14) \, (14)}$$

$$= \frac{28 \, (140) \, (140)}{14 \, (14) \, (14) \, (14)}$$

$$= \frac{548,800}{38,416}$$

$$\text{chi-square} = 14.29$$

Since both of these chi-square values are greater than 3.84, both tests produced a significant difference. Significantly more firstborns expressed a high need for affiliation in their stories than did later-borns, and this result held for males and for females.   (frames 10-11)

3.

	Received help	Did not receive help
Ill victim	62	3
Drunk victim	19	19

$$\text{chi-square} = \frac{103 (1178 - 57)^2}{65 (38) (81) (22)}$$

$$= \frac{103 (1121) (1121)}{65 (38) (81) (22)}$$

$$= \frac{129,434,023}{4,401,540}$$

$$\text{chi-square} = 29.41$$

Since this value for chi-square is greater than 3.84, there was a significant difference. Significantly more subjects helped the supposedly ill victim than the supposedly drunk victim.   (frames 10-11)

4. (a) Similar model condition:

	Returned the wallet	Did not return the wallet
Neutral or positive feeling	26	14
Negative feeling	2	18

$$\text{chi-square} = \frac{60 (468 - 28)^2}{40 (20) (28) (32)}$$

$$= \frac{60 (440) (440)}{800 (896)}$$

$$= \frac{11,616,000}{716,800}$$

$$\text{chi-square} = 16.21$$

Since the value for chi-square is larger than 3.84, there is a significant difference between the two experimental groups. This result can be summarized as follows: When subjects read a letter written in ordinary English, significantly more subjects returned the wallet when the letter expressed either a neutral or positive feeling toward the kind act than when the letter expressed a negative feeling toward the kind act.

(b) Dissimilar model condition:

	Returned the wallet	Did not return the wallet
Neutral or positive feeling	9	21
Negative feeling	6	9

$$\text{chi-square} = \frac{45 (81 - 126)^2}{30 (15) (15) (30)}$$

$$= \frac{45 (-45) (-45)}{30 (15) (15) (30)}$$

$$= \frac{91,125}{202,500}$$

$$\text{chi-square} = 0.45$$

Since this value for chi-square is less than 3.84, there is no significant difference between the two experimental groups. This result can be summarized as follows: When subjects read a letter written in broken English, there was no significant difference in the number of subjects who returned the wallet when the letter expressed either a neutral or positive feeling toward the kind act or when it expressed a negative feeling toward the kind act.   (frames 10-11)

5. (a) Floodlights petition:

	Agreed to sign the petition	Refused to sign the petition
Background person signs	14	1
Background person refuses to sign	9	21

$$\text{chi-square} = \frac{45 (294 - 9)^2}{15 (30) (23) (22)}$$

$$= \frac{45 (285) (285)}{15 (30) (23) (22)}$$

$$= \frac{3,655,125}{227,700}$$

$$\text{chi-square} = 16.05$$

Since this value for chi-square is larger than 3.84, significantly more subjects agreed to sign the petition when the background person had signed it than when the background person had refused to sign it.

(b)   Soft-drink machines petition:

	Agreed to sign the petition	Refused to sign the petition
Background person signs	10	20
Background person refuses to sign	0	15

$$\text{chi-square} = \frac{45\ (150 - 0)^2}{30\ (15)\ (10)\ (35)}$$

$$= \frac{45\ (150)\ (150)}{30\ (15)\ (10)\ (35)}$$

$$= \frac{1{,}012{,}500}{157{,}500}$$

chi-square =   6.43

Since this value for chi-square is larger than 3.84, significantly more subjects agreed to sign the petition when the background person had signed it than when the background person had refused to sign it.

(c)   Floodlights petition:

	Agreed to sign the petition	Refused to sign the petition
Background person signs	14	1
Control group	28	1

$$\text{chi-square} = \frac{44\ (14 - 28)^2}{15\ (29)\ (42)\ (2)}$$

$$= \frac{44\ (-14)\ (-14)}{15\ (29)\ (42)\ (2)}$$

$$= \frac{8{,}624}{36{,}540}$$

chi-square =   0.24

Since this value for chi-square is less than 3.84, there was no significant difference in the signing behavior of subjects in the control group and in the background person signs group.

(d)   Soft-drink machines petition:

	Agreed to sign the petition	Refused to sign the petition
Background person signs	10	20
Control group	4	25

$$\text{chi-square} = \frac{59\,(250 - 80)^2}{30\,(29)\,(14)\,(45)}$$

$$= \frac{59\,(170)\,(170)}{30\,(29)\,(14)\,(45)}$$

$$= \frac{1{,}705{,}100}{548{,}100}$$

$$\text{chi-square} = 3.11$$

Since this value for chi-square is not larger than 3.84, there was no significant difference in the signing behavior of subjects in the control group and in the background person signs group.

(e)   Floodlights petition:

	Agreed to sign the petition	Refused to sign the petition
Background person refuses to sign	9	21
Control group	28	1

$$\text{chi-square} = \frac{59\,(9 - 588)^2}{30\,(29)\,(37)\,(22)}$$

$$= \frac{59\,(-579)\,(-579)}{30\,(29)\,(37)\,(22)}$$

$$= \frac{19{,}779{,}219}{708{,}180}$$

$$\text{chi-square} = 27.93$$

Since this value for chi-square is larger than 3.84, significantly more subjects in the control group agreed to sign the petition than subjects in the group where the background person refused to sign the petition.

(f)   Soft-drink machines petition:

	Agreed to sign the petition	Refused to sign the petition
Background person refuses to sign	0	15
Control group	4	25

$$\text{chi-square} = \frac{44 \ (0 - 60)^2}{15 \ (29) \ (4) \ (40)}$$

$$= \frac{44 \ (-60) \ (-60)}{15 \ (29) \ (4) \ (40)}$$

$$= \frac{158,400}{69,600}$$

chi-square =   2.28

Since this value for chi-square is less than 3.84, there was no significant difference in signing behavior between the control group and the group in which the background person refused to sign the petition. (frames 10-11)

6.

	High scores for seeking social reinforcement	Low scores for seeking social reinforcement
Deprivation condition	20	14
Nondeprivation condition	12	22

$$\text{chi-square} = \frac{68 \ (440 - 168)^2}{34 \ (34) \ (32) \ (36)}$$

$$= \frac{68 \ (272) \ (272)}{34 \ (34) \ (32) \ (36)}$$

$$= \frac{5,030,912}{1,331,712}$$

chi-square =   3.78

Since this value for chi-square is less than 3.84, there was no significant difference in the social reinforcement scores of subjects in the Depriva-tion condition or in the Nondeprivation condition.   (frames 10-11)

CHAPTER THREE

Impact of an Attractive Model on Advertising Effectiveness

Chapter Three asks you to imagine that you are conducting a research study. You will be asked a series of questions which will require you to think through how you would analyze the data from the study. You do not actually have to do this research study in order to understand the chapter, though you may find it interesting to do so. You will not be asked to compute any statistical tests during this chapter. However, sample data based on this research study will be provided to you as part of the Self-Test for Chapters One through Three, which follows this chapter.

Now that you know how to analyze the data from a research study, let's try something different in this chapter. We'll plan an experiment which you can carry out yourself. This chapter will focus on the mechanics of conducting an experiment—how you would actually carry out an experiment— including its design, the procedures to use in collecting the data, and finally the analysis of the data that you have collected.

The research study we will develop in this chapter is based on a study described by Smith and Engel in a paper presented at the annual meeting of the American Psychological Association in 1968. In that study, the authors showed a photograph of an automobile to adults who lived in a housing development in East Brunswick, New Jersey. Half of the adults were shown a photograph of a medium-priced, two-door, hardtop automobile, while the other half of the adults were shown the identical photograph except that an attractive female model was standing in the foreground of the photograph with the car behind her.

The experimenters asked the subjects to rate the automobile on several characteristics—for example, ease of handling, desire to purchase. The authors were interested in answering the question: "Does sex sell?" Or, in other words, would the car be perceived differently when the model was present than when the model was absent? The results of studies like these are especially valuable to advertising executives who are interested in presenting a portrait of their product in such a way that the product will seem desirable to potential consumers—so desirable, in fact, that the consumer will rush out to purchase the product.

Published research studies of this type are seldom found in psychological journals, due largely, I suspect, to the desire of the companies who pay for this research to keep the results confidential so that the company can obtain maximum benefit from them. After all, if you were vice-president in charge of marketing for General Motors, and you had just spent $100,000 of your company's money for some potentially valuable research projects, would you want your competitors to find out what you had learned without having to invest a cent of their companies' funds?

The hypothetical research study which you will be thinking about in this chapter will consist of the following steps:

(1) *Overview of the experiment*—determining the purpose of the experiment.

(2) *Preparation for data collection*—finding an automobile to photograph, selecting a male and a female model to photograph, taking the photographs, preparing the photographs for use in the experiment, preparing copies of the questionnaire which the subjects will use to rate the photograph which they saw.

(3) *Selection of the subjects for the experiment*—using a table of random numbers, deciding where (in what location) to ask people if they will participate in the research study, preparing a standard invitation to use to ask people if they want to participate in the research study.

(4) *Data collection*—showing a photograph to a subject, having the subject fill out the questionnaire, coding the sex of the subject and the experimental condition which the subject was in.

(5) *Data analysis and interpretation of the results of the experiment*—using the data you have gathered to draw conclusions.

OVERVIEW OF THE EXPERIMENT

Let's plan a research study to test the attitudes of people toward a new automobile in terms of how they would be influenced by the presence of an adult model. The original study by Smith and Engel (1968) contained two experimental conditions: (1) an experimental group who saw a photograph of an automobile with an attractive female model standing to one side of the automobile, and (2) a control group who saw a photograph of an automobile only. If we were to do an exact replica of their study, we would need to use these same two experimental conditions; our study, then, would be an attempt to replicate their findings. (See Chapter One, frame 21, if you need to review the concept of replication.)

But let's *not* replicate their study. If you've been paying attention to television and magazine advertising of automobiles during the past two years, you undoubtedly have noticed a dramatic increase in the use of attractive male models in these advertisements. Famous personalities such as Rex

Harrison, Sergio Franchi, and Ricardo Montalbán are presented to us frequently in an attempt to influence our buying decisions. Instead of comparing the use of a female model to a control group without the model, as Smith and Engel did, let's do a different study. Let's compare the use of a female model to the use of a male model to see if the sex of the model influences a person's opinion of the dimensions that he perceives of the automobile.

PREPARATION FOR DATA COLLECTION

In this research study, we assume that you will be working on a shoestring budget. So, if you choose actually to carry out the experiment, you do not have to buy a brand-new automobile or hire your favorite entertainment personality to work with you on your project. (I'm sure that this will be a great relief to you!) To do this study you will need the following: a medium-priced, latest-model automobile that you can borrow from a friend long enough to take some pictures of it, a tripod (to guarantee that you use the *same* location of the camera for *all* of your photographs), a camera, some color film, an attractive male friend, and an attractive female friend. Once you have rounded up these things and people, you are ready to begin your research study.

Let's imagine that you had decided actually to conduct this research study. Think through the following questions, and write your answer in the space below each question. Take this opportunity to practice the careful thinking that is required to plan successfully a research study.

Can you think of someone you know who has a new car that would be suitable to photograph for this research project, if that person would agree to your photographing the car? If so, write that person's name below.

Think of an attractive male friend whom you would like to use as a model alongside the car in this research study, if he would agree to participate, and write his name below.

Now think of an attractive female friend whom you would like to use as a model alongside the automobile in this research study, if she would agree to participate, and write her name below.

Now think of someone who has a camera and a tripod and who is likely to allow you to borrow these, and write the name of that person below.

You will need to park the car in a place where there is an attractive setting in the background—some trees, a grassy field, a lake, an ocean—or whereever background provides a pleasant surrounding but does not distract the viewer from the automobile itself. Think of an attractive setting in which to photograph the automobile and the models, and describe below exactly where you would position the automobile and the models when you take your photographs.

Next, you would need to set up your camera on a tripod so that you can photograph the automobile from an angle where the car model and the name of the manufacturer are not obvious to the person who sees the photograph.

Now you are ready to shoot two types of photographs: (1) the automobile with an attractive male model in the foreground (the A-M condition), and (2) the automobile with an attractive female model in the foreground (the A-F condition).

The models should each stand in the same spot, and it is probably best if they are just presented in a decorative fashion rather than shown pointing out specific features of the automobile. Both models should be attractively dressed in up-to-date attire, and their dress should be comparable in style. For example, if one model is dressed in formal evening attire, the other should also be dressed in formal evening attire. If one model is dressed casually, the other should be dressed casually too. The people you ask to be models should be attractive, but they don't have to look like Rock Hudson or Ann-Margret! And the models should not be dressed in anything resembling cheesecake outfits. You can get some good ideas for appropriate dress for the models by looking at advertisements in the latest issues of best-selling magazines.

Have the photographs developed, and select the two photographs you want to use for your research study. Be sure they are of comparable quality. Once you have selected your A-M and A-F photographs, you should have them enlarged (8″ x 10″ is a convenient size) and pasted onto a matboard so that the photographs do not bend or become wrinkled.

Your next step is to design the questionnaire which you would ask the subjects to use to give their ratings of the dimensions of the automobile that you want them to rate. To simplify this step, we'll use the questionnaire that is given in Table 3.1. This questionnaire is based on the Smith and Engel study.

*Table 3.1. Rating Scale for Advertising Study**

Directions: For each of these rating scale items, circle a number from 1 to 7
to indicate your perception of the automobile based on the
photograph you were shown.

Question

1.

1	2	3	4	5	6	7
Very unappealing						Very appealing

2.

1	2	3	4	5	6	7
Dull						Lively

3.

1	2	3	4	5	6	7
Not youthful						Youthful

4.

1	2	3	4	5	6	7
Low horsepower						High horsepower

5.

1	2	3	4	5	6	7
Unsafe						Safe

6.

1	2	3	4	5	6	7
Difficult to handle						Easy to handle

7.

1	2	3	4	5	6	7
Would probably not purchase						Would probably purchase

M   F

A-M   A-F

---

*This rating scale is adapted from G. H. Smith and R. Engel, "Influence of a Female
Model on Perceived Characteristics of an Automobile," Proceedings of the 76th annual
convention. Copyright 1968 by the American Psychological Association. Reprinted by
permission.

Note that the coding scheme at the bottom of the questionnaire allows you to code two facts which describe the subject who filled out the questionnaire: (1) the sex of the subject—male (M) or female (F), and (2) the experimental condition the subject was in—automobile with a male model (the A-M condition) or automobile with a female model (the A-F condition). These two facts will become important when you reach the data-analysis phase of your experiment. If you have not coded the experimental condition on the questionnaire, for example, you will have a pile of completed questionnaires with no way to determine which ones belong to the subjects in the A-M condition and which ones belong to the subjects in the A-F condition. If you cannot determine this fact, you will be unable to analyze your data, and your experiment will have been a failure.

SELECTING THE SUBJECTS FOR THE EXPERIMENT

Let's stop a minute and review what we have accomplished so far in Chapter Three. We are thinking through the procedures necessary for conducting a research study to determine if the sex of a model who appears alongside an automobile in a photograph will affect the way a person perceives the dimensions of the automobile—how appealing the automobile was perceived to be; whether it was seen as lively or dull, safe or unsafe, and the like.

We have discussed the procedures for finding an automobile, selecting a male and female model, taking the photographs of the models and the automobile, preparing these photographs to be used in the experiment, and preparing copies of the questionnaire which the subjects would use to rate the photograph on various dimensions of the automobile.

Your next step is to decide on a procedure you would use in selecting the actual subjects who would participate in your experiment. You would need to find some subjects who would participate in your research study without pay (since you are working on a shoestring budget!). You can use your imagination to figure out where to locate your subjects, but some likely places are college campuses, shopping malls, and the sidewalks of the major streets of cities. There need not be an equal number of men and women available to choose from in the site you have selected at which to collect your data. Note also that if you are approaching people in a shopping mall or some similar public place, you would be wise to obtain permission from the management of the mall to do your study in that manner; this foresight may save you some embarrassment if a policeman asks you what you are doing while you are conducting your study!

Where would you go to find the subjects whom you would want to participate in this experiment? Think about this question, and then write your answer below.

Now let's talk about the procedure you will use when you collect the data for your study. You will need to establish a rule in your own mind for selecting subjects from among the people who cross your path. You could simply ask only those people to participate in the study who smile and say hello to you as you are walking toward them, but that would create a bias in your sample in favor of friendly people! To protect yourself against a biased sample, you should select a rule something like the following:

"I will ask a man and a woman alternately if they will participate in my research study. I will select the people in the following way: While walking on this side of the shopping mall, I will mentally create a path 8 feet in width to encompass the people walking toward me. I will ask the tenth person whom I count in that path who appears to be over 18 years of age and of the sex I'm looking for. My selection will be made as I scan visually from left to right within this 8-foot-wide boundary while I am walking. After I ask someone, whether they agree or refuse to act as a subject, I will wait 60 seconds before starting to look for my next subject."

Think about the rule you would use to decide whom to ask to participate in your research study, and write that procedure below.

You will need to develop a standardized "invitation" to each person you ask to participate in your research study. It should be similar to this: "Excuse me. I'm helping with an advertising study, and we are interested in your frank reaction to an advertisement we are working on for a new automobile. Could I show you a photograph of that automobile and ask you to rate that photograph in terms of seven dimensions?"

Think about the standard invitation you would use to ask people to participate in your research study, and write that invitation below.

Not everyone you ask will agree to participate in your research study. Whenever someone refuses to participate, you should continue to ask someone to participate who is of the same sex as the person who just refused, being careful to follow whatever procedure you are using to select subjects for your experiment.

Your final step in this phase of the experiment is to decide *which* of the two photographs you will show to each subject in your experiment. Since you could show each subject either of the two photographs, which one will you show to each subject? This question should really be answered by your using a table of random numbers. We will not disturb the flow of this chapter's discussion by explaining that procedure. The procedure for using a table of random numbers is explained in Appendix A; we recommend that you study Appendix A as a separate assignment after you have finished reading this chapter.

For now, let's suppose that you have already decided which of the two photographs to show to each of the subjects in your experiment, and that you are ready to proceed to the next step in the research study—data collection.

DATA COLLECTION

If the person you approach agrees to participate, you would then show the subject the photograph which corresponds to the experimental condition to which he or she has randomly been assigned (A-M or A-F). Then ask the subject to fill out a questionnaire like the one given in Table 3.1 by making the following request: "Would you please fill out this form by circling the number from 1 to 7 for each of these questions which corresponds to your opinion of the automobile." You would wait while the person filled out the form.

After the person hands the completed form back to you, you would circle at the bottom of that form either the letter M (for male) or the letter F (for female) and one of the sets of letters (A-M or A-F) which corresponds to the type of photograph that subject was shown. Thus you will have a record of the sex of each of your subjects and the experimental condition in which each participated.

DATA ANALYSIS

Let's suppose that you have finished collecting your data and that you are ready to analyze it. Take some time now to write out an answer to the following question: How would you test to see if the subjects who rated the photograph of the automobile with a male model (the A-M condition) differed in their perception of that automobile from the subjects who rated the photograph of the automobile with the female model (the A-F condition)? Take time now to write out *two* possible ways in which you could analyze the data from this experiment.

If you've drawn a blank in trying to answer this question, refresh your memory by going back to Chapter Two, frames 3–7, and review our discussion of the two ways you could analyze the data of the experiment discussed in that chapter before you go on to read the answer below.

If you are able to answer this question now, check your answer against the one given below.

Your answer should be something like this: There are two ways you could use to analyze the data for the experiment:

(1) Add up the rating for each subject on each of the seven items in Table 3.1 to obtain a *total score*; find the median of these total scores, and summarize these total scores in the following table:

		(Total scores)	
		Above the median	At or below the median
(Automobile photograph)	Male model		
	Female model		

If the resulting value for chi-square were greater than 3.84, there would be a significant difference between the two experimental groups in their overall perception of the automobile.

(2) Analyze the data for *each of the seven questions separately* by means of a chi-square test. For example, for question 1, set up the data in a chi-square table like the one below, where the average score is the median score for all of the subjects on that question.

		Question 1	
		Above average in appeal	At or below average in appeal
(Automobile photograph)	Male model		
	Female model		

Although you *could* analyze the data as described in method (1), a more appropriate way is method (2), using *each rating question separately* instead of establishing a single total score. This approach is preferred for two reasons: (a) the seven rating-scale items given in Table 3.1 do not really represent a *unidimensional* scale (see Chapter Two, frame 16, for a review of this concept), and (b) the use of a single total score masks the differences in perception between the two experimental groups on the *specific* rating-scale items that produced a significant difference. You would undoubtedly want to know in what specific ways the subjects' perception of the automobile was enhanced or depressed, and the total scores would not tell you that. Therefore, our recommendation is that you analyze the data following method (2).

A serious methodological flaw in the experiment described in this chapter is that the experimenters who show the photograph to the subjects are not "blind" to the experimental condition to which the subjects have been assigned; that is, since the experimenters know which photograph they are showing to each subject, the experimenters' biases toward the hypotheses of the research study may subtly influence their posture, their tone of voice, their expectancies, and the like, and these influences could affect the outcome of the experiment. One way to correct against some of these biases is to use as experimenters only those individuals who have not been told the hypotheses of the research study.

This chapter also provides a good basis for comment on the need for *replication* of research results (see Chapter One, frame 21) before we can be confident of our research findings. Here we describe an experiment which depends on the skill of one photographer, the type of physical beauty of only two models, the type of automobile chosen, and the subjects who happen to be chosen for the study (the amount of their education, their annual income, their occupations, and the like). If we did find a significant difference between the two experimental groups, we would need to repeat the experiment with different photographers, different models, and different subjects from different geographical locations in order to be confident that our results were not due to the specific photographer, models, or group of subjects who participated in our experiment. If several researchers in different parts of the country replicate the experiment and obtain the same results, then they are all more confident that the results of their research studies can be generalized beyond the particular subjects who participated in the original experiment.

In Smith and Engel's original study, the authors had only two experimental conditions: one was similar to our A-F group, and the other used a photograph of an automobile but without a model present. They found that subjects who saw a photograph of an automobile with a female model in the photograph saw the car as significantly more appealing, more lively, more youthful, less safe, and higher in horsepower. Interestingly enough, the authors found only minor sex differences in their data; the female model influenced women in almost the same way that she influenced men. An additional finding of their study was that in supplementary interviews conducted after the experiment was finished, the male subjects almost uniformly denied being influenced by the female model in the photograph in terms of their opinion of the automobile. (This can be called, facetiously, the "what girl?" phenomenon.) Some of our favorite quotes from these supplementary interviews were these:

"I don't let anything but the thing itself influence my judgments. The other is just propaganda."

"I never let myself be blinded by advertising; the car itself is what counts."

"The car itself. The other is just dressing."

"She could influence me, but not as far as the car is concerned!"

The Self-Test which follows is designed to check your understanding of the main points covered in the first three chapters of this book.

SELF-TEST FOR CHAPTERS ONE THROUGH THREE

This Self-Test is designed to show you whether you have mastered the key concepts and skills in Chapters One through Three. Answer each question to the best of your ability. Correct answers and review instructions are given at the end of the test.

When working on these problems, you might find it helpful to use the tear-out sheet for the chi-square test in Appendix E.

Whenever an article is cited in a problem, you will be working with the actual data of that published article, and you can check your answer against the actual results of that article. Whenever an article is not cited in a problem, we have created some hypothetical data to allow you to practice the skills you have learned.

1. Let's suppose that instead of the three-choice rating-scale items given for the warm-cold experiment in Chapter One frame 1, we decided instead to use seven-point scales for each question. The first three rating-scale items would then look like this:

   1. How would you rate Mr. Irving's knowledge of psychology?

   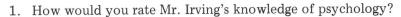

   | 1 | 2 | 3 | 4 | 5 | 6 | 7 |

   Doesn't know his stuff   No opinion   Knows his stuff

   2. How would you rate his consideration of others?

   | 1 | 2 | 3 | 4 | 5 | 6 | 7 |

   Self-centered   No opinion   Considerate of others

   3. Would you expect him to be formal or informal?

   | 1 | 2 | 3 | 4 | 5 | 6 | 7 |

   Informal   No opinion   Formal

   Now suppose that you used these questions to do the warm-cold experiment with a group of 15 college students and collected the following hypothetical data from them:

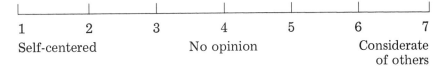

Question	"Warm" group								"Cold" group						
1	6	5	4	6	7	3	6	7	2	3	5	4	3	5	6
2	5	6	4	7	7	5	6	6	3	4	4	5	6	3	2
3	2	3	2	3	3	2	1	4	5	6	7	6	7	5	4

Let's make sure that you are reading this table correctly. For question 1, the eight subjects in the "warm" group gave these ratings, respectively: 6, 5, 4, 6, 7, 3, 6, 7; for question 1, the seven subjects in the "cold" group gave the ratings 2, 3, 5, 4, 3, 5, 6. Now you should use the above table to solve these problems:

(a) Which of the three questions produced a significant difference between the two experimental groups?
(b) For those questions that did produce a significant difference, in what way were the groups significantly different from one another?
(c) Write up the results of this research study.

2. Create a table to report the question number, the value for chi-square, and the significance level for questions 1-3 of problem 1 of this Self-Test.

3. Let's suppose that instead of the five-choice multiple-choice items given for the Joan-John Simpson experiment in Chapter Two, frame 1, we used a nine-point scale for each question. The first three rating-scale items would then look like this:

1. Based on this article, what would you judge Joan R. Simpson's professional competence to be?

| 1 | 2 | 3 | 4 | 5 | 6 | 7 | 8 | 9 |
| Incompetent | | | | Average competence | | | Superior competence | |

2. If you were to assign a grade to Joan R. Simpson's article, what would it be?

| 1 | 2 | 3 | 4 | 5 | 6 | 7 | 8 | 9 |
| Grade of F | | | | Grade of C | | | Grade of A | |

3. In her appeal, Joan R. Simpson was:

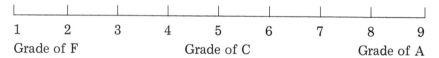

| 1 | 2 | 3 | 4 | 5 | 6 | 7 | 8 | 9 |
| Alarmist | | | | Emotional | | | Very rational | |

Now suppose that you used these three questions to do the Joan-John Simpson experiment with a group of 13 college students and collected the following data:

Question	"Joan" group							"John" group					
1	3	4	5	4	6	5	3	6	7	6	5	7	8
2	4	5	6	5	4	4	4	7	8	8	7	9	6
3	3	5	4	5	6	5	5	6	7	9	8	7	8

(a)   Which of the three questions produced a significant difference between the two experimental groups?
(b)   For those questions that did produce a significant difference, in what way were the groups significantly different from one another?
(c)   Write up the results of this research study.

4.   Let's suppose that you took the photographs required by the advertising experiment described in Chapter Three and collected the following data from fourteen subjects for the first two questions of the rating form given in Table 3.1 on page 95.

Question	Automobile plus male model (A-M group)							Automobile plus female model (A-F group)						
1	4	5	6	6	5	5	5	5	6	7	7	6	6	7
2	5	4	6	5	6	5	4	6	7	6	7	6	7	6

(a)   Did either of these two questions produce a significant difference between the automobile plus male model and the automobile plus female model groups?
(b)   If so, in what way were the groups significantly different from one another?
(c)   Write up the results of this study.

5.   Stanley Schachter wrote a book called *The Psychology of Affiliation* (1959) in which he summarized the results of an experiment related to the need to affiliate with other people. In that study, subjects were told either: (1) that the electric shocks that they were about to receive would be severe (the high-fear condition) or (2) that the electric shocks that they were about to receive would be very mild (the low-fear condition). He then told them that it would be a few minutes before the experiment would begin and gave them three choices for where they would like to wait in the meantime: (1) they could wait together with other subjects who were also waiting for the experiment to begin, (2) they could wait alone, or (3) they didn't care whether they were alone or with other subjects. (Actually, none of the subjects were shocked, and the experiment was over as soon as the subjects answered this question and some other questions; the subjects were then debriefed immediately by the experimenter.) The data produced by this experiment were the following ($N = 62$):

	Together	Alone *or* Don't care
High fear	20	12
Low fear	10	20

(a) Schachter summarized this table (on p. 18 of his book) as follows: "Some 63 percent of subjects in the high-anxiety condition wanted to be together with other subjects while they waited to be shocked. In the low-anxiety condition only 33 percent of the subjects wished to be together." Was there a significant difference between the two experimental groups?

(b) If so, in what way were the two groups significantly different from one another?

(c) Write up the results of this study.

6. Siegel and Siegel (1957) did a study with undergraduate women to find out the relationship between the authoritarianism scores of the women and their living arrangements. The women were divided into two groups: (1) those living in what were formerly sorority houses (the Sorority Row group), and (2) those living in non-sorority houses (the non-Row group). The experimenters summarized the data as follows:

(Authoritarianism test scores)

	Above-average scores	Below-average scores
Sorority Row subjects	166	137
Non-Row subjects	36	65

(a) Was there a significant difference between the two experimental groups on their authoritarianism scores?

(b) If so, in what way were the groups significantly different from one another?

(c) Write up the results of this study.

Answers for Self-Test for Chapters One through Three

Compare your answers to the questions on the Self-Test with the answers given below. If all of your answers are correct, you are ready to go on to Chapter Four. If you missed any questions, review the frames indicated in parentheses following the answer. If you miss several questions which refer to frames in the same chapter, you should probably carefully reread that entire chapter.

1. (a) For question 1, the median of all of the scores for all of the subjects is 5. In the "warm" group, five subjects have scores larger than 5, and three subjects have scores at or less than 5. One subject in the "cold" group has a score larger than 5, and six subjects have scores at or less than 5. Therefore, the chi-square table is:

Question 1

	Above average in knowledge of psychology	At or below average in knowledge of psychology
"Warm" group	5	3
"Cold" group	1	6

$$\text{chi-square} = \frac{15\,(30 - 3)^2}{(8)\,(7)\,(6)\,(9)}$$

$$= \frac{15\,(27)\,(27)}{(8)\,(7)\,(6)\,(9)}$$

$$= \frac{10{,}935}{3{,}024}$$

chi-square = 3.62

For question 2, the median of all the scores for all of the subjects is 5. In the "warm" group, five subjects have scores larger than 5, and three subjects have a score at or less than 5. In the "cold" group, one subject has a score larger than 5, and six subjects have scores at or less than 5.

Question 2

	Above average in consideration of others	At or below average in consideration of others
"Warm" group	5	3
"Cold" group	1	6

$$\text{chi-square} = \frac{15\,(30 - 3)^2}{(8)\,(7)\,(6)\,(9)}$$

$$= \frac{15\,(27)\,(27)}{(8)\,(7)\,(6)\,(9)}$$

$$= \frac{10{,}935}{3{,}024}$$

chi-square = 3.62

For question 3, the median of all the scores is 4. In the "warm" group, no subjects have a score above 4, and eight subjects have scores at or less than 4. In the "cold" group, six subjects have scores above 4, and one subject has a score at or less than 4.

Question 3

	Above average in formality	At or below average in formality
"Warm" group	0	8
"Cold" group	6	1

$$\text{chi-square} = \frac{15\,(0 - 48)^2}{(8)\,(7)\,(6)\,(9)}$$

$$= \frac{15\,(-48)\,(-48)}{(8)\,(7)\,(6)\,(9)}$$

$$= \frac{34{,}560}{3{,}024}$$

chi-square = 11.43

Since a chi-square value larger than 3.84 means that there is a significant difference between the two experimental groups, there is a significant difference for question 3 but not for questions 1 and 2.

(b) For question 3, six subjects in the "cold" group had scores above average, while one subject had a score at or below average; therefore, significantly more subjects in the "cold" group expected Mr. Irving to be formal than did subjects in the "warm" group.

(c) Your answer should be similar to this: Significantly more subjects in the "cold" group expected the guest speaker to be formal than did subjects in the "warm" group. The two experimental groups did not differ significantly in their expectation of the guest speaker's knowledge of psychology or in their opinion of his consideration of others.   (Chapter One, frames 5–8)

2.

Question	Chi-square	Significance level
1	3.62	n.s.
2	3.62	n.s.
3	11.43	$p < .05$

If you did not answer this question correctly, you should review the discussion presented earlier to be sure you understand how to create a table to summarize the results of a research study.   (Chapter One, frame 22)

3.   (a)   For question 1, the median of all the scores is 5. In the "Joan" group, one subject has a score larger than 5, and six subjects have scores at or less than 5. In the "John" group, five subjects have scores larger than 5, and one subject has a score at or less than 5.

Question 1

		Above-average competence	At or below-average competence
(Author of article)	Joan	1	6
	John	5	1

$$\text{chi-square} = \frac{13\,(1-30)^2}{7\,(6)\,(6)\,(7)}$$

$$= \frac{13\,(-29)\,(-29)}{7\,(6)\,(6)\,(7)}$$

$$= \frac{10{,}933}{1{,}764}$$

chi-square = 6.20

For question 2, the median of the scores of the subjects is 6. In the "Joan" group, no subjects have scores larger than 6, and seven subjects have scores at or less than 6. In the "John" group, five subjects have scores larger than 6, and one subject has a score at or less than 6.

Question 2

		Above-average grade	At or below-average grade
(Author of article)	Joan	0	7
	John	5	1

$$\text{chi-square} = \frac{13\,(0-35)^2}{(7)\,(6)\,(5)\,(8)}$$

$$= \frac{13\,(-35)\,(-35)}{(7)\,(6)\,(5)\,(8)}$$

$$= \frac{15{,}925}{1{,}680}$$

chi-square = 9.48

For question 3, the median of the scores is 6. No subjects in the "Joan" group had a score above 6, while seven subjects had scores at or less than 6. Five subjects in the "John" group had scores above 6, while one subject had a score at or less than 6.

Question 3

	Above-average in rationality	At or below-average in rationality
Joan	0	7
John	5	1

(Author of article)

$$\text{chi-square} = \frac{13\,(0 - 35)^2}{(7)\,(6)\,(5)\,(8)}$$

$$= \frac{13\,(-35)\,(-35)}{(7)\,(6)\,(5)\,(8)}$$

$$= \frac{15,925}{1,680}$$

$$\text{chi-square} = 9.48$$

Since the chi-square values for all three questions are larger than 3.84, all three questions produced a significant difference between the two experimental groups.

(b) For question 1, five subjects in the "John" group had above-average scores, while one subject had a score at or below average; therefore, significantly more subjects in the "John" group thought the male author to be competent than did subjects in the "Joan" group.

For question 2, five subjects in the "John" group had assigned an above-average grade, while one subject in this group had assigned a grade at or below average; therefore, significantly more subjects in the "John" group assigned a higher grade to the article than did subjects in the "Joan" group.

For question 3, five subjects in the "John" group had above-average scores in their ratings of the rationality of the article, while one subject in this group had a score at or below average; therefore, significantly more subjects in the "John" group thought the appeal of the author was rational than did subjects in the "Joan" group.

(c) Your answer should be similar to this: Significantly more subjects who thought that the article was written by a male thought that the author was competent, assigned a higher grade to the article, and thought that the appeal of the author was more rational than did subjects who thought that the article was written by a female. (Chapter One, frames 5–8)

4.   (a)   For question 1, the median of all the scores for the automobile plus male model group (A-M) and the automobile plus female model group (A-F) is 6. In the A-M group no subjects have scores larger than 6, and seven subjects have scores at or less than 6. In the A-F group three subjects have scores larger than 6 and four subjects have scores at or less than 6.

Question 1

	Above-average appeal	At or below-average appeal
A-M group	0	7
A-F group	3	4

$$\text{chi-square} = \frac{14\,(0-21)^2}{(7)\,(7)\,(3)\,(11)}$$

$$= \frac{14\,(-21)\,(-21)}{(7)\,(7)\,(3)\,(11)}$$

$$= \frac{6{,}174}{1{,}617}$$

$$\text{chi-square} = 3.82$$

For question 2, the median of all the scores is 6. In the A-M group, no subjects have scores larger than 6, and seven subjects have scores at or less than 6. In the A-F group, three subjects have scores larger than 6, and four subjects have scores at or less than 6.

Question 2

	Above-average liveliness	At or below-average liveliness
A-M group	0	7
A-F group	3	4

$$\text{chi-square} = \frac{14\,(0-21)^2}{(7)\,(7)\,(3)\,(11)}$$

$$= \frac{14\,(-21)\,(-21)}{(7)\,(7)\,(3)\,(11)}$$

$$= \frac{6{,}174}{1{,}617}$$

$$\text{chi-square} = 3.82$$

(b)   Since the chi-square value for both questions was less than 3.84, both questions failed to produce a significant difference between the A-M and the A-F groups.

(c)   There were no significant differences between subjects who were shown a photograph of an automobile with a female model in the foreground and subjects who were shown a photograph of the same automobile but with a male model in the foreground in their ratings of the automobile's appeal or liveliness, although both questions came close to producing a significant difference between these two experimental groups.   (Chapter One, frames 5–8)

5.   (a)

	Together	Alone or don't care
High fear	20	12
Low fear	10	20

$$\text{chi-square} = \frac{62\,(400 - 120)^2}{32\,(30)\,(30)\,(32)}$$

$$= \frac{62\,(280)\,(280)}{32\,(30)\,(30)\,(32)}$$

$$= \frac{4{,}860{,}800}{921{,}600}$$

$$\text{chi-square} = 5.27$$

(b)   Since this value for chi-square is larger than 3.84, there was a significant difference between the two experimental groups. Since 20 subjects in the high-fear group preferred to wait together while 12 subjects in this group either preferred to wait alone or did not care whether they waited alone or with others, significantly more subjects in the high-fear group preferred to wait together than subjects in the low-fear group.

(c)   When subjects were given a choice to wait alone or with other subjects who were also supposedly waiting to participate in an experiment that dealt with electric shock, significantly more subjects who were told that the shocks would be severe preferred to wait with other subjects than did subjects who were told that the shocks would be mild.   (Chapter One, frames 5–8)

6.　(a)

	(Authoritarianism test scores)	
	Above-average scores	Below-average scores
Sorority Row subjects	166	137
Non-Row subjects	36	65

$$\text{chi-square} = \frac{404 \, (10{,}790 - 4932)^2}{303 \, (101) \, (202) \, (202)}$$

$$= \frac{404 \, (5{,}858) \, (5{,}858)}{303 \, (101) \, (202) \, (202)}$$

$$= \frac{13{,}863{,}730{,}256}{1{,}248{,}724{,}812}$$

chi-square = 11.10

(b)　Since this value for chi-square is larger than 3.84, there was a significant difference between the two experimental groups. Since 166 of the 303 subjects who lived in the Sorority Row houses had above-average scores, while only 36 of the 101 subjects who did not live in these houses had above-average scores, significantly more subjects who lived in the Sorority Row houses had above-average scores on a test of authoritarianism than subjects who did not live in the Row houses.

(c)　Significantly more subjects who lived in the Sorority Row houses scored above average on a test of authoritarianism than subjects who did not live in the Row houses.　　(Chapter One, frames 5–8)

PART TWO

The Use of the *t*-Test in Psychological Research

Part II of this book focuses on how the *t*-test for independent samples can be used to analyze the data collected as part of various psychological experiments. Once again we will teach you how to use this test by taking you step-by-step through a series of experiments—from data collection to analysis of the data to interpretation of the results in terms of the experimental design and hypotheses of the study to the writing up of the results of the study.

Chapter Four focuses on the effect of social identity on achievement. It will introduce you to the types of experiments for which the data can be analyzed using the *t*-test. Chapter Five goes more deeply into the analysis of two experiments: one dealing with perception of the prestige and desirability of the occupation of accountant; the other dealing with first impressions of people. Chapter Six again focuses on a single experiment—the effectiveness of an advertisement based on the perceived expertness of the communicator. It stresses the process of actually conducting an experiment, giving you an experiment that you can do yourself.

By the time you complete Part II, you should have a good sense of how to apply the *t*-test to the data from a psychological experiment to determine the results of the experiment. You should also have made good progress in developing the skill of setting up and conducting simple research studies based on the ones which you have read in this book. When you finish Part II, you should be able to read simple research studies which have been published in psychological journals that have used the *t*-test, to perform the *t*-test on the data presented in the articles, to write up the results of your data analysis, and to compare your results with the author's conclusions.

Each of these chapters will include a Self-Test so that you can check your progress in terms of the following objectives.

Objectives

After completing Part II, you will be able to:

- compute the mean score and the standard deviation for a group of subjects.
- apply correctly the *t*-test for independent samples to determine if there was a significant difference between the responses of two groups of people.
- interpret correctly the results of an experiment by referring to the mean scores of the two groups of subjects to determine in what way the two groups were significantly different.
- summarize accurately, in writing, the results of a psychological experiment.
- apply the *t*-test for independent samples to actual data given in published psychological research studies to determine if your use of that statistical test produced the same conclusions and interpretations as those of the study's author.

CHAPTER FOUR

The Effect of Social Identity on Achievement

1.   Imagine for this chapter that you are a student in a course in educational psychology. Your professor has walked into class and announced that he will give a lecture on some important statistics in education and then will give a short quiz to assess the effectiveness of the lecture. He announces that he will hand out a set of instructions for the lecture to each member of the class so that the instructions will be clearly understood. A half-sheet of paper with some instructions on it is then handed to each member of the class, and your instructions read as follows:

> *Directions:* This is an experiment to determine the effect of a lecture on learning. At the end of the lecture, there will be a test. This test will not in any way affect your grade. The lecture is on some statistics related to educational practice; please try to listen.

After you have read these instructions, your professor launches into a 20-minute lecture which is packed with information about some important statistics in education: the number of school districts in the United States and their trend over the past 20 years; the number of teachers at the elementary- and secondary-school level; the percentage of male and female teachers in elementary and secondary schools; the average salaries of teachers in the elementary and secondary schools; the amount of education of elementary and secondary schoolteachers; the number of pupils enrolled in public and private elementary and secondary schools; the percentage of our gross national product spent each year on education by federal, state, and local authorities; the percentage of college-age population that are enrolled in college; the percentage of high-school graduates who enter a degree-credit program in a college or university; and many more facts. When he is finished, he says:

> What I tried to do today is summarize for you some of the important statistics in education that are found in the *Digest of Educational Statistics.* Let's see how effective this lecture was by having you answer this quiz.

He then hands out the quiz given in Table 4.1,* and you answer as best you can the eight questions given on that quiz. After you have answered these questions, your professor puts the answer key on the board, asks the students to score their own quizzes and to put the number of questions which they answered correctly at the top right-hand corner of their quizzes. When everyone is through, he says: "Now let's try to find out what happened during the lecture." He asks the person sitting next to you: "Would you please read aloud the instructions which you were given at the beginning of this lecture?" Your neighbor then reads the following instructions aloud:

> *Directions:* This is an experiment to determine the effect of a lecture on learning. At the end of the lecture, there will be a test. This test will not in any way affect your grade. The lecture is on some statistics related to educational practice; please try to listen as if you were an "A" student.

The class is buzzing now as several people are saying: "Those aren't the instructions I was given." Your professor asks you to read aloud the directions that you were given, and you do so. He then explains:

> Today we have tried to simulate a study done by Cullen (1973) in which he gave differing instructions to an experimental group and a control group of students. The experimental group was told to listen to the lecture as if they were "A" students. The control group was given identical instructions, except that they were not told to act like "A" students. Half of you in this class received the instructions given to the experimental group, and half of you received instructions given to the control group in Cullen's study.
>
> Cullen's hypothesis was that the experimental group would score significantly higher than the control group on a quiz given at the end of the lecture, and his results supported his hypothesis. He reasoned that if a student took on the social identity of an excellent student during a lecture, that student would be more highly motivated to do well on a task relevant to that social identity—namely, the quiz at the end of the lecture. In short, what you believe to be true about yourself, even when you are merely playing a role, can affect your behavior in important ways.
>
> Now, let's find out if our results are similar to the results obtained in Cullen's study. Would those of you who were told to act like an "A" student please write your scores on this blackboard, and those of you in the control group please write your scores on that blackboard?

The members of the class go up to the blackboard and write their scores on the board. The resulting (hypothetical) scores are shown in Table 4.2.

---

*I created this quiz for use in my educational psychology class when performing this experiment.

Table 4.1.   A Digest of Educational Statistics

_____ 1. How many students are there in the schools in America?
     A.   30 million
     B.   40 million
     C.   50 million
     D.   60 million

_____ 2. What amount of America's gross national product will be spent this school year on education by federal, state, and local authorities?
     A.   70 billion dollars
     B.   85 billion dollars
     C.   100 billion dollars
     D.   110 billion dollars

_____ 3. Approximately what percentage of the college-age (ages 18-24) population in this country are enrolled in college?
     A.   25%
     B.   35%
     C.   50%
     D.   60%

_____ 4. Approximately what percentage of the 210 million people in America are directly involved in the educational process?
     A.   10%
     B.   20%
     C.   30%
     D.   40%

_____ 5. What percentage of the elementary schoolteachers in America are female?
     A.   15%
     B.   40%
     C.   55%
     D.   85%

_____ 6. What percentage of the secondary schoolteachers in America are male?
     A.   30%
     B.   40%
     C.   55%
     D.   70%

_____ 7. Approximately how many public school districts are there in the United States?
     A.   10,000
     B.   13,000
     C.   18,000
     D.   21,000
     E.   24,000

_____ 8. Approximately what percentage of recent high-school graduates enter a degree-credit program in a college or univeristy?
     A.   25%
     B.   35%
     C.   50%
     D.   60%

Table 4.2.   *Hypothetical Test Scores of Experimental and Control Groups*

Experimental Group ("A" Student Role)	Control Group
7	6
8	5
6	4
5	2
7	6
8	4
5	3
7	4
7	5
	6

We could use the chi-square test to analyze these data, finding the median score for the experimental and control groups combined, and then counting the number of subjects who were either above or at or below this average to create the following table:

	Above-average scores	At or below-average scores
Experimental group		
Control group		

That type of analysis would be quite proper. However, instead let's learn to use another statistical test: the *t-test for independent samples.*

Sometimes the data from a psychological experiment are only in the form of categories. For example, the performance of a group of trainees can be summarized in two categories: pass or fail. However, sometimes the data are in the form of scores which can differ by a single point or only a few points. "The number of multiple-choice questions answered correctly on a final exam" would be an example of scores which can differ by a single point, while Scholastic Aptitude Test (SAT) scores typically differ by ten points (for example, 580, 590, 600).

Whenever the data do take the form of scores which can differ by a single point or only a few points, you could find the median score, create two categories for the scores (above average or below average), then analyze the data using the chi-square test based on these categories. The main difficulty with the chi-square test in such a case is that it ignores *how far* a score is above or below the median score. A score one point above the median and a score 100 points above are both in the "above-average" category. Such categorizing, then, ignores some important information—the value of the actual scores themselves. (We will have more to say about this important point in frame 31.) For now, we need a statistical test that uses the *value* of each score in the test itself without translating the score into a category. Fortunately, the *t*-test for independent samples, which is widely used in psychological research and which you will learn how to use in this chapter, does just that.

Whenever we use the *t*-test for independent samples, we are trying to answer these two questions: (1) Was there a significant difference between the two groups in the research study? and (2) if so, in what way were these two groups significantly different from one another? The *t*-test requires that no subject be in both of the two groups as given in the following rule:

Rule: The *t*-test for independent samples requires that no subject
be in both groups.

To use the formula for the *t*-test for independent samples, we need to be able to compute the following statistics:

(1)   The *mean* score of each of the two groups of subjects,
(2)   The *standard deviation* of each of the two groups of subjects, and
(3)   The *difference between the means* of the two groups of subjects.

Let's start by computing the *mean score* of each of the two groups of subjects. The mean score of a group of scores is a type of average score; it equals the sum of the scores divided by the number of subjects in that group. Notice that in Table 4.2 there are nine subjects in the experimental group and ten subjects in the control group. Try using the above definition of the mean score to answer the following question:

What is the mean score for the experimental group?

— — — — — — — — — — — — — — — —

The mean score for the experimental group is 7 + 8 + 6 + . . . + 7 + 7 divided by 9, or 60 ÷ 9 = 6.67.

2.   What is the mean score for the control group?

— — — — — — — — — — — — — — — —

The mean score for the control group is 6 + 5 + 4 + . . . + 5 + 6 divided by 10, or 45 ÷ 10 = 4.5.

3.   So far so good. To compute the mean scores for two groups of subjects is a simple process. Computing the standard deviation for each group is a little more complicated, but we can make it easy by following these six steps:

Step 1.   Square each score in the group.

Step 2.   Find the sum of these squared scores.
Step 3.   Divide this sum by the number of subjects in this group.
Step 4.   Square the mean score of this group.
Step 5.   Subtract the answer obtained in Step 4 from the answer obtained in step 3.
Step 6.   Take the square root of this answer.*

As you'll see, this is not difficult. (The arithmetic can be time-consuming. If you have access to a calculator, use it!) Let's apply these steps to find the *standard deviation* of the experimental group given in Table 4.2.

Let's go through the process of computing the standard deviation of the experimental group in Table 4.2 step by step. Square each score in the experimental group (Step 1), and then check your answers against the ones given below.

_ _ _ _ _ _ _ _ _ _ _ _ _ _ _ _

Step 1.   Square each score in the group. (Remember: to square a score, multiply it by itself.)

$$7^2 = 49$$
$$8^2 = 64$$
$$6^2 = 36$$
$$5^2 = 25$$
$$7^2 = 49$$
$$8^2 = 64$$
$$5^2 = 25$$
$$7^2 = 49$$
$$7^2 = 49$$

4.   Now find the sum of these squared scores (Step 2).

_ _ _ _ _ _ _ _ _ _ _ _ _ _ _

Step 2.   Find the sum of these squared scores.

$$49 + 64 + 36 + \ldots + 49 + 49 = 410$$

5.   Now divide this sum of the squared scores by the number of subjects in the experimental group (Step 3).

_ _ _ _ _ _ _ _ _ _ _ _ _ _ _

---

*If you need to review the procedure for taking the square root of a number, you can refer to Appendix B for an explanation of this procedure.

Step 3:   Divide this sum by the number of subjects in the group.

$$\frac{410}{9} = 45.56$$

6.   Next square the mean score of the experimental group (Step 4).

_ _ _ _ _ _ _ _ _ _ _ _ _ _ _ _ _ _

Step 4:   Square the mean score of this group.

$$6.67^2 = 44.49$$

7.   Now subtract the answer obtained in Step 4 from the answer you obtained in step 3 (the resulting answer is Step 5).

_ _ _ _ _ _ _ _ _ _ _ _ _ _ _ _ _ _

Step 5:   Subtract this squared mean score (found in Step 4) from the answer obtained by Step 3.

$$45.56 - 44.49 = 1.07$$

8.   Finally, find the square root of this answer (Step 6).

_ _ _ _ _ _ _ _ _ _ _ _ _ _ _ _ _

Step 6.   Take the square root of this answer.

$$\sqrt{1.07} = 1.03$$

Thus the standard deviation for the experimental group is 1.03.

9.   We have just calculated the standard deviation of the scores in the experimental group. To determine how closely together a set of scores is grouped, we found the mean and then measured how far each score deviates from this score. The *standard deviation* is an average of the deviations of each score from the mean. When the standard deviation is relatively small, it means that the scores are grouped fairly close together; when the standard deviation is relatively large, it means that the scores are spread out more and cover a wider range of score values.

In mathematical terms, the six steps for finding the standard deviation can be summarized by the following formula:

$$\text{s.d.} = \sqrt{\frac{\Sigma X^2}{N} - \bar{X}^2}$$

Where

s.d. = standard deviation

ΣX^2 = the sum of the squares of the scores of that group (Σ is the symbol for the sum of a set of scores; it is the Greek symbol *sigma*)

N = the number of scores in that group

$\bar{X}$ = the mean of the scores of that group (read "X bar")

$\bar{X}^2$ = the square of the mean of the scores of that group

Now try the whole procedure on your own. Compute the standard deviation of the *control group* of Table 4.2.

— — — — — — — — — — — — — — — — —

You should have obtained the following calculations:

Step 1. $6^2 = 36$
$5^2 = 25$
$4^2 = 16$
$2^2 = 4$
$6^2 = 36$
$4^2 = 16$
$3^2 = 9$
$4^2 = 16$
$5^2 = 25$
$6^2 = 36$

Step 2. $36 + 25 + 16 + \ldots + 25 + 36 = 219$

Step 3. $\dfrac{219}{10} = 21.9$

Step 4. $4.5^2 = 20.25$

Step 5. $21.9 - 20.25 = 1.65$

Step 6. $\sqrt{1.65} = 1.28$

Thus, the standard deviation of the control group is 1.28.

10. Let's summarize the computations thus far based on Table 4.2:

(a)   The nine subjects in the experimental group have a mean of 6.67 and a standard deviation of 1.03, and

(b)   The ten subjects in the control group have a mean of 4.5 and a standard deviation of 1.28.

We need to use this information to compute a value for the t-test. The formula for computing the t-test will use values based on the following definitions:

$$n_1 = \text{the number of subjects in the experimental group}$$

$$n_2 = \text{the number of subjects in the control group}$$

$$\frac{1}{n_1} + \frac{1}{n_2} = (1 \text{ divided by } n_1) \text{ plus } (1 \text{ divided by } n_2)$$

$$\bar{X}_1 = \text{the mean score of the subjects in the experimental group}$$

$$\bar{X}_2 = \text{the mean score of the subjects in the control group}$$

$\bar{X}_1 - \bar{X}_2 = $ the difference between the mean scores of the experimental group and the control group

$\text{s.d.}_1 = $ the standard deviation of the subjects in the experimental group

$\text{s.d.}_1{}^2 = $ the square of the standard deviation of the subjects in the experimental group

$\text{s.d.}_2 = $ the standard deviation of the subjects in the control group

$\text{s.d.}_2{}^2 = $ the square of the standard deviation of the subjects in the control group

Use the above definitions to fill in the values indicated below; then check your answers against ours.

$$n_1 =$$

$$n_2 =$$

$$\frac{1}{n_1} + \frac{1}{n_2} =$$

$$\bar{X}_1 =$$

$$\bar{X}_2 =$$

$$\bar{X}_1 - \bar{X}_2 =$$

$$\text{s.d.}_1 \ =$$

$$\text{s.d.}_1{}^2 \ =$$

$$\text{s.d.}_2 \ =$$

$$\text{s.d.}_2{}^2 \ =$$

$$n_1 \ = \ 9$$

$$n_2 \ = \ 10$$

$$\frac{1}{n_1} + \frac{1}{n_2} \ = \ \frac{1}{9} + \frac{1}{10} = 0.11 + 0.10 = 0.21$$

$$\bar{X}_1 \ = \ 6.67$$

$$\bar{X}_2 \ = \ 4.5$$

$$\bar{X}_1 - \bar{X}_2 \ = \ 6.67 - 4.5 = 2.17$$

$$\text{s.d.}_1 \ = \ 1.03$$

$$\text{s.d.}_1{}^2 \ = \ 1.06$$

$$\text{s.d.}_2 \ = \ 1.28$$

$$\text{s.d.}_2{}^2 \ = \ 1.64$$

11. If you have made it this far, you are ready for the big plunge. The formula for the t-test for independent samples is this:

$$t = \frac{\bar{X}_1 - \bar{X}_2}{\sqrt{\dfrac{(n_1)\,(\text{s.d.}_1)^2 \ + \ (n_2)\,(\text{s.d.}_2)^2}{n_1 \ + \ n_2 \ - \ 2} \left(\dfrac{1}{n_1} + \dfrac{1}{n_2}\right)}}\,.$$

That formula looks a lot more imposing at first glance than it will once you have had some practice using it. You've already found all the values you need to use it. Substitute the values from frame 10 into this formula; then check your answer for t against ours below.

$$t = \frac{2.17}{\sqrt{\frac{9\,(1.06) + 10\,(1.64)}{9 + 10 - 2}}\,(0.21)}\,.$$

$$= \frac{2.17}{\sqrt{\frac{9.54 + 16.4}{17}}\,(0.21)}\,.$$

$$= \frac{2.17}{\sqrt{\frac{25.94}{17}}\,(0.21)}\,.$$

$$= \frac{2.17}{\sqrt{(1.53)\,(0.21)}}\,.$$

$$= \frac{2.17}{\sqrt{0.32}}\,.$$

$$= \frac{2.17}{0.57}$$

$$t = 3.81$$

12. Congratulations! We did it! Right now, however, you are probably asking yourself: "What did we do? What have we accomplished?" Those are excellent questions and they deserve a straightforward answer. We have been trying to use a t-test for independent samples to answer the following two questions:

(1) *Was there* a significant difference between the experimental group and the control group in the test score data given in Table 4.2?
(2) If so, *in what way* were these two groups significantly different from one another?

To answer the first of these two questions, we need the following decision rule:

Rule: If the value obtained for t is larger than the value for t associated with $n_1 + n_2 - 2$ in Appendix D, there *is* a significant difference between the scores of the experimental group and the control group.

See if you can apply this rule now. Turn to Appendix D. How large must the value for t be in order for there to be a significant difference between these two groups?

__ __ __ __ __ __ __ __ __ __ __ __ __ __

Since $n_1 + n_2 - 2$ for this problem equals $9 + 10 - 2 = 17$, we note from Appendix D that the obtained value for t must be greater than 2.11 in order for there to be a significant difference between the two experimental groups.

13. Now that you know how large t would have to be in order for us to say there was a significant difference between these two groups, was there a significant difference?

———————————————————

Yes. Since the value of t which we obtained was 3.81, and since that value is larger than 2.11, the experimental group and the control group *did* differ significantly in their test performance after the lecture on educational statistics.

14. Now to the second question: *In what way* were the two groups significantly different from one another? The answer to that question is delightfully simple. You have only to look at the mean scores for the experimental group and the control group. Remembering that the scores represent the number of questions answered *correctly* on the quiz, the experimental group answered an average of 6.67 questions correctly, while the control group answered an average of 4.5 questions correctly; thus, the experimental group answered more questions correctly on the average than the control group. Since our value for t of 3.81 represents a significant difference, we can summarize our research study as follows: Subjects in an experimental group who were instructed to listen to a lecture as if they were an "A" student scored significantly higher on a test given immediately following the lecture than a control group of subjects who were not asked to assume the social identity of an "A" student during the lecture.

These results from our hypothetical research study are similar to the result found by Cullen (1973). These results also provide a good opportunity to point out the logic contained in any statement of the *direction* of a significant difference between two groups of subjects. Instead of recording the number of correct responses for each subject, Cullen chose instead to record the number of errors which each subject made. He then found that the experimental group which was instructed to listen to the lecture as if they were "A" students had significantly fewer errors than a control group which was not asked to assume the social identity of an "A" student during the lecture. You should note that the following two statements in the social identity study discussed in this chapter are *logically identical:*

    (1)   The experimental group answered significantly more questions correctly on the test than the control group.

    (2)   The experimental group made significantly fewer errors on the test than the control group.

If you are aware of the logical equivalence of statements such as these, you will be better able to understand the results of published research studies that you read. This example also points out the necessity of your remembering exactly how you set up your data when you are trying to interpret the meaning of the results of your own research studies.

Let's see if you can identify which statements are logically identical. Suppose that you gave a reading test to an experimental group and a control group and found by using the *t*-test that there was a significant difference between their scores ($p < .05$) based on the number of test questions which they answered correctly. The experimental group answered an average of 23 questions correctly, while the control group answered an average of 27 questions correctly. Which of the following statements is logically identical to this result?

A.   The experimental group made significantly fewer errors on the reading test than the control group.
B.   The control group made significantly fewer errors on the reading test than the experimental group.

B. Since the control group had a mean score of 27, while the experimental group had a mean score of 23, the control group scored significantly higher on the reading test than the experimental group. If the control group scored significantly higher in terms of the number of test questions answered correctly, then they also must have made fewer errors on the test.

15. Notice that we summarized the results of a research study differently when we used the chi-square test than when we used the *t*-test. When we used the chi-square test to analyze the data, we always wrote up the results in the following way: "*Significantly more subjects* in Group 1 had above average scores on the test than the subjects in Group 2."* In contrast, when we used the *t*-test for independent samples to analyze the data, we summarized the results in the following way: "Group 1 *scored significantly higher* than Group 2 on . . . ."

The two summaries differ because of the different types of data used in the two statistical tests. The chi-square test is based on the *number of subjects* in each of the two groups being compared on some characteristic; note that the chi-square test does not take into account *how far* above or *how far* below the median a subject's score actually is. However, the *t*-test is based on the *actual scores* of the subjects which are used to compute the means and the standard deviations of the two groups being compared. Since these two tests treat the data for the subjects differently, we reflect this difference in how we summarize the results of the research studies in this book.

---

*Another way to state this would be: "Subjects in Group 1 had above average scores on the test *significantly more often* than subjects in Group 2."

Now let's see if you can summarize the results of a research study correctly. Write out the results of the following research study based on the chi-square test applied to a spelling test:

	Above average	Below average
Group 1	18	6
Group 2	1	9

chi-square = 12.10

Since the value for chi-square is greater than 3.84, significantly more subjects in Group 1 had above average scores on the spelling test than the subjects in Group 2.

16. Now write out the results of the following research study based on the *t*-test applied to a mathematics test:

Group	N	$\bar{X}$	s.d.	t
Group 1	5	3.20	0.75	3.59*
Group 2	6	4.67	0.45	

*$p < .05$

Since Group 2 had a mean score of 4.67, while Group 1 had a mean score of 3.20, Group 2 scored significantly higher than Group 1 on the mathematics test.

17. You will find the *t*-test for independent samples used a great deal in your reading of published articles dealing with psychological research. Let's look at some more examples.

Suppose that you are hired as a research assistant by another professor who is teaching a course in social psychology. This professor has heard about the successful experiment on social identity conducted with your educational psychology class, and he wants to know if he can replicate the findings in his course. He hands out the same two sets of directions to his students, gives a lecture on some topic, has the students answer a short quiz at the end of the lecture, and then turns the answer sheets over to you. You find that the seven subjects in the experimental group (those subjects instructed to act like "A" students during the lecture) had a mean score of 6.3 and a standard deviation of 0.95; you also determine that the seven subjects in the control group had a mean score of 5.0 and a standard deviation of 1.05.

Here again are the two questions we want to answer:

(a) Was there a significant difference between the experimental and control groups?*

(b) If so, *in what way* were these two groups significantly different from one another?

First, answer question (a).

_ _ _ _ _ _ _ _ _ _ _ _ _ _ _ _

Since $n_1 + n_2 - 2$ for this problem equals $7 + 7 - 2 = 12$, we note from Appendix D that the obtained value for t must be greater than 2.18 in order for there to be a significant difference between the two experimental groups.

(a)

$$t = \frac{\bar{X}_1 - \bar{X}_2}{\sqrt{\frac{(n_1)(s.d._1)^2 + (n_2)(s.d._2)^2}{n_1 + n_2 - 2}\left(\frac{1}{n_1} + \frac{1}{n_2}\right)}}$$

$$= \frac{6.3 - 5.0}{\sqrt{\frac{7(0.95)^2 + 7(1.05)^2}{7 + 7 - 2}\left(\frac{1}{7} + \frac{1}{7}\right)}}$$

$$= \frac{1.3}{\sqrt{\frac{6.32 + 7.72}{12}(0.28)}}$$

$$= \frac{1.3}{\sqrt{\frac{14.04}{12}(0.28)}}$$

$$= \frac{1.3}{\sqrt{1.17(0.28)}}$$

$$= \frac{1.3}{\sqrt{.33}}$$

_____

*When working on problems which require you to use the formula for the *t*-test, you will find it helpful to use the tear-out sheet in Appendix E. With this tear-out sheet you won't have to memorize the formula or to locate it again each time you need it.

$$= \frac{1.3}{0.58}$$

$$t = 2.24$$

Since this value for t is larger than 2.18, there is a significant difference between the experimental group and the control group.

18. Now that we know that there was a significant difference between these two groups, answer question (b).

——————————————————

The mean for the experimental group was 6.3 questions answered correctly, while the mean for the control group was 5.0 questions answered correctly. Therefore, the experimental group answered significantly more questions correctly than the control group.

When you write up your summary this time, avoid terms like "experimental group," "control group," "Group 1," or "Group 2." Such terms are certainly acceptable and you will often find statements like: "Group 1 scored significantly higher on the achievement test than Group 2," or "The experimental group performed significantly better on the posttest than the control group" in your reading of published research articles. However, there are two reasons for avoiding them: (1) When you use these terms, you force the reader to recall your definitions of these terms as they apply to your particular research study. This task is frequently difficult for the reader. (2) When you use terms like these, *you* may become confused about the definitions of these terms (as unlikely as that sounds) and end up summarizing the results of your research study in a way which is not true from the data. Such mistakes have occurred! So in general we recommend that you spell out in detail the results *exactly* as they apply to the particular experimental and control groups that you have used. This will also make it easier for readers to understand the results of your study.

We have used both of these ways in summarizing the results of research studies in this book so that you could obtain experience in reading both kinds of summaries. You will come across both types of summaries in your reading of published journal articles, and you will, therefore, need to be able to understand both of these types of summaries.

19. Now try writing up the results of this experiment without using the terms *experimental group* or *control group*.

——————————————————

Your summary should read something like: Students who were instructed to act like "A" students during a lecture scored significantly higher on a quiz given at the end of the lecture than students who were not instructed to act like "A" students during a lecture.

20. To be sure that you have mastered the use of the *t*-test, try another example, starting with the raw data.

THE MR. WONDERFUL PROBLEM

Mr. Wonderful, a representative of Study Skills, Incorproated, is promoting a way to improve study skills for those students who would like to improve their performance in examinations. He convinces a college professor to try his home remedy and designs an experiment to test his hypothesis. Mr. Wonderful's hypothesis is that those students who do ten push-ups immediately before starting to work on an examination will score significantly higher on that examination than those students who do not do ten push-ups.

A cooperative group of students in a psychology course agrees to participate in a research study in order to advance the state of knowledge in the field of psychology, and Mr. Wonderful uses a table of random numbers (see Appendix A for an explanation of this procedure) to assign these students to two groups: Group 1 (the experimental group) and Group 2 (the control group). Immediately before starting to work on their examination, the students in the experimental group dutifully do 10 push-ups, while the control students sit quietly staring out the window.

The students' examinations are scored by a computer which does not know to which of the groups the students have been assigned (this acts as a control for possible experimenter bias). The computer presents the following hypothetical scores on the examination:

Group 1:   6, 8, 10, 12, 14, 15, 17, 18, 19, 20, 21, 22
Group 2:   12, 17, 19, 20, 23, 24, 26, 28, 30, 32, 33

We want to know: *Was* there a significant difference between the two groups? Let's take the process step by step.

What was the mean of Group 1?

— — — — — — — — — — — — — — — —

$n_1 = 12$

$$\bar{X}_1 = 6 + 8 + 10 + \ldots + 21 + 22 = \frac{182}{12} = 15.17$$

21. What was the standard deviation of Group 1?

— — — — — — — — — — — — — — — —

$$\text{s.d.}_1 = \sqrt{\frac{(6^2 + 8^2 + 10^2 + \ldots + 21^2 + 22^2)}{12} - 15.17^2}$$

$$= \sqrt{\frac{3064}{12} - 230.13}$$

$$= \sqrt{255.33 - 230.13}$$

$$= \sqrt{25.2}$$

$$\text{s.d.}_1 = 5.02$$

22. What is $(\text{s.d.}_1)^2$?

$$\text{s.d.}_1{}^2 = 25.20$$

23. What was the mean of Group 2?

$$n_2 = 11$$

$$\bar{X}_2 = 12 + 17 + 19 + \ldots + 32 + 33 = \frac{264}{11} = 24.0$$

24. What was the standard deviation of Group 2?

$$\text{s.d.}_2 = \sqrt{\frac{(12^2 + 17^2 + 19^2 + \ldots + 32^2 + 33^2)}{11} - 24^2}$$

$$= \sqrt{\frac{6772}{11} - 576}$$

$$= \sqrt{615.64 - 576}$$

$$= \sqrt{39.64}$$

$$\text{s.d.}_2 = 6.3$$

25. What is $(s.d._2)^2$?

_ _ _ _ _ _ _ _ _ _ _ _ _ _ _ _ _

$s.d._2{}^2 = 39.69$

26. How large must t be in order for there to be a significant difference between these two groups?

_ _ _ _ _ _ _ _ _ _ _ _ _ _ _ _ _

Since $n_1 + n_2 - 2$ for this problem equals $12 + 11 - 2 = 21$, we note from Appendix D that the obtained value for t must be greater than 2.08 in order for there to be a significant difference between the two experimental groups.

27. Now, use all of this information in the formula for the t-test to obtain a value for t, and then compare your answer against ours below.

_ _ _ _ _ _ _ _ _ _ _ _ _ _ _ _

$$t = \frac{\bar{X}_1 - \bar{X}_2}{\sqrt{\frac{(n_1)(s.d._1)^2 + (n_2)(s.d._2)^2}{n_1 + n_2 - 2}\left(\frac{1}{n_1} + \frac{1}{n_2}\right)}}$$

$$= \frac{15.17 - 24.0}{\sqrt{\frac{12(25.20) + 11(39.69)}{12 + 11 - 2}\left(\frac{1}{12} + \frac{1}{11}\right)}}$$

$$= \frac{-8.83}{\sqrt{\frac{302.4 + 436.59}{21}(0.17)}}$$

$$= \frac{-8.83}{\sqrt{\frac{738.99}{21}(0.17)}}$$

$$= \frac{-8.83}{\sqrt{35.19(0.17)}}$$

$$= \frac{-8.83}{\sqrt{5.98}}$$

$$= \frac{-8.83}{2.45}$$

$$t = -3.60$$

This answer for t of -3.60 is the first time we have had a negative value in our answer for t. Since the decision rule for the t-test states that there *is* a significant difference between the two groups whenever the value for t is greater than 2.08 for this problem, what do we do when the value for t is a negative value?

The answer to that question is quite simple:

Rule: Ignore the negative sign when trying to determine if there is a significant difference between the two groups.

When we ignore the negative sign, we find that 3.60 *is* larger than 2.08, and therefore there is a significant difference between these two groups.

Whenever we compute a value for t, the difference between the means will be positive whenever we subtract the smaller mean from the larger mean; and the difference between the means will be negative whenever we subtract the larger mean from the smaller mean. In either case, the magnitude of the difference between the two means will be identical, and the results will differ only in the sign. Only the *magnitude* of this difference matters, and not whether the sign of this difference is positive or negative.

28.   Now what were the results of this study? Write a summary of the results.

— — — — — — — — — — — — — — — —

Did you say that Group 1 scored significantly higher than Group 2? If you did, go back and rethink this question before you continue to read any further.

You should have noticed that Group 1 had a mean of 15.17, while Group 2 had a mean of 24.0. This means that *Group 2 scored significantly higher on the examination than Group 1.* Note that this result is exactly the opposite of Mr. Wonderful's claim! In other words, doing ten push-ups before the examination didn't raise their scores—it depressed them. Mr. Wonderful could benefit from a good course in psychological research.

29.   In most problems throughout this book, we have purposely used a small number of subjects to simplify the computations. That is, we have assumed that if you can apply a statistical test correctly using a small sample of subjects, you should be able to apply it correctly to a larger sample (though the calculations would take longer).

When you do your own research studies, however, you need to be aware of the handicaps that are associated with using just a small number of subjects. Whenever there are only a few subjects in an experiment, it is more difficult to obtain a significant difference than it is when the sample size is larger. See McNemar (1969) if you would like a further explanation of this point. Also, when you have a small sample, an extremely high or low score can drastically affect the mean score.

One way to "correct" for a small sample of subjects (and it is not really a very good way) is to require a more stringent level of significance (for example, you could require the difference to reach the .01 level of significance instead of merely the .05 level of significance). This would make it more difficult for you to obtain a significant difference.

However, it is best to avoid using small samples altogether—the larger the number of subjects in your sample, the better chance you will have of detecting a significant difference. As a good rule of thumb to use with the *t*-test, you should have at least 15 subjects in each of the two groups. That will give you a total of at least 30 subjects in your sample.

30.   In the published literature, statistical results for a research study using a *t*-test are often summarized in two main ways. The first type of summary uses a table which includes the value for *t* and the significance level of the result; such a table frequently includes the additional information of the number of people in each group (N), the mean score of each group ($\bar{X}$), and the standard deviation of each group of subjects (s.d.). For example, the results of the Mr. Wonderful problem in frame 20 of this chapter could be summarized in the following table:

Group	N	$\bar{X}$	s.d.	Group 1 vs. Group 2 *t*-value Significance level	
Group 1	12	15.17	5.02	–3.60	$p < .05$
Group 2	11	24.0	6.3		

A table such as the above in the summary of a research study gives the reader several advantages: (1) the table provides a summary of the *t*-value for the two groups being compared. (Note that when the value for *t* is reported, the reader could compute his or her own value for *t* to check its accuracy; authors occasionally make an error in computing the value for *t*.) (2) When more than two groups are being compared in the study, the reader can tell at a glance at the "significance level" column exactly *which* pairs of groups resulted in a significant difference between them. Remember, when the symbol "n.s." appears in this column, it means that there was not a significant difference between these two groups. The letter *p* stands for probability.

The expression "$p < .05$" means that the value you obtained for *t* was greater than the value required for the difference between the two groups to be significant at the .05 level.

The second way in which authors of published journal articles summarize their results is to include the value for *t* and the significance level as part of their written summary of the results of their study. Using the Mr. Wonderful problem again as an example, we could summarize the results of that study in this way:

Group 2 scored significantly higher on the examination than Group 1 $(t = -3.60, p < .05)$.

The symbols in parentheses serve the same function as the table which summarized the results for this problem; the t-value is reported along with the significance level so that the reader knows immediately whether there was a significant difference between the two groups being compared when the .05 level of significance is being used.

Keep in mind these two ways of summarizing the results of a research study when you are reading published journal articles.

You should also realize that .05 is not a sacred level of significance, but merely an agreed-upon convention among psychologists for deciding when the difference between two groups is large enough to be considered a significant difference.

Throughout this book, we have assumed that the desired level of significance for every problem is .05. If you were to ask all of the psychologists you know: "If you had to pick *one* level of significance for determining if there was a *significant* difference between two groups on some characteristic, what significance level would you pick?" the answer you would receive the great majority of the time would undoubtedly be: ".05." And, if you were to ask these same psychologists: "And what level of significance would you pick in order to say that there was a *highly significant* difference between two groups on some characteristic?" the answer you would undoubtedly receive would be: ".01."

However, a more sophisticated approach to answering these two questions would involve careful consideration of the following questions:

(1) What is the nature of the problem you are studying?
(2) What has past research in this area shown?
(3) How many subjects are you planning to use?
(4) What type of decision do you plan to make based on the results of your research?
(5) How serious are the consequences to other people if you make an incorrect decision based on the results of your research?

Ideally, the researcher needs to consider these types of questions *before* deciding what level of significance is most appropriate for his or her research. See Labovitz (1968) for an excellent discussion of these points. Unfortunately, as Morrison and Henkel (1970, p. 307) remind us: "The mathematical theory underlying significance tests provides no clue whatsoever as to the appropriate choice of level." What this means to us, in practice, is that there are no agreed-upon criteria among psychologists for deciding *how* to determine the appropriate significance level of a particular research study. In the absence of such criteria we have deliberately chosen throughout this book to select the .05 level of significance as that level of significance which is necessary in order to say that there is a significant difference between two groups of subjects on some characteristic.

As Skipper, Guenther, and Nass (1967, p. 16) put it:

> The choice of a statistical level of significance . . . apparently demands little psychic energy on the part of researchers. Casual examination of the literature discloses that the common, arbitrary, and virtually sacred levels of .05, .01, and .001 are almost universally selected regardless of the nature and type of problem. Of these three, .05 is perhaps most sacred.

We agree with Skipper, Guenther, and Nass (1967) that the best procedure for researchers to use would be to report the results of significance tests *at whatever level they occur* (.05, .10, .20, or whatever) and allow the reader to decide if the obtained significance level has any *practical significance* for his or her purposes. However, the procedures for determining the exact level of significance are beyond the scope of this book, and so we have chosen to apply the .05 level of significance throughout this book as the cutoff point for determining whether there is a significant difference between two groups of subjects.

31.   We have spent a lot of time learning how to apply the chi-square test and the *t*-test to research data. The chi-square test and the *t*-test were selected for this book because of three major reasons: (1) they are computationally simple—the mathematical computations of both tests are relatively easy to learn; (2) the logical meaning of these tests is relatively easy to understand; and (3) these tests are among the ones most frequently used by social scientists. As evidence for this latter point, Pollinger (1977) examined the statistical analysis procedures of a total of 472 articles which appeared in three major journals and found that almost 60 percent of these articles used some type of statistical analysis. Of these, more than 75 percent used either the chi-square test or the *t*-test.

Let's take a closer look at their special advantages. The two statistical tests are intended to help you determine if there is a significant difference between two groups of subjects on some characteristic. Both the chi-square test and the *t*-test can be used in comparing any two groups of subjects whenever the two groups of subjects are *independent* of one another (that is, no subject in one group is also in the other group). You can use both the chi-square test and the *t*-test whenever you are comparing an experimental group against a control group, or two experimental groups against one another, or two types of control groups against one another.

So how do we know *when* it is proper to use the *t*-test (discussed in Chapters Four through Six) and *when* it is proper to use the chi-square test (discussed in Chapters One through Three)? Whenever the two things being compared are only measured in terms of categories, the data cannot be analyzed by means of the *t*-test but must be analyzed by means of the chi-square test. For example, suppose you were developing an achievement test in reading for sixth graders and you wanted to identify which test items were

biased toward either boys or girls. In this case the chi-square test, not the
t-test, would be proper. You would apply the chi-square test to *each item
separately* to determine which items were biased in the responses which they
produced. So you would compute the chi-square value for the first item on
the test by using the following chi-square fourfold table:

Item 1

	Correct	Incorrect
Boys		
Girls		

The cells in this fourfold table would include the number of boys and
girls in the study who answered question 1 either correctly or incorrectly.
Whenever the chi-square value for any of the achievement test items was
greater than 3.84, it would mean that those test items were "sex-biased" in
the sense that there was a significant difference between how the boys and
the girls answered that test item. In this example, we would not apply the
t-test because it would make no sense to find a mean and standard deviation
for the "number correct" dimension. Since the data can only be summarized
in the form of categories, the chi-square test is the appropriate test to use on
these data.

However, when it *does* make sense to compute a mean and standard
deviation for data comparing two groups, the *t*-test has a special advantage
over the chi-square test: *the t-test makes use of all of the original raw data of
the subjects.* In contrast, using a chi-square test requires that all of the scores
be classified into one of only two categories: (1) above the median, and
(2) at or below the median. The two categories used do not take as full advantage of the differences between scores as does the *t*-test.

Some psychologists feel that you should never use the chi-square test
when it involves such a loss of the meaning of the original data and that only
the *t*-test should be used on data for which it makes sense to compute a mean
and standard deviation. Such a position, however, seems too extreme, because psychologists often disagree about whether the *t*-test or the chi-square
test is preferable for a particular set of data. When you are in doubt about
what test to use, your safest course is to ask a competent statistician for his
or her advice. But don't be surprised if a new and unfamiliar statistical test is
recommended. For example, while the chi-square test and the *t*-test for independent samples can be used only when the two groups are independent,
other statistical tests can be used when the two groups are not independent,
that is, when the same subjects are in both groups. Such a case occurs frequently in educational research. For example, you could give a reading test
to a group of students in the fall of the school year and then test these same
students again in the spring of that same school year to assess their improvement in reading skill during the year. One test that would be appropriate for
such a case would be the *t*-test for *correlated* samples; see, for example,
Bernstein (1964, p. 36).

Hundreds of statistical procedures can be applied to the analysis of data in psychology, and it takes a great deal of skill and experience to know when and how to apply each of these tests. This book can only give you a glimpse of the complexity involved in psychological research, but if it sparks your interest in the research process, it will have accomplished one of its major objectives.

Another question may have occurred to you: If we find a significant difference at the .05 level with one of these tests, will we also find a significant difference with the other when we apply it to the same data? Not always. It depends on the specific scores that you have. You might get a significant result from the t-test but a nonsignificant result using the chi-square test (or vice-versa). If the standard deviation is relatively large and the scores are well spread out over a large range of scores, then you may very well obtain a significant difference (or a nonsignificant difference) for *both* the chi-square and the t-test. It all depends on the data that you are working with.

The best way to solve this dilemma is to use the test which makes the most sense based on the form of the data in your particular research study. (Again, get some expert advice, if you can.) We have tried to describe a variety of types of research studies and types of data throughout this book so that you could develop your sense of which test to apply to the data of a particular experiment. You will have more opportunities to practice this skill as you continue to read through this book.

Let's look at a problem which would allow us to compare the results of these two tests using the same data. Do you remember The Chapel Green Problem in Chapter One, frames 23–31? That problem dealt with a Mr. Wizard who claimed that people who would run around the chapel green twice without stopping would be taller than those who ran around the gym. You applied the chi-square test to the hypothetical data and found a chi-square value of 5.24. Since that value of 5.24 was greater than 3.84, there was a significant difference between these two groups of subjects.

You might also remember that when you interpreted the fourfold table for that problem, that the results of the study turned out to be exactly the opposite of Mr. Wizard's claim. Instead of those subjects who ran around the chapel green being significantly taller than the subjects who ran around the gym, you found this result: Significantly more subjects who ran around the gym were above average in height than the subjects who ran around the chapel green.

Would we get the same result using the t-test on these data? Let's find out by working through the t-test step-by-step.

Go back to the original data in frame 1:23 and answer the following questions. Then check your answers against ours below.

What were the mean and standard deviation of Group 1?

- - - - - - - - - - - - - - -

$$\bar{X}_1 = \frac{1 + 3 + 5 + 7 + 9 + 10 + 12 + 13 + 14 + 15 + 16 + 17}{12} = \frac{122}{12} = 10.17$$

$$\text{s.d.}_1 = \sqrt{\frac{\Sigma X^2}{N} - \bar{X}^2}$$

$$\Sigma X^2 = 1^2 + 3^2 + 5^2 + \ldots + 17^2 = 1544$$

$$\text{s.d.}_1 = \sqrt{\frac{1544}{12} - (10.17)^2}$$

$$= \sqrt{128.67 - 103.43}$$

$$= \sqrt{25.24}$$

$$\text{s.d.}_1 = 5.02$$

32. What were the mean and standard deviation of Group 2?

- - - - - - - - - - - - - - - - - -

$$\bar{X}_2 = \frac{7 + 12 + 14 + 15 + 18 + 19 + 21 + 23 + 25 + 27 + 28}{11} = \frac{209}{11} = 19.0$$

$$\text{s.d.}_2 = \sqrt{\frac{\Sigma X^2}{N} - \bar{X}^2}$$

$$\Sigma X^2 = 7^2 + 12^2 + 14^2 + \ldots + 28^2 = 4407$$

$$\text{s.d.}_2 = \sqrt{\frac{4407}{11} - (19)^2}$$

$$= \sqrt{400.64 - 361}$$

$$= \sqrt{39.64}$$

$$\text{s.d.}_2 = 6.3$$

33. Now use the formula for the t-test to obtain an answer for t.

- - - - - - - - - - - - - - - - - -

$$t = \frac{\bar{X}_1 - \bar{X}_2}{\sqrt{\frac{(n_1)\,(\text{s.d.}_1)^2 + (n_2)\,(\text{s.d.}_2)^2}{n_1 + n_2 - 2}\left(\frac{1}{n_1} + \frac{1}{n_2}\right)}}.$$

$$t = \frac{10.17 - 19.0}{\sqrt{\dfrac{12\,(5.02)^2 + 11\,(6.3)^2}{12 + 11 - 2}\left(\dfrac{1}{12} + \dfrac{1}{11}\right)}}.$$

$$= \frac{-8.83}{\sqrt{\dfrac{12\,(25.2) + 11\,(39.69)}{21}\,(.08 + .09)}}.$$

$$= \frac{-8.83}{\sqrt{\dfrac{302.4 + 436.59}{21}\,(0.17)}}.$$

$$= \frac{-8.83}{\sqrt{\dfrac{738.99}{21}\,(0.17)}}.$$

$$= \frac{-8.83}{\sqrt{35.19\,(0.17)}}.$$

$$= \frac{-8.83}{\sqrt{5.98}}.$$

$$= \frac{-8.83}{2.45}$$

$$t = -3.60$$

34. Using Appendix D, how large must t be in order for there to be a significant difference between these two groups?

— — — — — — — — — — — — — —

Since $n_1 + n_2 - 2$ equals $12 + 11 - 2 = 21$, t must be greater than 2.08 in order for there to be a significant difference at the .05 level.

35. Was there a significant difference between these two groups? Explain.

— — — — — — — — — — — — — —

Yes. Ignoring the negative sign, 3.60 is larger than 2.08, and so there was a significant difference between the two groups.

36. Now for the hard part. Which group was significantly taller?

— — — — — — — — — — — — — — — — —

Group 2

37. Why?

— — — — — — — — — — — — — — — — —

Because it had the higher mean score of 19, while Group 1 only had a mean score of 10.17.

38. Was this the same result we obtained when we used the chi-square test?

— — — — — — — — — — — — — — — — —

Yes, it was. For *both* the chi-square test and the *t*-test (thank goodness!) we found that those subjects who ran around the gym were significantly taller than those who ran around the chapel green.

39. If you consult with any friends who have had courses in statistics, you may find that some of them use a different formula for the *t*-test for independent samples and standard deviation from the ones we have been using.
  If so, the formulas you find will be the following:

$$\text{s.d.} = \sqrt{\frac{N}{N-1}\left(\frac{\Sigma X^2}{N} - \bar{X}^2\right)}$$

$$t = \frac{\bar{X}_1 - \bar{X}_2}{\sqrt{\frac{(n_1 - 1)(\text{s.d.}_1)^2 + (n_2 - 1)(\text{s.d.}_2)^2}{n_1 + n_2 - 2}\left(\frac{1}{n_1} + \frac{1}{n_2}\right)}} .$$

  Note that this formula uses $(n_1 - 1)$ and $(n_2 - 1)$ instead of the n_1 and n_2 that are used in this book.
  If you do discover these two different formulas, there is no need for panic. These different formulas will produce the *identical* result for the *t*-test as the formulas which are used throughout this book. You can confirm this yourself by applying these two different formulas to any problem in this book for which the raw data are given to you.
  You have to be careful though. If you use the formula above to compute the standard deviation, you must use the formula above for the *t*-test; these two formulas above go together and must be used together. Similarly, if you use the different formula for computing the standard deviation that we have used throughout this book, then you must also use the formula for the *t*-test

which is used throughout this book; these two formulas that we are using throughout this book are also a matched pair and must be used together.

As an optional exercise, apply these two new formulas to the data given in Table 4.2 in frame 1. Recall that we obtained the following results for the data in that table:

Group	N	$\bar{X}$	s.d.	t
Experimental	9	6.67	1.03	3.81*
Control	10	4.50	1.28	

*$p < .05$

What results do you obtain when you use the new formulas for the standard deviation and the t-test which are given in frame 39? Do you obtain the same result for t with these new formulas?

_____

The new formula for the standard deviation is the following:

$$\text{s.d.} = \sqrt{\frac{N}{N-1}\left(\frac{\Sigma X^2}{N} - \bar{X}^2\right)}$$

We already computed the sum of the squares (ΣX^2) for the experimental group in frame 4 of this chapter where we found that $\Sigma X^2 = 410$. So the standard deviation of the experimental group using this new formula is:

$$\text{s.d.} = \sqrt{\frac{9}{9-1}\left(\frac{410}{9} - 6.67^2\right)}$$

$$= \sqrt{\frac{9}{8}(45.56 - 44.49)}$$

$$= \sqrt{(1.13)(1.07)}$$

$$= \sqrt{1.21}$$

$$\text{s.d.} = 1.10$$

Note that this value for the standard deviation of the experimental group is slightly different from the value which we obtained using the old formula.

Recall that we computed the sum of the squares (ΣX^2) for the control group in frame 9 of this chapter where we found that $\Sigma X^2 = 219$. So the standard deviation of the control group using this new formula is:

$$\text{s.d.} = \sqrt{\frac{10}{10-1}\left(\frac{219}{10} - 4.50^2\right)}$$

$$= \sqrt{\frac{10}{9}\,(21.90 - 20.25)}$$

$$= \sqrt{(1.11)\,(1.65)}$$

$$= \sqrt{1.83}$$

$$\text{s.d.} = 1.35$$

Note that this value for the standard deviation of the control group is slightly different from the value which we obtained using the old formula. We are now ready to compute the value for t using the new formula:

$$t = \frac{\bar{X}_1 - \bar{X}_2}{\sqrt{\dfrac{(n_1 - 1)\,(\text{s.d.}_1)^2 + (n_2 - 1)\,(\text{s.d.}_2)^2}{n_1 + n_2 - 2}\left(\dfrac{1}{n_1} + \dfrac{1}{n_2}\right)}}$$

$$= \frac{6.67 - 4.50}{\sqrt{\dfrac{(9-1)\,(1.10)^2 + (10-1)\,(1.35)^2}{9 + 10 - 2}\left(\dfrac{1}{9} + \dfrac{1}{10}\right)}}$$

$$= \frac{2.17}{\sqrt{\dfrac{8\,(1.21) + 9\,(1.82)}{17}\,(0.21)}}$$

$$= \frac{2.17}{\sqrt{\dfrac{9.68 + 16.38}{17}\,(0.21)}}$$

$$= \frac{2.17}{\sqrt{\dfrac{26.06}{17}\,(0.21)}}$$

$$= \frac{2.17}{\sqrt{(1.53)\,(0.21)}}$$

$$= \frac{2.17}{\sqrt{0.32}}$$

$$= \frac{2.17}{0.57}$$

$$t = 3.81$$

Note that this value for t of 3.81 is the same value that we obtained for t using the old formulas for the standard deviation and the t-test for independent samples. The old and new formulas produce slightly different values for the standard deviations, but they produce the identical result for t.

40. Let's try one final example which will ask you to apply all of the skills which you have learned in this chapter.

Scandura and Wells (1967) explored the effects of "advance organizers" (introductory material that organizes material that is to be learned) on achievement in abstract mathematics. Fifty-two college students were randomly assigned to two groups: 26 subjects in Group 1 studied a 1,000-word essay on topology after having been exposed to an advance organizer on the topic; 26 subjects in Group 2 read the same essay on topology after having read a 1,000-word historical sketch of Euler and Riemann, two famous mathematicians. At the end of the experimental period, each group was given an objective test on topological concepts. The following results were obtained:

Group 1 (advance organizer)	Group 2 (historical sketch)
$n_1 = 26$	$n_2 = 26$
$\bar{X}_1 = 7.65$	$\bar{X}_2 = 6.00$
s.d.$_1 = 2.55$	s.d.$_2 = 2.43$

(a) *Was there* a significant difference in the performance of these two experimental groups?

(b) If so, *in what way* were these two groups significantly different from one another?

Your first step is to determine how large the value for t must be in order for there to be a significant difference between these two groups. Based on

Appendix D, how large must t be in order for there to be a significant difference between these two groups?

– – – – – – – – – – – – – – – –

Since $n_1 + n_2 - 2$ for this problem equals $26 + 26 - 2 = 50$, we note from
Appendix D that the obtained value for t must be greater than 2.01 in order
for there to be a significant difference between the two experimental groups.

41.   Now, use the equation for the t-test to obtain a result for t, then check
your answer for t against ours below.

– – – – – – – – – – – – – – – –

$$t = \frac{\bar{X}_1 - \bar{X}_2}{\sqrt{\frac{(n_1)(\text{s.d.}_1)^2 + (n_2)(\text{s.d.}_2)^2}{n_1 + n_2 - 2}\left(\frac{1}{n_1} + \frac{1}{n_2}\right)}}$$

$$= \frac{7.65 - 6.00}{\sqrt{\frac{26(6.50) + 26(5.90)}{26 + 26 - 2}\left(\frac{1}{26} + \frac{1}{26}\right)}}$$

$$= \frac{1.65}{\sqrt{\frac{169 + 153.4}{50}(0.08)}}$$

$$= \frac{1.65}{\sqrt{\frac{322.4}{50}(0.08)}}$$

$$= \frac{1.65}{\sqrt{6.45(0.08)}}$$

$$= \frac{1.65}{\sqrt{0.52}}$$

$$= \frac{1.65}{0.72}$$

$$t = 2.29$$

42.   Now that you have a value for t, was there a significant difference between the two groups? Explain.

————————————————

Yes, Since this value for t is larger than 2.01, there was a significant difference between these two experimental groups.

43.   Now that we know that there was a significant difference between these two groups, which group scored significantly higher than the other? Explain.

————————————————

Group 1. The mean score for Group 1 was 7.65 problems answered correctly while the mean score for Group 2 was 6.0. Therefore, Group 1 answered significantly more questions correctly than Group 2.

44.   Now try writing up the results of this experiment without using the terms "Group 1" or "Group 2."

————————————————

Students who were in the advance organizer group answered significantly more questions correctly than the historical sketch group.

45.   Now write up a table to summarize the results of this study.

————————————————

Group	N	$\bar{X}$	s.d.	t
Group 1	26	7.65	2.55	2.29*
Group 2	26	6.00	2.43	

*$p < .05$

46.   Back in Chapter One we looked at some of the weaknesses of the "one group pretest-posttest design" (see frame 17 if you need to review this concept). The concept of "experimental design" is an extremely important one in psychological research. Campbell and Stanley, in their classic chapter on research designs, make this strong statement (1963, p. 172):

> This chapter is committed to the experiment: as the only means
> for settling disputes regarding educational practice, as the only way
> of verifying educational improvements, and as the only way of

establishing a cumulative tradition in which improvements can be introduced without the danger of a faddish discard of old wisdom in favor of inferior novelties.

Many of the research studies described in this book use a type of experimental design which is called the "posttest-only control group design." Campbell and Stanley present sixteen examples of major research designs and they say that this posttest-only control group design is (Campbell and Stanley, 1963, p. 196): ". . . greatly underused in educational and psychological research."

Campbell and Stanley classify the posttest-only control group design as a "true experimental design" in the sense that it is one of the currently recommended research designs in the methodological literature. The basic requirements of this experimental design are these:

(1)   The subjects used in the study should be randomly assigned to one of two groups: an experimental group and a control group. The purpose of random assignment is to attempt to achieve equality of the two groups (within statistical limits) before the treatment X is administered to the experimental group.

(2)   Some special treatment should be administered to the experimental group but not to the control group. The word "treatment" refers to some special procedure or situation which the researcher selects to be administered to the experimental group; some examples of a treatment would be: a special reading program, a film, a special article which the subjects are asked to read.

(3)   After the treatment is administered, some type of measurement of both groups is taken. The resulting data are then analyzed by means of some statistical test (for example, the chi-square test or the t-test).

This experimental design can be summarized graphically by the following diagram:

	Time 1	Time 2	Time 3
Group 1	R	X	O_1
Group 2	R		O_2

Where R means that the subjects were randomly assigned to this group.

X refers to the treatment which is to be administered to the experimental group.

O_1 and O_2 refer to the posttest measurements which are taken on groups 1 and 2 at approximately the same point in time after the treatment has been administered to the experimental group.

The alert reader might be tempted to feel that some type of pretest of the two groups before the treatment is administered is essential to a good experimental design. However, the use of a pretest is not essential to an experimental design *if* the subjects are randomly assigned to the two groups. Also, on many occasions a pretest is either unavailable, inconvenient, expensive, or reactive in the sense that it sensitizes the subjects to what is coming in the treatment, thus making it difficult to separate out the effect of the treatment from the effect of the pretest on the subjects' behavior.

To simplify the explanations and to allow for the use of simpler statistical techniques in the analysis of the data only simple experimental designs are used throughout this book. The reader who is interested in a more sophisticated explanation of the types of experimental design should read Campbell and Stanley (1963) and Marco, Murphy, and Quirk (1976).

We have covered a lot of ground in this chapter, but hopefully you are developing the confidence to know when and how to apply the *t*-test for independent samples to studies in psychological research. You should feel comfortable that you can compute a mean and standard deviation for each of two research groups, apply the *t*-test to these groups, check for a significant difference, and interpret the results correctly. The Self-Test at the end of Chapter Four will give you the opportunity to evaluate your skills in using the *t*-test.

After you finish the Self-Test, Chapter Five will show you how to apply the *t*-test to two different psychological experiments, and then Chapter Six will give you the opportunity to plan a research study carefully from start to finish so that you can sharpen your research planning skills.

SELF-TEST FOR CHAPTER FOUR

This Self-Test is designed to show you whether you have mastered the key concepts and skills in Chapter Four. Answer each question to the best of your ability. Correct answers and review instructions are given at the end of the test. When working on these problems, use the tear-out sheet in Appendix E for the formulas you need.

1. What is the mean of the following set of scores:

   3, 9, 4, 10, 1?

2. What is the standard deviation of the set of scores given in problem 1?

3. The final examination from one class of 16 introductory psychology students had a mean of 107 and a standard deviation of 10, while another class of 14 students had a mean of 112 and a standard deviation of 8. Was there a significant difference between the scores of these two groups? If so, how were these groups different?

4. Suppose you have been hired as a research assistant by a political science professor who is studying the effect of a film about the People's Republic of China on the attitude change of a group of undergraduates in one of his courses. You have designed a questionnaire in which the most important question asks the students to indicate their attitude toward China on an 11-point scale ranging from –5 to +5. You hand out the questionnaire a week before the film, and have the students answer it during class. You then show the film, and ask the students to complete the questionnaire again. Your preliminary analysis of the data for the key question indicates that the 35 students in the class had a mean score on the key question of 1.2 and a standard deviation of 0.62 on the original questionnaire, and a mean score of 2.3 with a standard deviation of 0.85 on the later questionnaire. Was there a significant change in the students' attitude toward China as the result of watching the film? If so, in what way did their attitude change?

Answers for Self-Test for Chapter Four

Compare your answers to the questions on the Self-Test with the answers given below. If all of your answers are correct, you are ready to go on to Chapter Five. If you missed any questions, review the frames indicated in parenthese following the answer. If you miss several questions, you should probably carefully reread the entire chapter.

1. $\dfrac{3 + 9 + 4 + 10 + 1}{5} = \dfrac{27}{5} = 5.40$ (Chapter Four, frame 2)

2.

$$\text{s.d.} = \sqrt{\dfrac{\Sigma X^2}{N} - \bar{X}^2}$$

$$= \sqrt{\dfrac{3^2 + 9^2 + 4^2 + 10^2 + 1^2}{5} - 5.4^2}$$

$$= \sqrt{\dfrac{9 + 81 + 16 + 100 + 1}{5} - 29.16}$$

$$= \sqrt{\dfrac{207}{5} - 29.16}$$

$$= \sqrt{41.4 - 29.16}$$

$$= \sqrt{12.24}$$

s.d. $= 3.5$ (Chapter Four, frames 3–9)

3.   Since $n_1 + n_2 - 2$ equals $16 + 14 - 2 = 28$, we note from Appendix D that the obtained value for t must be greater than 2.05 in order for there to be a significant difference between the two experimental groups.

$$t = \dfrac{\bar{X}_1 - \bar{X}_2}{\sqrt{\dfrac{(n_1)\,(\text{s.d.}_1)^2 + (n_2)\,(\text{s.d.}_2)^2}{n_1 + n_2 - 2} \left(\dfrac{1}{n_1} + \dfrac{1}{n_2}\right)}}$$

$$= \dfrac{107 - 112}{\sqrt{\dfrac{16\,(10)^2 + 14\,(8)^2}{16 + 14 - 2} \left(\dfrac{1}{16} + \dfrac{1}{14}\right)}}$$

$$= \dfrac{-5}{\sqrt{\dfrac{1600 + 896}{28}\,(0.13)}}$$

$$= \dfrac{-5}{\sqrt{\dfrac{2496}{28}\,(0.13)}}$$

$$= \frac{-5}{\sqrt{89.14 \, (0.13)}}$$

$$= \frac{-5}{\sqrt{11.59}}$$

$$= \frac{-5}{3.4}$$

$$t = -1.47$$

Once again, you need to *ignore* the negative sign in trying to determine if there is a significant difference between the two groups of subjects. Since 1.47 is not greater than 2.05, there is *not* a significant difference between the two groups of subjects.   (Chapter Four, frames 10–11)

4.   If you computed a value for *t*, read the problem again carefully. And remember that the *t*-test discussed in this book can only be used on *independent* samples of subjects. Since the same subjects filled out the questionnaire on both occasions, the two groups of subjects are not independent. The analysis of the data for this problem is beyond the scope of this book. Notice that even if we could have analyzed the data, we would not be able to answer the questions as asked, since we could not say *why* any change occurred—"as the result of watching the film" and not for any other reason. If you missed this question, you might want to review our discussion of the one-group pretest-posttest design in frame 17 of Chapter One.   (Chapter One, frame 17)

CHAPTER FIVE

Application of the *t*-Test in Two Experiments

Now that you know how to compute a mean, a standard deviation, and a value for *t* using the *t*-test, let's see if you can apply these skills to two experiments. The first experiment deals with the problem of how people perceive the prestige of an occupation based on the percentage of women who are employed in that occupation. The second experiment deals with how we develop our impressions of other people. It asks the question: if a person is first described as acting friendly toward others and then described as acting withdrawn from others, will people develop a different impression of that person than if that person is first described as withdrawn and then described as acting friendly toward others? In other words, does the *order* in which we receive information about other people affect our impressions of their personalities?

OCCUPATIONAL PRESTIGE AND DESIRABILITY

1. For the first experiment, assume that you have decided to conduct your own research study to see if you can obtain results similar to that obtained in an interesting article by Touhey (1974) you have read. In that study Touhey studied the impact of increasing the percentages of women in certain occupations on people's perception of the prestige and desirability of those occupations. Subjects were asked to read an information sheet describing the occupations of architect, college professor, lawyer, physician, and scientist. The descriptions had been abstracted from the occupation descriptions contained in the *Occupational Outlook Handbook* produced by the United States Department of Labor. The information sheet described each occupation in terms of the nature of the work, places of employment, training and other qualifications, employment outlook, earnings and working conditions, and additional opportunities. The information sheet of the experimental group predicted, under the heading of additional opportunities, that the proportion of women in that occupation would sharply increase over the next 30

years. The additional opportunities section of the information sheet for the control group indicated that the proportion of women in the particular profession had stabilized and was likely to remain unchanged over the next 30 years.

Undergraduates at the University of Tulsa read these information sheets and then rated the occupations in terms of their prestige and desirability. These students rated the occupations of architect, college professor, physician, and scientist as significantly lower in prestige and significantly less desirable when the information sheet predicted a sharp increase in the proportion of women in those occupations. No significant difference occurred in the students' ratings of the prestige or desirability of the occupation of lawyer between the experimental and control groups.

Suppose that you have decided, after reading this study, that you would like to explore further the psychological effects of an increasing proportion of women in occupations in terms of people's perceptions of these occupations. You go to the library and find the *Occupational Outlook for College Graduates: 1974-75 Edition* (U.S. Department of Labor, 1974). Now you have to decide which occupation to study. Perhaps you recently read an article by Fleming (1976) which gave you some insight into why the occupation of accountant is an especially useful one for women. Let's assume that you decide to use the occupation of accountant in your research study.

If you would like actually to do this experiment, look at the *Occupational Outlook for College Graduates: 1974-75 Edition*; from the description of an accountant (pp. 21-23), create an abstract, a description of that occupation in terms of the nature of the work, places of employment, training and other qualifications, employment outlook, and earnings and working conditions, and then compare it to our abstract, given below.

———————————————

ACCOUNTANT*

Nature of the Work: Accountants prepare and analyze reports that furnish financial information to managers. Accountants often specialize in auditing (reviewing financial records for their reliability), taxes, or budgeting. Accountants who work for the federal government often work as bank examiners, investigators, or Internal Revenue agents. Public accountants work for accounting firms or as independent businessmen. Management accountants are responsible for the financial records of their companies. Government accountants examine the financial records of government agencies and audit businesses or individuals who are subject to government regulations.

Places of Employment: More than 700,000 people worked as accountants in 1972; about 20 percent of these were Certified Public Accountants (CPAs). More than 60 percent of accountants work as management accountants. Another 20 percent work as public accountants. Others work for local, state, and federal agencies, while a small

———————

*Adapted from the *Occupational Outlook for College Graduates: 1974-75 Edition*.

number teach in colleges and universities. Most accountants work in large cities where accounting firms and central offices of large businesses are found.

Training and Other Qualifications: A person can be trained in accounting in an accounting and business school, a correspondence school, or at a college or university. Most large accounting and business firms require applicants to have at least a bachelor's degree in accounting or a closely related field. For teaching positions, most colleges and universities require a master's degree or a doctorate. Anyone working as a CPA must hold a certificate issued by the state board of accountancy. Almost all states require at least two years of public accounting experience for a CPA certificate. People who are thinking seriously about a career in accounting should have an aptitude for mathematics; neatness and accuracy are also important. Accountants who can accept responsibility and who can work effectively with little supervision are sought out by employers.

Employment Outlook: The need for accountants is expected to increase rapidly through the 1980s as business and government agencies continue to expand. Accountants with college degrees will be in more demand than those without this training as accounting practices in business become more complex. The data processing aspects of financial systems are expected to increase the complexity of accounting procedures.

Earnings and Working Conditions: Starting salaries of beginning accountants in private industry were $9,100 a year in 1972 in urban areas. Earnings of experienced accountants range between $12,000 and $17,500. Chief accountants who are responsible for the accounting program of their company earn between $15,000 and $27,000, depending upon the complexity of their responsibility. Salaries are generally higher for accountants holding a graduate degree or a CPA certificate and for those who are required to travel a great deal. Experienced accountants in the federal government earn about $20,000 a year. Accountants often work very long hours, especially during tax season.

2.   The *Occupational Outlook for College Graduates: 1974-75 Edition* states (p. 22) that: "About 3 percent of the CPAs and 22 percent of all accountants are women." You are confident that people in general will not know the percentage of accountants who are women, and so you decide that the occupation of accountant is ideal for your research study.

Suppose you then decide to add a paragraph on "additional opportunities" to your description of accountant which will distinguish the experimental and control groups. Both of these groups will receive the identical description of an accountant given in frame 1. However, the *experimental group* will have the following additional paragraph included in their description:

Additional Opportunities: Approximately 7 percent of the accountants in the United States are women. However, current patterns of recruitment indicate that the percentage of women accountants will increase to 35 percent during the next 15 years, and that women will comprise a majority of accountants in 25 to 30 years.

The *control group* will have the following additional paragraph included in their description:

Additional Opportunities: Approximately 7 percent of the accountants in the United States are women. Current patterns of recruitment indicate that the percentage of women accountants will stabilize at between 6 and 8 percent during the next 25 to 30 years.

You then include the rating scales given below* with each description of the occupation of accountant.

RATING SCALES FOR THE OCCUPATION OF ACCOUNTANT**

This study is concerned with the way people evaluate different occupations.

1. How would you rate the *prestige* of the occupation of accountant?

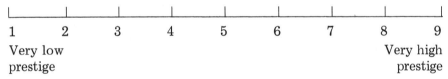

1	2	3	4	5	6	7	8	9
Very low prestige							Very high prestige	

2. How would you rate the *desirability* of the occupation of accountant?

1	2	3	4	5	6	7	8	9
Very undesirable							Very desirable	

You are now ready to collect your data. Let's suppose that you have rounded up a group of fifteen subjects and that you have randomly assigned each subject either to the experimental group or to the control group.† Your subjects fill out the rating scales, and produce the hypothetical data with regard to prestige and desirability of the occupation of accountant summarized in the following table.

---

*Touhey (1974) used 60-point scales which ranged from 0 (that is, very low prestige) to 60 (that is, very high prestige) in 10-point intervals. We have chosen to use 9-point scales which range from 1-9, but either procedure would be acceptable.

**These rating scales are adapted from J. C. Touhey, "Effects of Additional Women Professionals on Ratings of Occupational Prestige and Desirability," *Journal of Personality and Social Psychology*, 1974, vol. 29, pp. 86-89. Copyright 1974 by the American Psychological Association. Reprinted by permission.

†See Appendix A for an explanation of this procedure.

Prestige Ratings		Desirability Ratings	
Experimental Group	Control Group	Experimental Group	Control Group
8	6	7	6
9	5	6	7
8	4	5	5
7	5	6	7
7	6	7	6
8	3	5	5
6	4	6	7
7		6	

You should be able to analyze the data, using the *t*-test for independent samples, to answer the following three questions:

(1) Was there a significant difference between the experimental and control groups in their ratings of the prestige of the occupation of accountant?

(2) Was there a significant difference between the experimental and control groups in their ratings of the desirability of the occupation of accountant?

(3) What were the results of this study? (Write up the summary of the answers to questions 1 and 2.)

First, what are the mean and standard deviation of the experimental group on their ratings of the prestige of an accountant?

— — — — — — — — — — — — — — — —

The experimental group has eight subjects. Their mean score is:

$$\frac{8 + 9 + 8 + \cdots + 6 + 7}{8} = \frac{60}{8} = 7.5$$

Their standard deviation is:

$$\text{s.d.} = \sqrt{\frac{\Sigma X^2}{N} - \bar{X}^2}$$

$$= \sqrt{\frac{(8^2 + 9^2 + 8^2 + \cdots + 6^2 + 7^2)}{8} - 7.5^2}$$

$$= \sqrt{\frac{456}{8} - 56.25}$$

$$= \sqrt{57 - 56.25}$$

$$= \sqrt{0.75}$$

s.d. $= 0.87$

Thus, the eight subjects in the experimental group had a mean rating of prestige of 7.5 with a standard deviation of 0.87.

3.   What are the mean and standard deviation of the control group on their ratings of the prestige of an accountant?

_ _ _ _ _ _ _ _ _ _ _ _ _ _ _ _ _ _ _

The control group has seven subjects. Their mean score is:

$$\frac{6 + 5 + 4 + \cdots + 3 + 4}{7} = \frac{33}{7} = 4.71$$

Their standard deviation is:

$$\text{s.d.} = \sqrt{\frac{\Sigma X^2}{N} - \bar{X}^2}$$

$$= \sqrt{\frac{(6^2 + 5^2 + \cdots + 3^2 + 4^2)}{7} - 4.71^2}$$

$$= \sqrt{\frac{163}{7} - 22.18}$$

$$= \sqrt{23.29 - 22.18}$$

$$= \sqrt{1.11}$$

s.d. $= 1.05$

Thus, the seven subjects in the control group had a mean rating of prestige of 4.71 with a standard deviation of 1.05.

4.   Using Appendix D, how large must t be in order for there to be a significant difference between these two groups?

— — — — — — — — — — — — — — —

Since $n_1 + n_2 - 2$ for this problem equals $8 + 7 - 2 = 13$, we note from Appendix D that the obtained value for t must be greater than 2.16 in order for there to be a significant difference between the two groups.

5.   Now use the formula for the *t*-test to obtain an answer for t.

— — — — — — — — — — — — — — —

$$t = \frac{\bar{X}_1 - \bar{X}_2}{\sqrt{\frac{(n_1)\,(\text{s.d.}_1)^2 + (n_2)\,(\text{s.d.}_2)^2}{n_1 + n_2 - 2}\left(\frac{1}{n_1} + \frac{1}{n_2}\right)}}$$

$$= \frac{7.5 - 4.71}{\sqrt{\frac{8\,(0.87)^2 + 7\,(1.05)^2}{8 + 7 - 2}\left(\frac{1}{8} + \frac{1}{7}\right)}}$$

$$= \frac{2.79}{\sqrt{\frac{6.06 + 7.72}{13}\,(0.27)}}$$

$$= \frac{2.79}{\sqrt{\frac{13.78}{13}\,(0.27)}}$$

$$= \frac{2.79}{\sqrt{0.29}}$$

$$= \frac{2.79}{0.54}$$

$$t = 5.17$$

6.   Was there a significant difference between these two groups? Explain.

— — — — — — — — — — — — — — —

Yes. Because the value for t of 5.17 is larger than 2.16.

7.   Now that we know that there was a significant difference between the two groups, which group rated the occupation of accountant significantly higher in prestige? Explain.

_ _ _ _ _ _ _ _ _ _ _ _ _ _ _ _ _ _

The experimental group. The mean prestige rating for the experimental group was 7.5, while the mean prestige rating for the control group was 4.71. Therefore, subjects in the experimental group rated the occupation of accountant significantly higher in prestige than subjects in the control group.

8.   Try writing up the summary of the results of this study without using the terms "experimental group" or "control group."

_ _ _ _ _ _ _ _ _ _ _ _ _ _ _ _ _ _

Your summary should read something like this: Subjects who read a description of the occupation of accountant which stated that the percentage of women accountants would increase dramatically over the next 25 to 30 years rated that occupation significantly higher in prestige than subjects who read a description which stated that the percentage of women accountants would remain at about its present level.

9.   Now let's analyze the data for the second question, which dealt with the desirability of the occupation of accountant.
    What are the mean and standard deviation of the experimental group on their ratings of the desirability of the occupation of accountant?

_ _ _ _ _ _ _ _ _ _ _ _ _ _ _ _ _ _

The experimental group has eight subjects. Their mean score is:

$$\frac{7 + 6 + 5 + \cdots + 6 + 6}{8} = \frac{48}{8} = 6.0$$

Their standard deviation is:

$$\text{s.d.} = \sqrt{\frac{\Sigma X^2}{N} - \bar{X}^2}$$

$$= \sqrt{\frac{(7^2 + 6^2 + \cdots + 6^2 + 6^2)}{8} - 6^2}$$

$$= \sqrt{\frac{292}{8} - 36}$$

$$= \sqrt{36.5 - 36}$$

$$= \sqrt{0.5}$$

s.d. $= 0.71$

Thus, the eight subjects in the experimental group had a mean rating of desirability of 6.0 and a standard deviation of 0.71.

10.   What are the mean and standard deviation of the control group on their ratings of the desirability of the occupation of accountant?

— — — — — — — — — — — — — — — — — —

The control group has seven subjects. Their mean score is:

$$\frac{6 + 7 + 5 + \cdots + 5 + 7}{7} = \frac{43}{7} = 6.14$$

Their standard deviation is:

$$\text{s.d.} = \sqrt{\frac{\Sigma X^2}{N} - \bar{X}^2}$$

$$= \sqrt{\frac{(6^2 + 7^2 + \cdots + 5^2 + 7^2)}{7} - 6.14^2}$$

$$= \sqrt{\frac{269}{7} - 6.14^2}$$

$$= \sqrt{38.43 - 37.70}$$

$$= \sqrt{0.73}$$

s.d. $= 0.85$

Thus, the seven subjects in the control group had a mean rating of desirability of 6.14 and a standard deviation of 0.85.

11.   Using Appendix D, how large must t be in order for there to be a significant difference between these two groups?

— — — — — — — — — — — — — — — — — —

As in frame 4 above, since $n_1 + n_2 - 2$ for this problem equals $8 + 7 - 2 = 13$, we note from Appendix D that the obtained value for t must be greater than 2.16 in order for there to be a significant difference between the two experimental groups.

12. Now use the formula for the t-test to obtain an answer for t.

$$t = \frac{\bar{X}_1 - \bar{X}_2}{\sqrt{\dfrac{(n_1)\,(\text{s.d.}_1)^2 + (n_2)\,(\text{s.d.}_2)^2}{n_1 + n_2 - 2}\left(\dfrac{1}{n_1} + \dfrac{1}{n_2}\right)}}$$

$$= \frac{6.0 - 6.14}{\sqrt{\dfrac{8\,(0.71)^2 + 7\,(0.85)^2}{8 + 7 - 2}\left(\dfrac{1}{8} + \dfrac{1}{7}\right)}}$$

$$= \frac{-0.14}{\sqrt{\dfrac{4.03 + 5.06}{13}\,(0.27)}}$$

$$= \frac{-0.14}{\sqrt{\dfrac{9.09}{13}\,(0.27)}}$$

$$= \frac{-0.14}{\sqrt{0.19}}$$

$$= \frac{-0.14}{0.44}$$

$$t = -0.32$$

13. Was there a significant difference between these two groups? Explain.

No. Ignoring the negative sign, 0.32 is less than 2.16, and therefore there is no significant difference between the groups in their rating of the desirability of the occupation.

14. Now try writing up the results of the data analysis for the desirability of the occupation of accountant without using the terms "experimental group" or "control group."

Your summary should read something like this: There was no significant dif-ference in their ratings of the desirability of the occupation of accountant between subjects who read a description which stated that the percentage of women accountants would increase dramatically over the next 25 to 30 years and subjects who read a description which stated that the percentage of women accountants would remain at about its present level.

15. The third and last step is to summarize the results of this hypothetical study for both of the rating-scale items. Write a summary of this study which is concise and which summarizes the results for both of the rating-scale items.

— — — — — — — — — — — — — — — — —

Subjects who read a description of the occupation of accountant which predicted a sharp increase in the proportion of women in that occupation over the next 30 years rated that occupation as significantly higher in prestige than a control group of subjects who read that the proportion of women in that occupation would stabilize at about its present level over the next 30 years. There was no significant difference between the two groups in their rating of the desirability of the occupation of accountant.

IMPRESSION FORMATION

16. Now let's shift gears to a second experiment. For this second experiment, we will focus on what social psychologists like to call "impression formation." This concept deals with the impressions we form about other people's personalities based on their behavior. Let's suppose that you have spent some time researching this topic deep in the recesses of a large university library and that you have stumbled across a chapter by Luchins in a book by Hovland (1957) which deals directly with impression formation. That chapter by Luchins discusses how the kinds and sequences of information about an individual affects our impression of what that person is "really like." Luchins was especially interested in the effect of a description of two quite different behavior patterns which are inconsistent with one another. Do we give more weight to the first behavior pattern (the primacy effect) or the second behavior pattern (the recency effect)?

Luchins did a study which used mimeographed paragraphs describing a fictitious person named Jim. One paragraph described Jim as exhibiting friendly, outgoing behavior; Luchins called this the *extrovertive (E) description.* The other paragraph described Jim as exhibiting more withdrawn behavior in similar situational contexts; this paragraph was called the *introvertive (I) description.* The two paragraphs are given below.

EXTROVERTIVE AND INTROVERTIVE DESCRIPTION*

Extrovertive Description: Jim left the house to get some stationery. He walked out into the sun-filled street with two of his friends, basking in the sun as he walked. Jim entered the stationery store, which was full of people. Jim talked with an acquaintance while he waited for the clerk to catch his eye. On his way out, he stopped to chat with a school friend who was just coming into the store. Leaving the store, he walked toward school. On his way out he met the girl to whom he had been introduced the night before. They talked for a short while, and then Jim left for school.

Introvertive Description: After school Jim left the classroom alone. Leaving the school, he started on his long walk home. The street was brilliantly filled with sunshine. Jim walked down the street on the shady side. Coming down the street toward him, he saw the pretty girl whom he had met on the previous evening. Jim crossed the street and entered a candy store. The store was crowded with students, and he noticed a few familiar faces. Jim waited quietly until the counterman caught his eye and then gave his order. Taking his drink, he sat down at a side table. When he had finished his drink, he went home.

Luchins first tested the two paragraphs separately and found that 95 percent of the subjects who were presented only with the E (extrovertive) paragraph rated Jim as friendly; only 3 percent of those presented only with the I (introvertive) paragraph rated him as friendly. For those presented with both paragraphs, 78 percent of those given the E-I sequence rated Jim as friendly, compared to 18 percent of those who received the I-E sequence.

The main purpose of the experiment was to answer this question: Does the *sequence* in which a person reads these two paragraphs affect the person's impression of Jim? If all of the subjects in the experiment read both paragraphs, then any difference in their impression of Jim should be due to the fact that one group of subjects read the extrovertive description followed by the introvertive description, while the other group of subjects read the introvertive description followed by the extrovertive description.

Luchins put these two paragraphs in two different sequences to test their order effect in personality impression. Half of the subjects read the E-I sequence of paragraphs, while the other half of the subjects read the I-E sequence of paragraphs; Luchins did not indent the second paragraph in either of these sequences, so that all of the subjects would read one long paragraph containing a description of two inconsistent behavioral patterns. Thus, all of the subjects read the same words about Jim but in two different sequences of behavior patterns.

---

*Reprinted by permission of Yale University Press from Abraham Luchins, "Primacy-Recency in Impression Formation," *The Order of Presentation in Persuasion,* by Carl I. Hovland. Copyright © 1957 by Yale University Press, Inc., pp. 34-35.

Luchins introduced his experiment to the subjects with the following words (1957, p. 35):

> In everyday life we sometimes form impressions of people based on what we read or hear about them. You will be given a paragraph about someone named Jim. Please read the paragraph through only once and then answer the question (or questions) about Jim.

The subjects were then handed a two-page booklet. The first page contained the description of Jim, while the second page contained some questions about Jim's personality.

Let's suppose that you are intrigued with this study and that you decide to carry out your own study on impression formation. Your first task is to design the questions that you will ask the subjects about Jim. Assume that you have decided to use a two-step approach in testing the subjects' impressions of Jim:

(1) You will ask the subjects to write out a paragraph with a maximum of 30 words about Jim at the top of the second page of the booklet so that they will form a definite impression about Jim before you ask them any specific questions about him, and

(2) You will ask the subjects to answer the set of questions on the second page of the booklet which are given below.*

SECOND PAGE OF IMPRESSION FORMATION BOOKLET

Directions: Select from each question the word or phrase that best fits your impression of Jim, and circle the number which corresponds to your choice.

1. How friendly or unfriendly a person is Jim?

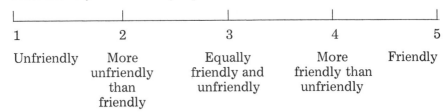

1	2	3	4	5
Unfriendly	More unfriendly than friendly	Equally friendly and unfriendly	More friendly than unfriendly	Friendly

---

*Adapted by permission of Yale University Press from Abraham S. Luchins, "Primacy-Recency in Impression Formation," *The Order of Presentation in Persuasion* by Carl I. Hovland. Copyright © 1957 by Yale University Press, Inc., p. 41. The questions given are the same ones that Luchins asked (1957, p. 41). He asked these questions in multiple-choice format with the "middle response" of each question (for example, "equally friendly and unfriendly") given as the last choice in a five-choice multiple-choice item. We have arranged the responses to the questions in rating-scale format so that the "equally" response is in the middle of a five-point rating scale. We prefer the rating-scale format given above, because we feel that it is easier to read.

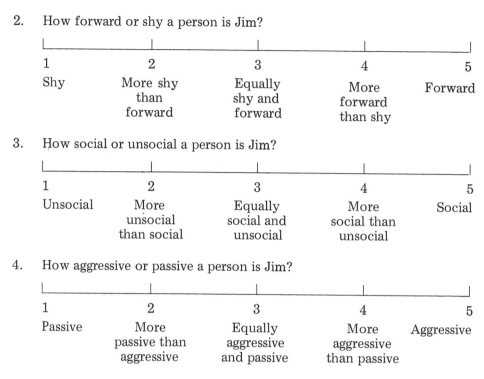

2.   How forward or shy a person is Jim?

1	2	3	4	5
Shy	More shy than forward	Equally shy and forward	More forward than shy	Forward

3.   How social or unsocial a person is Jim?

1	2	3	4	5
Unsocial	More unsocial than social	Equally social and unsocial	More social than unsocial	Social

4.   How aggressive or passive a person is Jim?

1	2	3	4	5
Passive	More passive than aggressive	Equally aggressive and passive	More aggressive than passive	Aggressive

Suppose you then find a group of 11 people to serve as subjects in your experiment (11 is an arbitrary number of people; we deliberately chose a small number in order to simplify the mathematics). You then mix together the two different descriptions of Jim (I-E and E-I) in a random order* and hand these descriptions to your subjects. Let's suppose that your subjects generate the hypothetical data regarding personality impression which is summarized below.

Question number	I-E group					E-I group					
1	3	4	4	3	2	5	4	5	4	5	5
2	2	3	4	3	2	4	5	4	4	5	4
3	3	3	3	2	3	5	4	4	3	5	5
4	3	4	3	2	2	4	5	5	5	5	5

Now analyze the data for the first two ratings using the *t*-test for independent samples. (We will analyze the other questions later.) Remember, we want to answer these two questions: (1) Were there any significant differences between the two experimental groups? (2) If so, in what way were the groups significantly different from one another?

_____

*See Appendix A for a description of this procedure.

By now you should be able to answer these questions without our taking you through the solution on a step-by-step basis. In trying to answer these questions, try to act like a research assistant who has been hired to answer them, work through what you consider to be a complete answer to these questions, and then write your summary of the results.

_ _ _ _ _ _ _ _ _ _ _ _ _ _ _ _ _

Rating 1:

The I-E group has five subjects. Their mean score is:

$$\frac{3 + 4 + 4 + 3 + 2}{5} = \frac{16}{5} = 3.2$$

Their standard deviation is:

$$\text{s.d.} = \sqrt{\frac{\Sigma X^2}{N} - \bar{X}^2}$$

$$= \sqrt{\frac{3^2 + 4^2 + 4^2 + 3^2 + 2^2}{5} - 3.2^2}$$

$$= \sqrt{\frac{54}{5} - 10.24}$$

$$= \sqrt{10.8 - 10.24}$$

$$= \sqrt{0.56}$$

$$\text{s.d.} = 0.75$$

Thus the five subjects in the I-E group have a mean of 3.2 and a standard deviation of 0.75 for rating 1.

The E-I group has six subjects. Their mean score is:

$$\frac{5 + 4 + 5 + 4 + 5 + 5}{6} = \frac{28}{6} = 4.67$$

Their standard deviation is:

$$\text{s.d.} = \sqrt{\frac{\Sigma X^2}{N} - \bar{X}^2}$$

$$= \sqrt{\frac{5^2 + 4^2 + 5^2 + 4^2 + 5^2 + 5^2}{6} - 4.67^2}$$

$$= \sqrt{\frac{132}{6} - 21.8}$$

$$= \sqrt{22 - 21.8}$$

$$= \sqrt{0.20}$$

s.d. = 0.45

Thus, the six subjects in the E-I group have a mean of 4.67 and a standard deviation of 0.45 for question 1.

Since $n_1 + n_2 - 2$ equals $5 + 6 - 2 = 9$, we note from Appendix D that the obtained value for t must be greater than 2.26 in order for there to be a significant difference between the two experimental groups. The formula for the t-test gives us:

$$t = \frac{\bar{X}_1 - \bar{X}_2}{\sqrt{\frac{(n_1)(s.d._1)^2 + (n_2)(s.d._2)^2}{n_1 + n_2 - 2}\left(\frac{1}{n_1} + \frac{1}{n_2}\right)}}$$

$$= \frac{3.2 - 4.67}{\sqrt{\frac{5(0.75)^2 + 6(0.45)^2}{5 + 6 - 2}\left(\frac{1}{5} + \frac{1}{6}\right)}}$$

$$= \frac{-1.47}{\sqrt{\frac{2.81 + 1.22}{9}(0.37)}}$$

$$= \frac{-1.47}{\sqrt{\frac{4.03}{9}(0.37)}}$$

$$= \frac{-1.47}{\sqrt{0.45(0.37)}}$$

$$= \frac{-1.47}{\sqrt{0.17}}$$

$$= \frac{-1.47}{0.41}$$

$$t = -3.59$$

Ignoring the negative sign, 3.59 is larger than 2.26, and so there is a significant difference between the two experimental groups on rating 1. Since the I-E group had a mean of 3.2, while the E-I group had a mean of 4.67, the E-I group saw Jim as significantly more friendly than the I-E group.

Rating 2:

The I-E group has five subjects. Their mean score is:

$$\frac{2 + 3 + 4 + 3 + 2}{5} = \frac{14}{5} = 2.8$$

Their standard deviation is:

$$\text{s.d.} = \sqrt{\frac{\Sigma X^2}{N} - \bar{X}^2}$$

$$= \sqrt{\frac{(2^2 + 3^2 + 4^2 + 3^2 + 2^2)}{5} - 2.8^2}$$

$$= \sqrt{\frac{42}{5} - 7.84}$$

$$= \sqrt{8.4 - 7.84}$$

$$= \sqrt{0.56}$$

$$\text{s.d.} = 0.75$$

Thus, the five subjects in the I-E group have a mean of 2.8 and a standard deviation of 0.75 for question 2.

The E-I group has six subjects. Their mean score is:

$$\frac{4 + 5 + 4 + 4 + 5 + 4}{6} = \frac{26}{6} = 4.33$$

Their standard deviation is:

$$\text{s.d.} = \sqrt{\frac{\Sigma X^2}{N} - \bar{X}^2}$$

$$= \sqrt{\frac{4^2 + 5^2 + 4^2 + 4^2 + 5^2 + 4^2}{6} - 4.33^2}$$

$$= \sqrt{\frac{114}{6} - 18.75}$$

$$= \sqrt{19 - 18.75}$$

$$= \sqrt{0.25}$$

$$\text{s.d.} = 0.5$$

Thus, the six subjects in the E-I group have a mean of 4.33 and a standard deviation of 0.5 for question 2.

Since $n_1 + n_2 - 2$ equals $5 + 6 - 2 = 9$, we note from Appendix D that the obtained value for t must be greater than 2.26 in order for there to be a significant difference between the two experimental groups.

The formula for the t-test gives us:

$$t = \frac{\bar{X}_1 - \bar{X}_2}{\sqrt{\frac{(n_1)(s.d._1)^2 + (n_2)(s.d._2)^2}{n_1 + n_2 - 2} \left(\frac{1}{n_1} + \frac{1}{n_2}\right)}}$$

$$= \frac{2.8 - 4.33}{\sqrt{\frac{5(0.75)^2 + 6(0.5)^2}{5 + 6 - 2} \left(\frac{1}{5} + \frac{1}{6}\right)}}$$

$$= \frac{-1.53}{\sqrt{\frac{2.81 + 1.5}{9} (0.37)}}$$

$$= \frac{-1.53}{\sqrt{\frac{4.31}{9} (0.37)}}$$

$$= \frac{-1.53}{\sqrt{0.48 (0.37)}}$$

$$= \frac{-1.53}{\sqrt{0.18}}$$

$$= \frac{-1.53}{0.42}$$

$$t = -3.64$$

Ignoring the negative sign, 3.64 is larger than 2.26, and so there is a significant difference between the two experimental groups on rating 2. Since the I-E group had a mean of 2.8 while the E-I group had a mean of 4.33, the E-I group saw Jim as significantly more forward than the I-E group.

For our hypothetical data, then, subjects who read an extrovertive description of Jim first, followed by an introvertive description, rated Jim as significantly more friendly and more forward than subjects who read these two descriptions in the opposite sequence. This means that for these hypothetical data, at least, subjects who first read a description of a person in which that person was described as friendly and outgoing tended to maintain an impression of that person as friendly and outgoing even when they read a later description which described that person as exhibiting the opposite of these qualities. In other words, our first impressions of other people often stick in our memory, even though the people may act in a very different way later on.

SELF-TEST FOR CHAPTER FIVE

This Self-Test is designed to show you whether you have mastered the key concepts and skills in Chapter Five. Answer each question to the best of your ability. Correct answers and review instructions are given at the end of the test.

When working on these problems, use the tear-out sheet in Appendix E for any formulas you need.

Whenever an article is cited in a problem, you will be working with the actual data of that published article, and you can check your answer against the actual results of that article. Otherwise, the data are hypothetical and created just for this book.

1.   You will recall that we analyzed the data for the table in frame 16 for only the first two ratings, and that the E-I group saw Jim as significantly more friendly and significantly more forward than the I-E group. What result do you get when you use the t-test for independent samples on ratings 3 and 4 of that table?

2.   Greenspoon (1955) did a classic study in which he studied the effect of an experimenter's saying "mmm-hmm" on the number of plural nouns which a subject would state aloud during a 25-minute test period. He was interested in determining the effectiveness of this special form of reinforcement on the subjects' verbal behavior. A control group of subjects did not receive any type of reinforcement sound during their 25-minute test period. Greenspoon kept a record of the number of plural nouns stated by the subjects during the 25-minute test period, and analyzed the data for each 5-minute interval of this 25-minute period. Let's analyze the data for his third 5-minute interval: the 14 subjects in the experimental group had a mean of 22.43 plural responses and a standard deviation of 16.9 plural responses during this 5-minute interval; the 15 subjects in the control group had a mean of 11.0 plural responses and a standard deviation of 6.83 plural responses during the same 5-minute interval. Was there a significant difference in the number of plural nouns generated between the experimental and control groups? If there was a significant difference, in what way were the two groups significantly different from one another?

Answers to Self-Test for Chapter Five

Compare your answers to the questions on the Self-Test with the answers given below. If all of your answers are correct, you are ready to go on to Chapter Six. If you missed any questions, review the frames indicated in parentheses following the answer. If you miss several questions, you should probably carefully reread the entire Chapter Five.

1.   *Rating 3 of the table in frame 16:*

The I-E group has five subjects. Their mean score is:

$$\frac{3 + 3 + 3 + 2 + 3}{5} = \frac{14}{5} = 2.8$$

Their standard deviation is:

$$\text{s.d.} = \sqrt{\frac{\Sigma X^2}{N} - \bar{X}^2}$$

$$= \sqrt{\frac{3^2 + 3^2 + 3^2 + 2^2 + 3^2}{5} - 2.8^2}$$

$$= \sqrt{\frac{40}{5} - 7.84}$$

$$= \sqrt{8 - 7.84}$$

$$= \sqrt{0.16}$$

$$\text{s.d.} = 0.4$$

Thus, the five subjects in the I-E group had a mean of 2.8 and a standard deviation of 0.4 on question 3.

The E-I group has six subjects. Their mean score is:

$$\frac{5 + 4 + 4 + 3 + 5 + 5}{6} = \frac{26}{6} = 4.33$$

Their standard deviation is:

$$\text{s.d.} = \sqrt{\frac{\Sigma X^2}{N} - \bar{X}^2}$$

$$= \sqrt{\frac{5^2 + 4^2 + 4^2 + 3^2 + 5^2 + 5^2}{6} - 4.33^2}$$

$$= \sqrt{\frac{116}{6} - 18.75}$$

$$= \sqrt{19.33 - 18.75}$$

$$= \sqrt{0.58}$$

s.d. $= 0.76$

Thus, the six subjects in the E-I group had a mean of 4.33 and a standard deviation of 0.76 on question 3.

Since $n_1 + n_2 - 2$ equals $5 + 6 - 2 = 9$, we note from Appendix D that the obtained value for t must be greater than 2.26 in order for there to be a significant difference between the two experimental groups.

$$t = \frac{\bar{X}_1 - \bar{X}_2}{\sqrt{\frac{(n_1)(s.d._1)^2 + (n_2)(s.d._2)^2}{n_1 + n_2 - 2} \left(\frac{1}{n_1} + \frac{1}{n_2}\right)}}$$

$$= \frac{2.8 - 4.33}{\sqrt{\frac{5(0.4)^2 + 6(0.76)^2}{5 + 6 - 2} \left(\frac{1}{5} + \frac{1}{6}\right)}}$$

$$= \frac{-1.53}{\sqrt{\frac{0.8 + 3.47}{9} (0.37)}}$$

$$= \frac{-1.53}{\sqrt{\frac{4.27}{9} (0.37)}}$$

$$= \frac{-1.53}{\sqrt{0.47 (0.37)}}$$

$$= \frac{-1.53}{\sqrt{0.17}}$$

$$= \frac{-1.53}{0.41}$$

$t = -3.73$

Ignoring the negative sign, 3.73 is larger than 2.26, and so there is a significant difference between the two experimental groups on rating 3.

Since the I-E group had a mean of 2.8, while the E-I group had a mean of 4.33, this means that the E-I group saw Jim as significantly more social than the I-E group.

Rating 4 of the table in frame 16:

The I-E group has five subjects. Their mean score is:

$$\frac{3 + 4 + 3 + 2 + 2}{5} = \frac{14}{5} = 2.8$$

Their standard deviation is:

$$\text{s.d.} = \sqrt{\frac{\Sigma X^2}{N} - \bar{X}^2}$$

$$= \sqrt{\frac{3^2 + 4^2 + 3^2 + 2^2 + 2^2}{5} - 2.8^2}$$

$$= \sqrt{\frac{42}{5} - 7.84}$$

$$= \sqrt{8.4 - 7.84}$$

$$= \sqrt{0.56}$$

$$\text{s.d.} = 0.75$$

Thus, the five subjects in the I-E group had a mean of 2.8 and a standard deviation of 0.75 on question 4.

The E-I group has six subjects. Their mean score is:

$$\frac{4 + 5 + 5 + 5 + 5 + 5}{6} = \frac{29}{6} = 4.83$$

Their standard deviation is:

$$\text{s.d.} = \sqrt{\frac{\Sigma X^2}{N} - \bar{X}^2}$$

$$= \sqrt{\frac{4^2 + 5^2 + 5^2 + 5^2 + 5^2 + 5^2}{6} - 4.83^2}$$

$$= \sqrt{\frac{141}{6} - 23.33}$$

$$= \sqrt{23.5 - 23.33}$$

$$= \sqrt{0.17}$$

$$\text{s.d.} = 0.41$$

Thus, the six subjects in the E-I group had a mean of 4.83 and a standard deviation of 0.41 on question 4.

Since $n_1 + n_2 - 2$ equals $5 + 6 - 2 = 9$, we note from Appendix D that the obtained value for t must be greater than 2.26 in order for there to be a significant difference between the two experimental groups.

The formula for the t-test gives us:

$$t = \frac{\bar{X}_1 - \bar{X}_2}{\sqrt{\frac{(n_1)\,(\text{s.d.}_1)^2 + (n_2)\,(\text{s.d.}_2)^2}{n_1 + n_2 - 2}\left(\frac{1}{n_1} + \frac{1}{n_2}\right)}}$$

$$= \frac{2.8 - 4.83}{\sqrt{\frac{5\,(0.75)^2 + 6\,(0.41)^2}{5 + 6 - 2}\left(\frac{1}{5} + \frac{1}{6}\right)}}$$

$$= \frac{-2.03}{\sqrt{\frac{2.81 + 1.01}{9}\,(0.37)}}$$

$$= \frac{-2.03}{\sqrt{\frac{3.82}{9}\,(0.37)}}$$

$$= \frac{-2.03}{\sqrt{0.42\,(0.37)}}$$

$$= \frac{-2.03}{\sqrt{0.16}}$$

$$= \frac{-2.03}{0.4}$$

$$t = -5.08$$

Ignoring the negative sign, 5.08 is larger than 2.26, and so there is a significant difference between the two experimental groups on rating 4.

Since the I-E group had a mean of 2.8, while the E-I group had a mean of 4.83, the E-I group saw Jim as significantly more aggressive than the I-E group.

The summary of the data analyses for all four ratings of the table in frame 16 would be as follows: Subjects who read a description of a person in which that person acted first in an extroverted manner and second in an introverted manner thought that that person was significantly more friendly, more forward, more social, and more aggressive than subjects who read a description of a person in which that person acted first in an introverted manner and second in an extroverted manner.   (frames 4-8)

2.   Remember that the 14 subjects in the experimental group had a mean of 22.43 plural responses and a standard deviation of 16.9 plural responses; the 15 subjects in the control group had a mean of 11.0 plural responses and a standard deviation of 6.83 plural responses.

Since $n_1 + n_2 - 2$ equals $14 + 15 - 2 = 27$, we note from Appendix D that the obtained value for t must be greater than 2.05 in order for there to be a significant difference between the two experimental groups.

$$t = \frac{\bar{X}_1 - \bar{X}_2}{\sqrt{\dfrac{(n_1)\,(\text{s.d.}_1)^2 + (n_2)\,(\text{s.d.}_2)^2}{n_1 + n_2 - 2} \left(\dfrac{1}{n_1} + \dfrac{1}{n_2}\right)}}$$

$$= \frac{22.43 - 11.0}{\sqrt{\dfrac{14\,(16.9)^2 + 15\,(6.83)^2}{14 + 15 - 2} \left(\dfrac{1}{14} + \dfrac{1}{15}\right)}}$$

$$= \frac{11.43}{\sqrt{\dfrac{3998.54 + 699.73}{27}}\,(0.14)}$$

$$= \frac{11.43}{\sqrt{\dfrac{4698.27}{27}}\,(0.14)}$$

$$= \frac{11.43}{\sqrt{174.01\,(0.14)}}$$

$$= \frac{11.43}{\sqrt{24.36}}$$

$$= \frac{11.43}{4.94}$$

$$t = 2.31$$

Since this value for t is larger than 2.05, this means that there was a significant difference between the two groups. And, since the experimental group had a mean of 22.43 plural responses, while the control group had a mean of 11.0 plural responses, the experimental group produced significantly more plural responses than the control group. (frames 4-6)

CHAPTER SIX

Impact of the Expertness
of the Communicator
on Advertising Effectiveness

Chapter Six will give you some additional practice in thinking through the mechanics of an experiment—how you would actually carry out an experiment—including its design, the procedures to use in collecting the data, and finally the analysis of the data that you have collected.

Imagine that you are conducting a research study. You will be asked a series of questions which will require you to think through how you would analyze the data from the study. You do not actually have to do this research study in order to understand the chapter, though you may find it interesting to do so.

Suppose that you have been hired by the advertising department of one of America's largest tire manufacturing companies. You have been asked to help the advertising department plan a television commercial to point out the advantages of a new product that has been developed in the company's research laboratories. This product uses a new combination of man-made fibers which has strengthened the durability of a newly created tire well beyond the present capabilities of your competitors' tires. Your company is very excited about the possible market sales that can come from the sale of this product if the advertising for the product is effective.

The hypothetical research study which you will be thinking about in this chapter will consist of the following steps:

(1) Overview of the experiment—determining the purpose of the experiment.
(2) Preparation for data collection—preparing copies of the questionnaire.
(3) Selection of the subjects for the experiment—using a table of random numbers, deciding where (in what location) to ask people if they will participate in the research study, preparing a standard invitation to use to ask people if they want to participate in the research study.

(4) Data collection—handing the questionnaire to the subjects, having the subjects fill out the questionnaire, coding the experimental condition which the subject was in.

(5) Data analysis and interpretation of the results of the experiment.

OVERVIEW OF THE EXPERIMENT

Your initial problem is to decide on the type of communicator to use in the television commercial. How should factors such as the communicator's attractiveness, credibility, and expertness be taken into account in the design of the television commercial?

Your advertising research group has decided to concentrate initially on the importance of the expertness of the communicator in the advertising message. You have been given the responsibility of designing and conducting a pilot study to test out some of the basic ideas in the commercial. Now what do you do?

After considerable thought and extensive research in a local university library of the literature on attitude change in social psychology, you decide to try out a simple pilot test with the communicator's expertness as a variable. To conserve budget funds on this initial pilot study, you decide to use written communications instead of video communications. If the written communications prove to be effective, you plan to write a script for the television commercial designed to take into account the results of your pilot test.

You have decided to concentrate on the following research question in your pilot study: What type of communicator is more likely to be perceived by people as more believable—a research expert or a marketing expert?

To answer that question, you decide to present your subjects with an identical message except that for the first experimental group, the message will be attributed to your company's vice-president for marketing, while for the second experimental group, it will be attributed to the director of your company's research laboratories. The specific design for the study calls for the first experimental group to receive the following information on the cover page of their informational booklet:

You are being asked to evaluate the message which follows. The speaker is the marketing vice-president of the Stronger Tire Company. He is speaking to a local group of businessmen about a new product which his company has developed. His intention is to persuade them of the usefulness and excellence of this product which has just recently been developed and tested in his company's laboratories.

The second experimental group will receive the following information on the cover page of their informational booklet:

You are being asked to evaluate the message which follows. The speaker is the director of research for the Stronger Tire Company. He holds a Ph.D. in chemistry from one of the country's largest universities. He is speaking to a local group of businessmen about a new product which his company has developed. His intention is to persuade them of the usefulness and excellence of this product which has just recently been developed and tested in his company's laboratories.

Both experimental groups will receive the following identical second page of the informational booklet:

I am speaking to you today because I think you will be very interested in this discussion of new information on a product which all of us use every day.

All of us want to use tires which are not only safe but also durable. Recent research in our laboratories has made an important discovery regarding the materials which are used to manufacture automobile tires. Our laboratories have discovered a new combination of materials which increases the tensile strength of our tires so that the tires are pound-for-pound stronger than steel. We are very excited about this product, and we feel that the tire which we have just recently developed will be the tire of the future. . . .

PREPARATION FOR DATA COLLECTION

Your first step is to design the questionnaire which you would ask the subjects to use to give their ratings of the message that they have read. In order to simplify this step, suppose that you have decided to use the following questionnaire as the third page of the booklet.

MESSAGE RATING SCALES

Question

1.

| 1 | 2 | 3 | 4 | 5 | 6 | 7 |

Unbelievable   Believable

2.

| 1 | 2 | 3 | 4 | 5 | 6 | 7 |

Fictitious   Factual

3.

| 1 | 2 | 3 | 4 | 5 | 6 | 7 |

Slanted   Objective

4.

1	2	3	4	5	6	7

Ineffective   Effective

5.

1	2	3	4	5	6	7

Unreasonable   Reasonable

                 MVP   DR

Both experimental groups will receive the identical third page of the informational booklet—the Message Rating Scales, which is a set of *semantic differential* rating scales. As you see from the scales, the phrase "semantic differential" refers to a *range* of meanings. The subject is to rate the message on a 7-point scale which contains adjectives which are polar opposites anchored at either end of the scale.

Note that the coding scheme at the bottom of the questionnaire allows you to code the experimental condition the subject was in—marketing vicepresident (MVP) or director of research (DR). This fact will become important when you reach the data-analysis phase of your experiment. If you have not coded the experimental condition on the questionnaire, you will have a pile of completed questionnaires with no way to determine which belong to the subjects in the MVP condition and which belong to the subjects in the DR condition. And if you cannot determine this fact, you will be unable to analyze your data, and your experiment will have been a failure.

The rating scales which we have been using throughout this book are arranged differently than you should arrange them in your own research. To simplify data analysis, we have purposely put the "positive" end of the scale on the same end of the scale for *all* of the items in the rating scale. In the table on page 181, for example, all of the positive adjectives (for example, "believable," "factual") are on the right end of each rating scale item.

In published research studies, however, the rating scale items have not usually been arranged this way during the data-collection phase of the study. Instead, the positive adjective would sometimes be on the right and sometimes on the left end of the scale. This varied placement is done in an attempt to correct for the tendencies of some subjects to rate all items positively (or negatively) based on their overall attitude toward the thing they are rating. This tendency to rate all questions the same is called a *response set*. Changing the positive end of the rating scale from one side to the other of the scale encourages the subject to read each rating item carefully, since he or she is forced to rate items using both sides of the scale by this technique.

In this book, we have put the positive adjective on the same end for every item in the rating scale to simplify the data analyses. Varying the positive and negative ends of the scale is a good idea in your own research studies. However, be very careful to assign the point value correctly (such as 7 points for the most positive rating, 6 points for the next most positive rating, . . . , 1 point for the least positive (or most negative). Otherwise, your scoring will be inaccurate.

SELECTING THE SUBJECTS FOR THE EXPERIMENT

Now you must decide on the procedure you would use in selecting the subjects who will participate in your research study without pay (since you are working on a shoe-string budget!).

Where would you go to find the subjects that you would want to participate in this experiment? Think about this question, and then write your answer down.

Let's talk about the procedure you will use when you collect the data for your study. You will need to establish a rule in your own mind for selecting subjects from among the people who cross your path.

Think about the rule you would use to decide whom to ask to participate in your research study, and write that procedure down. (If you have trouble answering this question, you might want to review pages 96–98.)

You need to develop a standard invitation to each person you ask to participate in your research study. Think about the standard invitation you would use to ask people to participate in your research study, and write that invitation down.

Not everyone will agree to participate in your research study, and whenever someone refuses to participate, you should continue to ask someone of the same sex as the person who just refused to participate, being careful to follow whatever procedure you are using to select subjects for your experiment.

Your final step in this phase of the experiment is to decide which of the descriptions of the two experts (MVP or DR) you will give to each subject in your experiment. Which one will you give to each subject? In order to answer this question, you should really use a table of random numbers in Appendix A. For now, suppose that you have already decided which of the two descriptions to give to each of the subjects in your experiment, and that you are ready to proceed to the next step in the research study—data collection.

DATA COLLECTION

If the person agrees to participate, you would show the subject the description which corresponds to the experimental condition to which he or she has randomly been assigned (MVP or DR) and ask him or her to fill out the questionnaire like the one given on page 181 by making a request like the following: Would you please fill out this form by circling the number from one to seven for each of these questions which corresponds to your opinion of the message which you just read. You would wait until the person filled out the form. After the person has handed the completed form back to you, you would circle either the letters MVP (for marketing vice-president) or DR (for director of research) which corresponds to the experimental treatment that subject was in. Thus you will have a record of this important fact.

DATA ANALYSIS

Suppose, further, that you have mixed together these two types of informational booklets*, and you have asked each of 13 passersby in a local shopping mall to read one of these booklets and to fill out the semantic differential rating scales.** You then obtain the hypothetical data summarized below.

Question	First Experimental Group (Marketing vice-president)							Second Experimental Group (Director of research)					
1	3	4	2	4	3	3	4	5	6	6	5	6	6
2	2	3	4	3	2	2	3	6	6	5	5	6	5
3	3	4	3	3	3	2	3	5	5	5	6	6	6
4	4	3	2	2	2	3	3	6	6	5	4	6	6
5	3	3	3	4	3	3	3	5	4	4	5	4	6

1.   Now you have finished collecting your data, and you are ready to analyze it. Take some time now to write out an answer to the following question: How would you test to see if the subjects in the MVP condition rated the message differently from the subjects in the DR condition? Take time now to write out *two* possible ways in which you could analyze the data from this experiment using the *t*-test for independent samples.

— — — — — — — — — — — — — — — —

If you've drawn a blank in trying to answer this question, go back to frames 2:3-7 and review our discussion of the two ways you could analyze the data of the experiment discussed in that chapter by using the chi-square test; then see if you can apply the same concepts to the *t*-test.
        If you are able to answer this question now, check your answer against the one given below.

— — — — — — — — — — — — — — — —

Your answer should be something like this: There are two ways you could analyze the data for this experiment:

(1)   For each subject, add up the rating on each of the five items listed in the table above to obtain a *total score* for each subject. Then use

---

*See Appendix A for how you could do this.
        **As we mentioned in Chapter Three, it is best if the person who is handing out the questionnaires does not know the hypotheses of the study so that he or she does not consciously (or unconsciously) influence the responses of the subjects in the experiment through tone of voice, posture, voice inflection, and so forth.

that score to compute the mean and standard deviation for each of the two groups of subjects. Apply the *t*-test to the data, and interpret the results.

(2) Analyze the data for *each of the five questions separately*. Find the mean and standard deviation for each question for each of the two experimental groups, apply the *t*-test to each question; then interpret the results for each question separately.

2. We could add up the ratings for the five questions in the table on page 184 for each subject to obtain a total score for each subject and then compute a *t*-test between the two experimental groups based on these total scores. If we did that, however, we might lose valuable information that was contained in each question separately. In designing a commercial, it is very important that *every* important dimension of the commercial affect the audience in the desired way. The use of a total score would mask the impact of the individual rating-scale items and you might miss the opportunity to determine how *each* rating dimension was perceived by the subjects.

For example, if some of the rating-scale items were perceived positively, while others were perceived negatively within one of the two experimental groups, these differences would blend together and be hidden within the total score. It may then result in a significant difference between the two experimental groups based on their total scores. However, the commercial might be even more effective if it were redesigned so that *every one* of the important rating dimensions was perceived positively by the subjects; the only way you could check to see if this were true would be to analyze the data separately using a *t*-test for each question in the rating scale. For this reason we will analyze the data separately for each question in the table under discussion.

Let's analyze the data using the *t*-test for independent samples for questions 3 and 5 now. (We'll save the analysis of the data for questions 1, 2, and 4 until later.) Be sure to answer the following questions in your analysis of the data for questions 3 and 5:

(1) Were there any significant differences between the two experimental groups?

(2) If so, in what way were these groups significantly different from one another?

_ _ _ _ _ _ _ _ _ _ _ _ _ _ _ _

Question 3: The first experimental group has seven subjects. Their mean score is:

$$\frac{3 + 4 + 3 + 3 + 3 + 2 + 3}{7} = \frac{21}{7} = 3.0$$

Their standard deviation is:

$$\text{s.d.} = \sqrt{\frac{\Sigma X^2}{N} - \bar{X}^2}$$

$$= \sqrt{\frac{3^2 + 4^2 + 3^2 + 3^2 + 3^2 + 2^2 + 3^2}{7} - 3^2}$$

$$= \sqrt{\frac{65}{7} - 9}$$

$$= \sqrt{9.29 - 9}$$

$$= \sqrt{0.29}$$

s.d. $= 0.54$

Thus, the seven subjects in the first experimental group have a mean of 3.0 and a standard deviation of 0.54 on question 3.

The second experimental group has six subjects. Their mean score is:

$$\frac{5 + 5 + 5 + 6 + 6 + 6}{6} = \frac{33}{6} = 5.5$$

Their standard deviation is:

$$\text{s.d.} = \sqrt{\frac{\Sigma X^2}{N} - \bar{X}^2}$$

$$= \sqrt{\frac{5^2 + 5^2 + 5^2 + 6^2 + 6^2 + 6^2}{6} - 5.5^2}$$

$$= \sqrt{\frac{183}{6} - 30.25}$$

$$= \sqrt{30.5 - 30.25}$$

$$= \sqrt{0.25}$$

s.d. $= 0.5$

Thus, the six subjects in the second experimental group have a mean of 5.5 and a standard deviation of 0.5 on question 3.

Since $n_1 + n_2 - 2$ equals $7 + 6 - 2 = 11$, we note from Appendix D that the obtained value for t must be greater than 2.20 in order for there to be a significant difference between the two experimental groups.

The formula for the *t*-test gives us:

$$t = \frac{\bar{X}_1 - \bar{X}_2}{\sqrt{\frac{(n_1)(\text{s.d.}_1)^2 + (n_2)(\text{s.d.}_2)^2}{n_1 + n_2 - 2}\left(\frac{1}{n_1} + \frac{1}{n_2}\right)}}$$

$$= \frac{3.0 - 5.5}{\sqrt{\frac{7(0.54)^2 + 6(0.5)^2}{7 + 6 - 2}\left(\frac{1}{7} + \frac{1}{6}\right)}}$$

$$= \frac{-2.5}{\sqrt{\frac{2.04 + 1.5}{11}(0.31)}}$$

$$= \frac{-2.5}{\sqrt{\frac{3.54}{11}(0.31)}}$$

$$= \frac{-2.5}{\sqrt{0.32(0.31)}}$$

$$= \frac{-2.5}{\sqrt{0.10}}$$

$$= \frac{-2.5}{0.32}$$

$$t = -7.81$$

Ignoring the negative sign, 7.81 is larger than 2.20, so there is a significant difference between the two experimental groups. Since the mean for the first experimental group was 3.0, while the mean for the second experimental group was 5.5, subjects who read a message attributed to the director of research rated that message as significantly more objective than subjects who read a message attributed to the marketing vice-president.

Question 5: The first experimental group has seven subjects. Their mean score is:

$$\frac{3 + 3 + 3 + 4 + 3 + 3 + 3}{7} = \frac{22}{7} = 3.14$$

Their standard deviation is:

$$\text{s.d.} = \sqrt{\frac{\Sigma X^2}{N} - \bar{X}^2}$$

$$= \sqrt{\frac{3^2 + 3^2 + 3^2 + 4^2 + 3^2 + 3^2 + 3^2}{7} - 3.14^2}$$

$$= \sqrt{\frac{70}{7} - 9.86}$$

$$= \sqrt{10 - 9.86}$$

$$= \sqrt{0.14}$$

$$\text{s.d.} = 0.37$$

Thus, the seven subjects in the first experimental group have a mean of 3.14 and a standard deviation of 0.37 on question 5.

The second experimental group has six subjects. Their mean score is:

$$\frac{5 + 4 + 4 + 5 + 4 + 6}{6} = \frac{28}{6} = 4.67$$

Their standard deviation is:

$$\text{s.d.} = \sqrt{\frac{\Sigma X^2}{N} - \bar{X}^2}$$

$$= \sqrt{\frac{5^2 + 4^2 + 4^2 + 5^2 + 4^2 + 6^2}{6} - 4.67^2}$$

$$= \sqrt{\frac{134}{6} - 21.81}$$

$$= \sqrt{22.33 - 21.81}$$

$$= \sqrt{0.52}$$

$$\text{s.d.} = 0.72$$

Thus, the six subjects in the second experimental group have a mean of 4.67 and a standard deviation of 0.72 on question 5.

Since $n_1 + n_2 - 2$ equals $7 + 6 - 2 = 11$, we note from Appendix D that the obtained value for t must be greater than 2.20 in order for there to be a significant difference between the two experimental groups.

The formula for the t-test gives us:

$$ t = \frac{\bar{X}_1 - \bar{X}_2}{\sqrt{\dfrac{(n_1)\,(\text{s.d.}_1)^2 + (n_2)\,(\text{s.d.}_2)^2}{n_1 + n_2 - 2} \cdot \left(\dfrac{1}{n_1} + \dfrac{1}{n_2}\right)}} $$

$$ = \frac{3.14 - 4.67}{\sqrt{\dfrac{7\,(0.37)^2 + 6\,(0.72)^2}{7 + 6 - 2} \left(\dfrac{1}{7} + \dfrac{1}{6}\right)}} $$

$$ = \frac{-1.53}{\sqrt{\dfrac{0.96 + 3.11}{11}\,(0.31)}} $$

$$ = \frac{-1.53}{\sqrt{\dfrac{4.07}{11}\,(0.31)}} $$

$$ = \frac{-1.53}{\sqrt{(0.37)\,(0.31)}} $$

$$ = \frac{-1.53}{\sqrt{0.12}} $$

$$ = \frac{-1.53}{0.35} $$

$$ t = -4.37 $$

Ignoring the negative sign, 4.37 is larger than 2.20, so there is a significant difference between the two experimental groups. Since the mean for the first experimental group was 3.14 while the mean for the second experimental group was 4.67, subjects who read a message attributed to the director of research rated that message as significantly more reasonable than subjects who read a message attributed to the marketing vice-president.

SELF-TEST FOR CHAPTERS FOUR THROUGH SIX

This Self-Test is designed to show you whether you have mastered the key concepts and skills in Chapters Four through Six. Answer each question to the best of your ability. Correct answers and review instructions are given at the end of the test.

When working on these problems, you might find it helpful to use the tear-out sheet in Appendix E for any formulas you need.

Whenever an article is cited in a problem, you will be working with the actual data of that published article, and you can check your answer against the actual results of that article. Whenever an article is not cited in a problem, we have created some hypothetical data to allow you to practice the skills you have learned.

1. You will recall that your data analyses of the material in the table on page 184 for questions 3 and 5 revealed that subjects who read a message attributed to the director of research rated that message as significantly more objective and more reasonable than subjects who read a message attributed to the marketing vice-president. At that time we said we would save the data analyses for questions 1, 2, and 4 for the Self-Test. Analyze the data for those three questions now, using the t-test for independent samples. Were there any significant differences between the two experimental groups? If so, in what way were the groups significantly different from one another?

2. Aronson and Linder (1965) studied the effect of gain and loss of esteem and how these variables affected interpersonal attraction. The authors hypothesized that if the behavior of a confederate toward a subject was initially negative but gradually became more positive, the subject would like the confederate more than she would have if the behavior of the confederate had been uniformly positive. Undergraduate females (the subjects) at the University of Minnesota were led to believe that they were assisting the experimenter in a verbal conditioning experiment. Actually, the person they were observing through a one-way mirror (that is, the subjects could see the confederate, but the confederate could not see them) was a paid confederate programmed to act in certain ways after a series of conversations with the subjects. In the positive-positive condition, the confederate, throughout the entire experiment, made uniformly positive statements about the subject (which the subject overheard). In the negative-positive condition, the confederate expressed a negative impression of the subject (which the subject overheard) during the first three interviews and then gradually became more and more favorable in her impression of the subject through the next four interviews. After the experiment was over, the subjects rated their liking of the confederate somewhere on a 21-point scale from –10 to +10. The 20 subjects in the positive-positive group had a mean liking score

for the confederate of 6.42 with a standard deviation of 1.42; the 20 subjects in the negative-positive group had a mean liking score for the confederate of 7.67 with a standard deviation of 1.51. Was there a significant difference between these two groups in their liking for the confederate? If there was, which group liked the confederate more?

3.   Herman (1967) compared the teaching attitudes of male athletes and nonathletes who were senior physical education majors and minors at Colorado State College on the *Minnesota Teacher Attitude Inventory* (MTAI). The students were categorized as either successful in athletics (athletes) or unsuccessful in athletics (nonathletes). The 14 athletes had a mean of 116 and a standard deviation of 31.11 on the MTAI, while the 28 nonathletes had a mean of 119.54 and a standard deviation of 32.41 on the MTAI. Was there a significant difference between the MTAI scores of the athletes and nonathletes?

4.   Samuels (1967) conducted an experiment to determine the effect of pictures on the ability of children to learn words. Children who were enrolled in a pre-first-grade summer program were randomly assigned to either an experimental group (which was asked to learn words that were illustrated with simple pictures in the form of black-and-white drawings) or a control group (which was asked to learn the same words but without the aid of pictures). After several learning trials, the children were tested on their knowledge of the words that they were taught. The 10 children in the experimental group had a mean of 11.30 and a standard deviation of 5.79, while the 10 children in the control group had a mean of 19.20 and a standard deviation of 7.93. Was there a significant difference between the experimental and control groups in the number of words that they remembered correctly (that is, did the presence of the pictures facilitate learning or inhibit learning)?

Answers to Self-Test for Chapters Four through Six

Compare your answers to the questions on the Self-Test with the answers given below. If all of your answers are correct, you are ready to go on to Chapter Seven. If you missed any questions, review the frames indicated in parentheses following the answer. If you miss several questions which refer to frames in the same chapter, you should probably carefully reread that entire chapter.

1.   *Question 1:* The first experimental group has seven subjects. Their mean score is:

$$\frac{3 + 4 + 2 + 4 + 3 + 3 + 4}{7} = \frac{23}{7} = 3.29$$

Their standard deviation is:

$$\text{s.d.} = \sqrt{\frac{\Sigma X^2}{N} - \bar{X}^2}$$

$$= \sqrt{\frac{79}{7} - 3.29^2}$$

$$= \sqrt{11.29 - 10.82}$$

$$= \sqrt{0.47}$$

$$\text{s.d.} = 0.69$$

Thus, the seven subjects in the first experimental group had a mean of 3.29 and a standard deviation of 0.69 on question 1.

The second experimental group has six subjects. Their mean score is:

$$\frac{5 + 6 + 6 + 5 + 6 + 6}{6} = \frac{34}{6} = 5.67$$

Their standard deviation is:

$$\text{s.d.} = \sqrt{\frac{\Sigma X^2}{N} - \bar{X}^2}$$

$$= \sqrt{\frac{5^2 + 6^2 + 6^2 + 5^2 + 6^2 + 6^2}{6} - 5.67^2}$$

$$= \sqrt{\frac{194}{6} - 32.15}$$

$$= \sqrt{32.33 - 32.15}$$

$$= \sqrt{0.18}$$

$$\text{s.d.} = 0.42$$

Thus, the six subjects in the second experimental group had a mean of 5.67 and a standard deviation of 0.42 on question 1.

Since $n_1 + n_2 - 2$ equals $7 + 6 - 2 = 11$, we note from Appendix D that the obtained value for t must be greater than 2.20 in order for there to be a significant difference between the two experimental groups.

The formula for the t-test gives us:

$$t = \frac{\bar{X}_1 - \bar{X}_2}{\sqrt{\frac{(n_1)(s.d._1)^2 + (n_2)(s.d._2)^2}{n_1 + n_2 - 2} \left(\frac{1}{n_1} + \frac{1}{n_2}\right)}}$$

$$= \frac{3.29 - 5.67}{\sqrt{\frac{7(0.69)^2 + 6(0.42)^2}{7 + 6 - 2} \left(\frac{1}{7} + \frac{1}{6}\right)}}$$

$$= \frac{-2.38}{\sqrt{\frac{3.33 + 1.06}{11}(0.31)}}$$

$$= \frac{-2.38}{\sqrt{\frac{4.39}{11}(0.31)}}$$

$$= \frac{-2.38}{\sqrt{0.40(0.31)}}$$

$$= \frac{-2.38}{\sqrt{0.12}}$$

$$= \frac{-2.38}{0.35}$$

$$t = -6.8$$

Ignoring the negative sign, 6.8 is larger than 2.20, and so there is a significant difference between the two experimental groups. Since the mean for the first experimental group was 3.29 while the mean for the second experimental group was 5.67, subjects who read a message attributed to the director of research rated that message as significantly more believable than subjects who read a message attributed to the marketing vice-president.

Question 2: The first experimental group has seven subjects. Their mean score is:

$$\frac{2 + 3 + 4 + 3 + 2 + 2 + 3}{7} = \frac{19}{7} = 2.71$$

Their standard deviation is:

$$\text{s.d.} = \sqrt{\frac{\Sigma X^2}{N} - \bar{X}^2}$$

$$= \sqrt{\frac{2^2 + 3^2 + 4^2 + 3^2 + 2^2 + 2^2 + 3^2}{7} - 2.71^2}$$

$$= \sqrt{\frac{55}{7} - 7.34}$$

$$= \sqrt{7.86 - 7.34}$$

$$= \sqrt{0.52}$$

$$\text{s.d.} = 0.72$$

Thus, the seven subjects in the first experimental group had a mean of 2.71 and a standard deviation of 0.72 on question 2.

The second experimental group has six subjects. Their mean score is:

$$\frac{6 + 6 + 5 + 5 + 6 + 5}{6} = \frac{33}{6} = 5.5$$

Their standard deviation is:

$$\text{s.d.} = \sqrt{\frac{\Sigma X^2}{N} - \bar{X}^2}$$

$$= \sqrt{\frac{6^2 + 6^2 + 5^2 + 5^2 + 6^2 + 5^2}{6} - 5.5^2}$$

$$= \sqrt{\frac{183}{6} - 30.25}$$

$$= \sqrt{30.5 - 30.25}$$

$$= \sqrt{0.25}$$

s.d. $= 0.5$

Thus, the six subjects in the second experimental group had a mean of 5.5 and a standard deviation of 0.5 on question 2.

Since $n_1 + n_2 - 2$ equals $7 + 6 - 2 = 11$, we note from Appendix D that the obtained value for t must be greater than 2.20 in order for there to be a significant difference between the two experimental groups.

The formula for the t-test gives us:

$$t = \frac{\bar{X}_1 - \bar{X}_2}{\sqrt{\frac{(n_1)(\text{s.d.}_1)^2 + (n_2)(\text{s.d.}_2)^2}{n_1 + n_2 - 2} \left(\frac{1}{n_1} + \frac{1}{n_2}\right)}}$$

$$= \frac{2.71 - 5.5}{\sqrt{\frac{7(0.72)^2 + 6(0.5)^2}{7 + 6 - 2} \left(\frac{1}{7} + \frac{1}{6}\right)}}$$

$$= \frac{-2.79}{\sqrt{\frac{3.63 + 1.5}{11} (0.31)}}$$

$$= \frac{-2.79}{\sqrt{\frac{5.13}{11} (0.31)}}$$

$$= \frac{-2.79}{\sqrt{0.47 (0.31)}}$$

$$= \frac{-2.79}{\sqrt{0.15}}$$

$$= \frac{-2.79}{0.39}$$

$t = -7.15$

Ignoring the negative sign, 7.15 is larger than 2.20, so there is a significant difference between the two experimental groups. Since the mean for the first experimental group was 2.71 while the mean for the second experimental group was 5.5, subjects who read a message attributed to the director of research rated that message as significantly more factual than subjects who read a message attributed to the marketing vice-president.

Question 4: The first experimental group has seven subjects. Their mean score is:

$$\frac{4 + 3 + 2 + 2 + 2 + 3 + 3}{7} = \frac{19}{7} = 2.71$$

Their standard deviation is:

$$\text{s.d.} = \sqrt{\frac{\Sigma X^2}{N} - \bar{X}^2}$$

$$= \sqrt{\frac{4^2 + 3^2 + 2^2 + 2^2 + 2^2 + 3^2 + 3^2}{7} - 2.71^2}$$

$$= \sqrt{\frac{55}{7} - 7.34}$$

$$= \sqrt{7.86 - 7.34}$$

$$= \sqrt{0.52}$$

$$\text{s.d.} = 0.72$$

Thus, the seven subjects in the first experimental group had a mean of 2.71 and a standard deviation of 0.72 on question 4.

The second experimental group has six subjects. Their mean score is:

$$\frac{6 + 6 + 5 + 4 + 6 + 6}{6} = \frac{33}{6} = 5.5$$

Their standard deviation is:

$$\text{s.d.} = \sqrt{\frac{\Sigma X^2}{N} - \bar{X}^2}$$

$$= \sqrt{\frac{6^2 + 6^2 + 5^2 + 4^2 + 6^2 + 6^2}{6} - 5.5^2}$$

$$= \sqrt{\frac{185}{6} - 30.25}$$

$$= \sqrt{30.83 - 30.25}$$

$$= \sqrt{0.58}$$

$$\text{s.d.} = 0.76$$

Thus, the six subjects in the second experimental group had a mean of 5.5 and a standard deviation of 0.76 on question 4.

Since $n_1 + n_2 - 2$ equals $7 + 6 - 2 = 11$, we note from Appendix D that the obtained value for t must be greater than 2.20 in order for there to be a significant difference between the two experimental groups.

The formula for the t-test gives us:

$$t = \frac{\bar{X}_1 - \bar{X}_2}{\sqrt{\frac{(n_1)(\text{s.d.}_1)^2 + (n_2)(\text{s.d.}_2)^2}{n_1 + n_2 - 2}\left(\frac{1}{n_1} + \frac{1}{n_2}\right)}}$$

$$= \frac{2.71 - 5.5}{\sqrt{\frac{7(0.72)^2 + 6(0.76)^2}{7 + 6 - 2}\left(\frac{1}{7} + \frac{1}{6}\right)}}$$

$$= \frac{-2.79}{\sqrt{\frac{3.63 + 3.47}{11}(0.31)}}$$

$$= \frac{-2.79}{\sqrt{\frac{7.1}{11}(0.31)}}$$

$$= \frac{-2.79}{\sqrt{0.65(0.31)}}$$

$$= \frac{-2.79}{\sqrt{0.20}}$$

$$= \frac{-2.79}{0.45}$$

$$t = -6.2$$

Ignoring the negative sign, 6.2 is larger than 2.20, so there is a significant difference between the two experimental groups. Since the mean for the first experimental group was 2.71 while the mean for the second experimental group was 5.5, this means that subjects who read a message attributed to the director of research rated that message as significantly more effective than subjects who read a message attributed to the marketing vice-president.

The complete summary of the data analyses of the responses in the table on page 184 would, therefore, be as follows: subjects who read a message attributed to the director of research rated that message as significantly more believable, more factual, more objective, more effective, and more reasonable than subjects who read a message attributed to the marketing vice-president. If the results of your other research studies are similar to the results of this pilot study, it looks like the television script will be written around the director of research instead of the marketing vice-president!   (Chapter Five, frames 4–8)

2. Remember that the 20 subjects in the negative-positive group had a mean liking score for the confederate of 7.67 with a standard deviation of 1.51; the 20 subjects in the positive-positive group had a mean liking score for the confederate of 6.42 with a standard deviation of 1.42.

Since $n_1 + n_2 - 2$ equals $20 + 20 - 2 = 38$, we note from Appendix D that the obtained value for t must be greater than 2.02 in order for there to be a significant difference between the two experimental groups.

$$t = \frac{\bar{X}_1 - \bar{X}_2}{\sqrt{\frac{(n_1)(s.d._1)^2 + (n_2)(s.d._2)^2}{n_1 + n_2 - 2} \left(\frac{1}{n_1} + \frac{1}{n_2}\right)}}$$

$$= \frac{7.67 - 6.42}{\sqrt{\frac{20(1.51)^2 + 20(1.42)^2}{20 + 20 - 2} \left(\frac{1}{20} + \frac{1}{20}\right)}}$$

$$= \frac{1.25}{\sqrt{\frac{45.60 + 40.33}{38} (0.10)}}$$

$$= \frac{1.25}{\sqrt{\frac{85.93}{38} (0.10)}}$$

$$= \frac{1.25}{\sqrt{2.26 (0.10)}}$$

$$= \frac{1.25}{\sqrt{0.23}}$$

$$= \frac{1.25}{0.48}$$

$$t = 2.60$$

Since this value for t is larger than 2.02, there is a significant difference between the two groups of subjects. Since the negative-positive group had a mean rating of the confederate of 7.67, while the positive-positive group had a mean rating of 6.42, subjects in the negative-positive group rated their liking of the confederate significantly higher than subjects in the positive-positive group. In this study confederates who started out saying negative things but who switched to saying positive things about the subjects were liked significantly more by the subjects than confederates who said positive things about the subjects consistently throughout the experiment.

Perhaps the moral to this experiment is: If you want someone to like you, you should start out your acquaintance by saying negative things about him or her. Then, when you later say positive things about him or her, you will be seen as a discriminating observer of character who has obvious good taste in your choice of friends! (Chapter Four, frames 10–11)

3.

$$t = \frac{\bar{X}_1 - \bar{X}_2}{\sqrt{\frac{(n_1)\,(\text{s.d.}_1)^2 + (n_2)\,(\text{s.d.}_2)^2}{n_1 + n_2 - 2}\left(\frac{1}{n_1} + \frac{1}{n_2}\right)}}$$

$$= \frac{119.54 - 116}{\sqrt{\frac{28\,(32.41)^2 + 14\,(31.11)^2}{28 + 14 - 2}\left(\frac{1}{28} + \frac{1}{14}\right)}}$$

$$= \frac{3.54}{\sqrt{\frac{28\,(1050.41) + 14\,(967.83)}{40}\,(.04 + .07)}}$$

$$= \frac{3.54}{\sqrt{\frac{29{,}411.48 + 13{,}549.62}{40}\,(.11)}}$$

$$= \frac{3.54}{\sqrt{\frac{42{,}961.10}{40}\,(.11)}}$$

$$= \frac{3.54}{\sqrt{1074.03 \ (.11)}}$$

$$= \frac{3.54}{\sqrt{118.14}}$$

$$= \frac{3.54}{10.87}$$

$$t = 0.33$$

Since $n_1 + n_2 - 2 = 40$, and since Appendix D requires a value for t greater than 2.02 to obtain a significant difference, there was no significant difference between the MTAI scores of the athletes and nonathletes. (Chapter Four, frames 10–11)

4.

$$t = \frac{\bar{X}_1 - \bar{X}_2}{\sqrt{\frac{(n_1) \ (\text{s.d.}_1)^2 + (n_2) \ (\text{s.d.}_2)^2}{n_1 + n_2 - 2} \left(\frac{1}{n_1} + \frac{1}{n_2} \right)}}$$

$$= \frac{11.30 - 19.20}{\sqrt{\frac{10 \ (5.79)^2 + 10 \ (7.93)^2}{10 + 10 - 2} \left(\frac{1}{10} + \frac{1}{10} \right)}}$$

$$= \frac{-7.9}{\sqrt{\frac{10 \ (33.52) + 10 \ (62.88)}{18} \ (.10 + .10)}}$$

$$= \frac{-7.9}{\sqrt{\frac{335.2 + 628.8}{18} \ (.20)}}$$

$$= \frac{-7.9}{\sqrt{\frac{964}{18} \ (.20)}}$$

$$= \frac{-7.9}{\sqrt{53.56 \ (.20)}}$$

$$= \frac{-7.9}{\sqrt{10.71}}$$

$$= \frac{-7.9}{3.27}$$

$$t \ = \ -2.42$$

Since $n_1 + n_2 - 2 = 18$, and since Appendix D requires a value for t greater than 2.10 to obtain a significant difference, there was a significant difference between the experimental and control groups. Children who learned the words without pictures remembered significantly more words than children who learned the words with pictures.
(Chapter Four, frames 10–11)

The Use of the Rank-Order Correlation in Psychological Research

Part III of this book focuses on the relationship between two variables—how closely related the rank orders of one group of subjects are on the two variables under study. You will learn how to compute a rank-order correlation step-by-step, and once again you will be asked to show that you understand the meaning of the mathematical computations by writing up the results of your data analyses.

By the time you complete Part III, you should have a good sense of how to apply the rank-order correlation to data in order to determine the results of an experiment. Thus, you will have gained a valuable tool which you can apply to research data to determine "how the data came out."

Part III includes a Self-Test so that you can check your progress in terms of the following objectives.

Objectives

After completing Part III, you will be able to:

- compute a rank-order correlation, rho.
- distinguish between a positive correlation and a negative correlation.
- classify values of a correlation as near-zero, low, moderate, or high.
- assign ranks to tied scores when computing a rank-order correlation.
- compute a median correlation.

CHAPTER SEVEN

Rank-Order Correlation

1. This book concentrates on teaching you three statistical techniques:

   - the chi-square test for a fourfold table (Chapters One through Three),
   - the *t*-test for independent samples (Chapters Four through Six), and
   - the rank-order correlation.

You already know how to use these first two statistical tests to answer the following two questions:

   (1) Was there a significant difference between the two experimental groups?
   (2) If so, in what way were the two groups significantly different from one another?

Chapter Seven concentrates on the third statistical technique—the rank-order correlation. A *rank-order correlation* is a number between –1 and +1 which summarizes the degree of relationship between two variables for *one* group of subjects. It does *not* tell you if there is a significant difference between two experimental groups. It does *not* compare two groups of subjects; rather it tells us how closely related two variables are for one group of subjects.

To clarify the meaning of a correlation, let's look at some examples of questions that can be answered by means of a rank-order correlation:

   - How closely related are the SAT-verbal scores and the freshmen grade-point average for last year's freshman class at our university?
   - How closely related are the final grades in geometry of this year's geometry students and their grades last year in Algebra I?
   - How closely related are the aptitude test scores of that company's pilots to their subsequent performance ratings as pilots?
   - How closely related are the scores on this employment screening test to the actual ratings of job performance for everyone we hired three years ago?

- How closely related are the high school rank-in-class scores and the freshman grade-point average scores of last year's freshman class at our college?

Are you getting the idea of the kind of question a correlation is designed to answer? We can compute a correlation whenever we have scores on two variables for one group of subjects. As we have seen, a *variable* is a quantity which can "vary" from one person to another in such a way that it can be assigned a numerical value. A variable must be readily *measurable* in some quantitative way so that scores can be assigned to the subjects. Some common examples of variables would be the following:

> height
> weight
> annual salary
> grade-point average
> aptitude test scores
> amount of insurance sold last year
> high school rank-in-class
> Graduate Record Examination scores
> amount of education
> number of college degrees obtained

You could probably add many other variables to that list based on your own experience.

Now let's see how to compute a rank-order correlation. After we've done that and given you a chance to practice that skill, we'll return to explain more about what a rank-order correlation means.

You can compute a rank-order correlation by following these nine steps:

Step 1: Make a list of the names of every subject in your sample. Write each person's score for both variables beside his or her name. Cross out the name of any subject who does not have a score on *both* variables.

Step 2. Look at the scores of each subject on the *first* variable only. Find the largest score, and give that score a rank of 1 by writing the number "1" next to the score. Find the second-largest score, and write the number "2" next to it; find the third-largest score, and write the number "3" beside it; and so on, until every score has been assigned a rank-order number.

What happens when two or more scores are *tied* for the same rank? In that case, we follow this decision rule:

Rule: Whenever two or more subjects have the same score within the variable being ranked, assign to each of these tied scores the *mean value of the ranks* that would have been assigned if these scores had not been tied.

For example, let's suppose we had the following four scores:

29, 18, 20, 29.

Two subjects have the same score, 29. Since 29 is the largest score, the first score of 29 would receive a rank of 1 and the second score of 29 a rank of 2, had they not been tied. The *average* of the ranks of the tied scores is $\frac{1 + 2}{2} = 1.5$. Therefore the two scores of 29 would each receive a rank of 1.5. The score of 20 would receive a rank of 3 (since we have already used the rank of 2 in computing our average rank for the two scores tied at 29). The score of 18 would receive a rank of 4.

Step 3. Look at the scores of each subject on the *second* variable only. Find the largest score, and give that score a rank of 1 by writing the number "1" next to that score; find the second-largest score, and write the number "2" next to it; find the third-largest score, and write tne number "3" next to it, and so on, until every score has been assigned a rank-order. In the event of tied scores, assign the ranks according to the decision rule of Step 2.

Step 4. Find the difference of the two ranks for each subject (*d*) by subtracting the rank on the second variable from the rank on the first variable. Retain the resulting plus or minus signs, because these will be important later. (A good rule of thumb that you can use to check your arithmetic is this: The sum of all the *d* scores that are *positive* (for example, +2, +3, +0.5, and the like) should *equal* the sum of all of the *d* scores that are *negative* (-2, -1, -0.5, and so on); if these two sums are not equal, you made a mistake somewhere in your computations.)

Step 5. Square the difference of the two ranks for each subject by multiplying the difference by itself. (Since each number is being multiplied by itself, the results will all be positive numbers.)

Step 6. Find the sum of the squared difference scores for all subjects.

Step 7. Multiply the answer found in Step 6 by the number 6.

Step 8. Divide the answer of Step 7 by $N(N^2 - 1)$ where N is the number of subjects for whom you have scores on *both* variables.

Step 9. Subtract the answer of Step 8 from the number 1, and the resulting number is the value of the rank-order correlation.

The rank-order correlation is symbolized by the word "rho."* In mathematical terms, the nine steps for computing a rank-order correlation can be summarized by the following formula:

---

*The Greek letter ρ (rho) is frequently used in published research studies to stand for this rank-order correlation. You need to be aware of this Greek symbol ρ so that you can recognize it in your reading of journal articles.

$$rho = 1 - \frac{6\Sigma d^2}{N(N^2 - 1)}$$

where

N = The number of subjects for whom you have scores for both of the variables

d = The difference of the ranks for each subject

d^2 = The square of the difference of the ranks for each subject

Σd^2 = The sum of the squares of the difference of the ranks for each subject (Σ is the symbol for sum).

One part of the computational process—the procedure for assigning ranks to tied scores—deserves some special attention. Let's practice that procedure now with two examples to make sure you have mastered it.

Example 1. Suppose the eight subjects given below have the given grade-point averages (GPA). Fill in the rank of each subject in the table below, and then check your ranks against the correct ones given below the dashed line.

Subject	Grade-point Average (GPA)	Rank of GPA
1	3.8	———
2	3.6	———
3	3.5	———
4	3.5	———
5	3.5	———
6	3.3	———
7	3.1	———
8	3.1	———

- - - - - - - - - - - - - - - -

Subject	Grade-point Average (GPA)	Rank of GPA
1	3.8	1
2	3.6	2
3	3.5	4
4	3.5	4
5	3.5	4
6	3.3	6
7	3.1	7.5
8	3.1	7.5

Subjects 3, 4, and 5 each are tied at the same GPA of 3.5, which would be ranked 3, 4, 5 if the scores were not tied. Therefore, each of these three subjects should receive the average of these ranks: $\frac{3 + 4 + 5}{3} = 4$.

Subjects 7 and 8 are each tied at the same GPA of 3.1 which would be ranked 7, 8 if the scores were not tied. Therefore, each of these two subjects should receive the average of these ranks: $\frac{7 + 8}{2} = 7.5$

2.   Notice that we made the above example simpler by arranging the grade-point averages in descending order from highest to lowest. We won't do that for the second example, which more closely simulates what you would normally do with some actual data.

Example 2. Suppose that the 10 subjects given below have the given reading test scores. Fill in the rank of each subject in the table below, and then check your ranks against the correct ones given.

Subject	Reading Test Score	Rank of Reading Test Score
1	60	_____
2	70	_____
3	65	_____
4	80	_____
5	65	_____
6	50	_____
7	75	_____
8	65	_____
9	40	_____
10	65	_____

Subject	Reading Test Score	Rank of Reading Test Score
1	60	8
2	70	3
3	65	5.5
4	80	1
5	65	5.5
6	50	9
7	75	2
8	65	5.5
9	40	10
10	65	5.5

Subjects 3, 5, 8, and 10 each are tied at the same reading score of 65, which would be ranked 4, 5, 6, 7 if the scores were not tied. Therefore, each of these four subjects should receive the average of these ranks: $\frac{4 + 5 + 6 + 7}{4}$ = $\frac{22}{4}$ = 5.5.

3.   Let's do a sample problem to practice computing a value for rho. Suppose that we have a sample of seven subjects for whom we have hypothetical scores on two variables: their SAT-math scores as high school seniors (the familiar "College Board" math scores) and their grade-point average at our college for their freshman year. These scores are summarized in Table 7.1.

Table 7.1. SAT-Math Scores and Freshman Grade-Point Averages for a Group of Seven Students

Student	SAT-Math Score	Freshman GPA (4-point scale)
John Jones	520	3.00
Sally Smith	650	2.60
Betsy Foreman	680	3.65
Erik Appleman	580	3.15
Samantha Jones	600	2.75
George Johnson	750	3.75
Mac Friend	610	3.10

Let's compute the value for rho for the scores given in Table 7.1 by using the nine steps:

Step 1. Do you have a score on *both* variables for every subject in the sample?

— — — — — — — — — — — — — — — —

Yes.

4.   Is it necessary to cross any of these subjects off of your list?

— — — — — — — — — — — — — — — —

No, since you have a score on both variables for every subject in the sample.

5.   *Step 2.* Rank the subjects on the first variable.

— — — — — — — — — — — — — — — —

The first variable of Table 7.1 is the SAT-math scores. The largest score is 750, so that score gets a rank of 1; the second-largest score of 680 gets a rank of 2; 650 gets a rank of 3; 610 gets a rank of 4; 600 gets a rank of 5; 580 gets a rank of 6; and 520 gets a rank of 7. There are no tied scores, so we do not need to average any of these ranks.

6.   *Step 3.*   Rank the subjects on the second variable.

— — — — — — — — — — — — — — — —

The second variable in Table 7.1 is the freshman GPA scores. The largest score of 3.75 gets a rank of 1; 3.65 gets a rank of 2; 3.15 gets a rank of 3; 3.10 gets a rank of 4; 3.00 gets a rank of 5; 2.75 gets a rank of 6; and 2.60 gets a rank of 7. There are no tied scores, so we do not need to average any of these ranks.

7.   Summarize these rank scores in the table below; then check your ranks against those given below the table.

Student	Rank of SAT-Math Score	Rank of Freshman GPA
John Jones	_____	_____
Sally Smith	_____	_____
Betsy Foreman	_____	_____
Erik Appleman	_____	_____
Samantha Jones	_____	_____
George Johnson	_____	_____
Mac Friend	_____	_____

— — — — — — — — — — — — — — — —

Student	Rank of SAT-Math Score	Rank of Freshman GPA
John Jones	7	5
Sally Smith	3	7
Betsy Foreman	2	2
Erik Appleman	6	3
Samantha Jones	5	6
George Johnson	1	1
Mac Friend	4	4

8.   *Step 4.* Find the difference (*d*) between the ranks of each subject, and write your result in the following table:

Student	Rank of SAT-Math Score	Rank of Freshman GPA	*d*
John Jones	7	5	———
Sally Smith	3	7	———
Betsy Foreman	2	2	———
Erik Appleman	6	3	———
Samantha Jones	5	6	———
George Johnson	1	1	———
Mac Friend	4	4	———

The difference of the two ranks for each subject would be:

	Difference (*d*)
John	7 - 5 = 2
Sally	3 - 7 = -4
Betsy	2 - 2 = 0
Erik	6 - 3 = 3
Samantha	5 - 6 = -1
George	1 - 1 = 0
Mac	4 - 4 = 0

Student	Rank of SAT-Math Score	Rank of Freshman GPA	*d*
John Jones	7	5	2
Sally Smith	3	7	-4
Betsy Foreman	2	2	0
Erik Appleman	6	3	3
Samantha Jones	5	6	-1
George Johnson	1	1	0
Mac Friend	4	4	0

9. *Step 5.* Find the square of d for each subject, and write your answers in the following table:

Student	Rank of SAT-Math Score	Rank of Freshman GPA	d	d^2
John Jones	7	5	2	_____
Sally Smith	3	7	-4	_____
Betsy Foreman	2	2	0	_____
Erik Appleman	6	3	3	_____
Samantha Jones	5	6	-1	_____
George Johnson	1	1	0	_____
Mac Friend	4	4	0	_____

_ _ _ _ _ _ _ _ _ _ _ _ _ _ _ _ _ _

The square of the difference of the two ranks for each subject would be:

	d^2
John	$2^2 = 4$
Sally	$(-4)^2 = 16$
Betsy	$0^2 = 0$
Erik	$3^2 = 9$
Samantha	$(-1)^2 = 1$
George	$0^2 = 0$
Mac	$0^2 = 0$

Student	Rank of SAT-Math Score	Rank of Freshman GPA	d	d^2
John Jones	7	5	2	4
Sally Smith	3	7	-4	16
Betsy Foreman	2	2	0	0
Erik Appleman	6	3	3	9
Samantha Jones	5	6	-1	1
George Johnson	1	1	0	0
Mac Friend	4	4	0	0

10. *Step 6.* Find the sum of d^2, and write it in the table below:

Student	Rank of SAT-Math Score	Rank of Freshman GPA	d	d^2
John Jones	7	5	2	4
Sally Smith	3	7	-4	16
Betsy Foreman	2	2	0	0
Erik Appleman	6	3	3	9
Samantha Jones	5	6	-1	1
George Johnson	1	1	0	0
Mac Friend	4	4	0	0
			Σd^2 =	

The sum of the squared difference scores for all seven subjects is:

Student	Rank of SAT-Math Score	Rank of Freshman GPA	d	d^2
John Jones	7	5	2	4
Sally Smith	3	7	-4	16
Betsy Foreman	2	2	0	0
Erik Appleman	6	3	3	9
Samantha Jones	5	6	-1	1
George Johnson	1	1	0	0
Mac Friend	4	4	0	0
			Σd^2 =	30

11. *Step 7.* What is the sum of d^2 multiplied by 6?

6 (30) = 180

12. *Step 8.* Divide the answer from Step 7 by N ($N^2 - 1$).

$$\frac{180}{7\,(7^2 - 1)} = \frac{180}{7\,(48)} = \frac{180}{336} = 0.54$$

13. *Step 9.* Subtract the answer in Step 8 from the number 1; then check your result below.

— — — — — — — — — — — — — — — — —

1 – 0.54 = 0.46

14. Thus, the rank-order correlation between the SAT-math scores and the freshman GPA of our hypothetical group of seven students is 0.46.

Now see if you can obtain this same result using the mathematical formula for rho, and check your computations against the correct ones below.*

— — — — — — — — — — — — — — — — —

If we double check our computation by the mathematical formula for rho, we obtain:

$$\text{rho} = 1 - \frac{6\Sigma d^2}{N(N^2 - 1)}$$

$$= 1 - \frac{6(30)}{7(7^2 - 1)}$$

$$= 1 - \frac{180}{336}$$

$$= 1 - 0.54$$

$$\text{rho} = 0.46$$

15. Once again, the rank-order correlation between the SAT-math scores and the freshman GPA for the seven subjects given in Table 7.1 is 0.46. We'll talk about what that value means in a few pages. First, try another sample problem on your own to check out your skill in computing a rank-order correlation. Using the data given in Table 7.2, answer this question: what is the rank-order correlation between the high-school GPA and the college GPA of the eight subjects given in Table 7.2?

————————————

*When you are working on problems that require you to compute a rank-order correlation, you will find it helpful to use the tear-out sheet given in Appendix E. It will save you the time of memorizing this formula.

Table 7.2. *High School GPA and College GPA for a Hypothetical Group of Eight Subjects*

Student Number	High School GPA (4-point scale)	College GPA (8-point scale)
1	2.0	6.8
2	3.5	6.6
3	2.7	5.8
4	3.8	6.8
5	3.0	6.8
6	3.9	6.0
7	3.5	6.5
8	3.5	7.0

Use the table given below to work out your answer to this question.

Student Number	High School GPA (4-point scale)	College GPA (8-point scale)	Rank of High School GPA	Rank of College GPA	d	d^2
1	2.0	6.8				
2	3.5	6.6				
3	2.7	5.8				
4	3.8	6.8				
5	3.0	6.8				
6	3.9	6.0				
7	3.5	6.5				
8	3.5	7.0				
					$\Sigma d^2 =$	

$$\text{rho} = 1 - \frac{6\Sigma d^2}{N(N^2 - 1)}$$

Student Number	High School GPA (4-point scale)	College GPA (8-point scale)	Rank of High School GPA	Rank of College GPA	d	d^2
1	2.0	6.8	8	3	5	25
2	3.5	6.6	4	5	−1	1
3	2.7	5.8	7	8	−1	1
4	3.8	6.8	2	3	−1	1
5	3.0	6.8	6	3	3	9
6	3.9	6.0	1	7	−6	36
7	3.5	6.5	4	6	−2	4
8	3.5	7.0	4	1	3	9
					$\Sigma d^2 = 86$	

$$\text{rho} = 1 - \frac{6\,(86)}{8\,(8^2 - 1)}$$

$$= 1 - \frac{516}{8\,(63)}$$

$$= 1 - \frac{516}{504}$$

$$= 1 - 1.02$$

$$\text{rho} = -0.02$$

16. Whenever you are assigning ranks to two variables for a group of subjects, it is advisable that you assign the ranks for *both* variables in a similar way. For example, let's suppose that you collected the following data on height and weight from five students.

Student	Height	Weight
1	6′5″	210
2	6′4″	200
3	6′3″	190
4	6′2″	195
5	6′1″	180

If you assign a rank of one to the *tallest* person, you should also assign a rank of one to the *heaviest* person; conversely, if you assign a rank of one to the *smallest* person, you should also assign a rank of one to the *lightest* person.

If we assigned a rank of one to the tallest person and to the heaviest person, we would obtain the following value for rho:

Student	Height	Weight	Rank of Height	Rank of Weight	d	d^2
1	6'5''	210	1	1	0	0
2	6'4''	200	2	2	0	0
3	6'3''	190	3	4	-1	1
4	6'2''	195	4	3	1	1
5	6'1''	180	5	5	0	0

$$\Sigma d^2 = 2$$

$$\text{rho} = 1 - \frac{6\Sigma d^2}{N(N^2 - 1)}$$

$$= 1 - \frac{6(2)}{5(5^2 - 1)}$$

$$= 1 - \frac{12}{120}$$

$$= 1 - 0.10$$

$$\text{rho} = 0.90$$

This value of 0.90 for rho means that there is a very similar relationship between the rank orders of this group of five people on their height and on their weight, and this conclusion can be verified by a glance at the heights and weights of our sample of subjects.

If we had, instead, assigned a rank of one to the tallest person (height of 6'5'') and a rank of one to the lightest person (weight of 180), this ranking would have been improper. It would produce a value for Σd^2 equal to 38 and a value for rho of –.90. This might lead us to the mistaken conclusion that those individuals who were the tallest were also the lightest in weight, a conclusion which we know to be incorrect from a glance at the distribution of heights and weights for our sample of subjects. For this reason you need to be careful to assign the ranks on both variables in a similar way, and to remember exactly *how* you ranked both variables so that you interpret the resulting correlation correctly.

17. Now you know how to compute a rank-order correlation. You will have a chance to practice and sharpen your skill in computing rank-order correlations in the Self-Test at the end of this chapter.

But let's leave the mathematics aside for a moment and talk about the meaning of a correlation. A rank-order correlation is a number that summarizes the answer to the following question: For this group of subjects, how does the rank-order of the subjects on one variable compare to their rank-order on the other variable? If we assigned the rank of 1 to the highest score on both variables, and if the subjects were in the *identical* rank-order on both variables, the rank-order correlation would be equal to +1.0. If the rank-order of the subjects on one of the variables were in exactly the *opposite* order of the rank-order of the subjects on the other variable (for example, the subject who ranked first on one variable was ranked last on the other variable, the subject who ranked second on one variable was ranked second-to-last on the other variable, and so on), the rank-order correlation would be equal to –1.0. A rank-order correlation can never be less than –1.0, nor larger than +1.0.

But what does a positive correlation or a negative correlation *mean*? A *positive correlation* (rho is between zero and +1.0) means that the rank-orders of the subjects are similar in that subjects who have high ranks on one variable tend to have high ranks on the other variable, while subjects who have low ranks on one variable tend to have low ranks on the other variable.

A *negative correlation* (rho is between –1.0 and zero) means that the rank-orders of the subjects are *not similar* in that subjects who have high ranks on one variable tend to have low ranks on the other variable, while subjects who have low ranks on one variable tend to have high ranks on the other variable.

If rho is near .00, a person's score on one variable gives no indication of what his score will be on the other variable.

Another way to summarize what a rank-order correlation means is to define a rule-of-thumb procedure for determining *when* a correlation is near-zero, low, moderate, or high. Statisticians love to argue about the cut-off points, but for our purposes let's arbitrarily define these terms as follows:

(1) A correlation is *near-zero* if rho is between –.09 and +.09.
(2) A correlation is *low* if rho is between either –.29 and –.10 *or* +.10 and +.29.
(3) A correlation is *moderate* if rho is between either –.59 and –.30 *or* +.30 and +.59.
(4) A correlation is *high* if rho is between either –.99 and –.60 *or* +.60 and +.99.

Note that the *sign* of rho (positive or negative) is irrelevant to determining the degree of correlation rho represents: near-zero, low, moderate, or high. However, the sign of rho is extremely important in indicating the *type* of correlation. For example, a "high, positive correlation" (rho is between +.60 and +.99) means that the subjects in the sample are in very *similar* rank-orders on both of the variables. However, a "high, negative correlation" (rho is between –.99 and –.60) means that subjects who have low ranks on one variable tend to have high ranks on the other variable, that is, the ranks are very dissimilar.

We can summarize these categories in the following chart. You may want to refer to this chart when you are working with rank-order correlations.

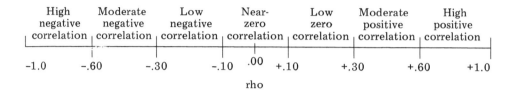

| High negative correlation | Moderate negative correlation | Low negative correlation | Near-zero correlation | Low zero correlation | Moderate positive correlation | High positive correlation |

```
-1.0      -.60       -.30       -.10  .00  +.10      +.30       +.60      +1.0
                                       rho
```

A rho of +.80 between some aptitude test X and success on the job compared to a rho of –.80 between a different aptitude test Y and success on the job means that tests X and Y are *equally good predictors* of success on the job. In the former case, subjects with high scores on test X are likely to be successful on the job, while, in the latter case, subjects with low scores on test Y are likely to be successful on the job.

Here's a chance to practice using these terms: high, moderate, low, near-zero, positive, negative. Look at the 10 correlations given below, and decide for each of these ten values for rho:

(1)   Is the correlation positive or negative?
(2)   Is the correlation near-zero, low, moderate, or high?

Question	Rho
1	+.43
2	−.65
3	−.83
4	+.95
5	−.05
6	+.10
7	−.25
8	+.30
9	+.70
10	−.15

- - - - - - - - - - - - - - - -

1.   +.43 is a moderate positive correlation
2.   –.65 is a high negative correlation
3.   –.83 is a high negative correlation
4.   +.95 is a high positive correlation

5. −.05 is a near-zero negative correlation
6. +.10 is a low positive correlation
7. −.25 is a low negative correlation
8. +.30 is a moderate positive correlation
9. +.70 is a high positive correlation
10. −.15 is a low negative correlation

18. You should now be able to recognize whether a correlation is positive or negative and whether it is near-zero, low, moderate, or high. When you are reporting the results of a research study, however, you should always report the *exact value* of rho in summarizing your results because others may have different standards for what value of rho represents a near-zero, low, moderate, or high correlation.

Correlations are used a great deal in psychological research. One of the most frequent uses of correlations is to summarize the ability of one test to *predict* some future performance for a group of students. All of the following questions can be answered by computing a rank-order correlation:

- How well do SAT-verbal scores predict freshman GPA scores at our college?
- How well do Graduate Record Examinations scores predict GPA scores in graduate school?
- How well does this pilot aptitude test predict the ability to become a successful pilot for a major airline?
- How well does this clerical aptitude test predict on-the-job ratings by clerical supervisors?
- How well do grades in first-year algebra predict grades in second-year algebra in high school?
- How well do scores on the National Teacher Examinations taken by college seniors predict success in teaching as measured by ratings of their school principals during their first and second year of full-time teaching? (You might enjoy reading an article by Quirk, Witten, and Weinberg (1973) which summarizes over 30 years of research on the National Teacher Examinations; that article contains dozens of correlations, and it would give you a lot of practice in interpreting correlation coefficients.)

All of these questions involve two things:

(1) a test which is taken at one point in time (the *predictor test*), and
(2) a test score of some kind that is developed at some later point in time (the *criterion score*).

In all cases, we would like to find a value for rho that is at least a "moderate correlation" and we would be delighted if we could find a "high correlation." That would show that the test we have selected as our predictor test does, in fact, predict very well the criterion score in which we are interested. Now you might ask, But how high should a correlation be? The answer to that question is: As high as possible. You may think that that answer is too vague, but in fact we always want to find the best predictors we can.

The typical correlation between SAT-verbal scores and freshman GPA, for example, ranges between .40 to .60. Suppose someone tried to convince you to use a special aptitude test he or she had developed to select the freshman class at your college. You could test the validity of his or her claim of the test's usefulness for that purpose by administering it to some high school seniors who had applied to your college and later correlating their scores on that aptitude test with their freshman GPA. If you found that correlation to be 0.25, for example, you would never substitute that new aptitude test for the use of SAT-verbal scores because that aptitude test is a poorer predictor of freshman GPA than SAT-verbal scores are. (We are assuming that the correlation between SAT-verbal scores and freshman GPA at your college is larger than 0.25.) On the other hand, if the highest correlation you can find between a battery of aptitude tests and some important criterion in which you are interested is 0.25, you might make limited use of that particular aptitude test in your selection process, since it is the best predictor you have been able to find.

Another way to answer the question: How large should a rank-order correlation be?, is to ask this specific question: How large should a rank-order correlation be in order for me to be confident that it is significantly different from a zero correlation? Using the .05 level of significance to answer this question, we find that the answer varies considerably depending on the size of your sample of subjects. If you only had 12 subjects in your study, your rank-order correlation would have to be greater than .59 in order for you to be confident that the correlation you obtained was significantly different from zero; if you had 30 subjects in your study, your rank-order correlation would have to be greater than .36 in order for you to be confident that the correlation you obtained was significantly different from zero (Ullman, 1972, p. 559). Because the rank-order correlation is so sensitive to differences in the number of subjects under study, we recommend that you have at least 30 subjects in your comparison whenever you use the rank-order correlation.

Correlations are frequently cited in court cases dealing with job discrimination for both racial discrimination and sex discrimination. If a company requires a certain test for all applicants for a certain job but is unable to find anything except near-zero correlations between that test and ratings of job performance, for example, the company may have a very difficult time proving in court that it should be permitted to use that test as a screening device for job applicants.

Many other kinds of correlations can be computed, each appropriate for certain types of data. The type of rank-order correlation which you have learned to compute in this chapter is the Spearman rank-difference correlation coefficient. We will not go into other types of correlation in this book. However, any good statistics book will probably include the following types of correlations: multiple correlation, partial correlation, Pearson product-moment correlation, Kendall rank correlation coefficient, Kendall partial rank correlation coefficient, point biserial correlation, biserial correlation, fourfold point correlation, part correlation, tetrachoric correlation, and others.

Caution! When interpreting a rank-order correlation, keep in mind that:

(1) The value for rho is not a percent. Be careful that you do not interpret it as a percent.

(2) You cannot average a set of correlations to find their mean correlation. For example, if you found that the correlations between high school GPA and college freshman GPA for the last three entering classes of your college were 0.65, 0.47, and 0.56, you could not average those three numbers. Instead, put the set of correlations in rank-order, and choose the one in the "middle" of the rank-order as the "average correlation." The value of rho chosen this way would be the *median correlation*; for our sample of freshman classes, the median correlation between high school GPA and college freshman GPA would be 0.56.

Let's try an example to make sure you understand how to determine an average correlation.

What is the average correlation between high school GPA and college GPA in the following correlations from seven hypothetical colleges:

.56, .60, .45, .55, .72, .63, .48?

——————————————————

In determining an average correlation, *always* put the correlations in rank-order as your first step. When we do that, we obtain this rank-order:

.72
.63
.60
.56
.55
.48
.45

Since there are seven correlations, the median correlation is the fourth correlation in the rank-order of correlations. Therefore, the average correlation is .56.

19. Now try writing a one-sentence summary of the results of this hypothetical research study, using these correlations which would include the range of the correlations (that is, the lowest and highest correlation) and the average correlation.

——————————————————

Your summary should read something like this: The rank-order correlations for the seven colleges between high school GPA and college GPA ranged from .45 to .72, with a median correlation of .56.

THE CAUSE-EFFECT DILEMMA IN CORRELATION

20. When trying to interpret a correlation, you must keep in mind that it summarizes a *relationship* between two variables, but this relationship may or may not be a cause-effect relationship between these two variables. A high correlation may *suggest* a cause-effect relationship, but it does not establish one. The only way to establish a cause-effect relationship is by conducting an experiment.

Whenever you find a high correlation between two variables, X and Y, there are always three possible meanings for this relationship: (1) X causes Y, (2) Y causes X, or (3) some third variable, W, causes both X and Y. To give a concrete example, suppose that you found a correlation of .80 between the self-concept of third-graders and their mathematics achievement test scores. This could mean one of three things: (1) a higher self-concept leads to higher math achievement; (2) higher math achievement increases self-concept; or (3) parental encouragement, aptitude, interest (or some other factors) strongly affect both the child's self-concept and his or her achievement in school. The "true" explanation cannot be determined through a correlational study, but only through an experiment.

It is frequently tempting to conclude that, because two variables have a high, positive correlation, that one of them causes the other. If the rho for achievement test scores in physics and achievement test scores in mathematics is +.80, for example, we might conclude that a good way to improve one's knowledge of physics would be to take more mathematics courses. However, it might be equally plausible to conclude, instead, that a good way to improve one's knowledge of mathematics is to take more physics courses. It is also possible that some third variable, such as the development of one's reasoning ability through a special course in problem-solving, might improve both one's knowledge of physics *and* one's knowledge of mathematics. But unless an actual experiment is done controlling one's exposure to physics or mathematics, there is no way to be certain which subject area causes an improvement in one's ability in the other subject area.

Some further examples may help to clarify further the cause-effect dilemma:

(1)   If there is a negative correlation between income level and the number of children in a family, it does not follow that as your income increases, you will have fewer children.

(2)   If there is a high, positive correlation between head size and hat size, it does not follow that a good way to develop people with larger heads is to create larger hats.

(3)   If there is a moderate, negative correlation between the number of books per pupil in the nation's high school libraries and the percent of high school dropouts in each school, this does not mean that all we have to do to reduce the dropout rate is to put more books in the school libraries.

(4)   If there is a moderate, positive correlation between the average salary of teachers in the nation's high schools and the proportion of the schools' graduates who enter college immediately following high school graduation, this does not mean that the percent of high school graduates entering college would increase if we raised the salaries of teachers. The financial condition of a community affects its ability *both* to pay teachers' salaries and college tuitions; and the amount and type of encouragement given at home to the student would also affect the student's desire to attend college in the first place.

Let's test your understanding of the cause-effect dilemma with two examples.

Suppose rho = .50 between age and reading comprehension. Is there likely to be a cause-effect relationship?

— — — — — — — — — — — — — —

No. This does *not* mean that if we increase a person's reading comprehension, he will get older! Nor does it mean that age itself *causes* reading comprehension. Other factors associated with age (such as education, experience, maturity) are more likely causes of reading-comprehension scores.

21.   Suppose rho = .60 between the amount of time students spend using a typewriter and their grade-point average. What does this correlation mean?

— — — — — — — — — — — — — —

If you find a correlation of .60 between the amount of time students spend using a typewriter and their grade-point average, this does not mean that all you have to do to get better grades is to increase the amount of time that you spend typing. The high correlation indicates that the better students do use typewriters more often than the poorer students, but the better students would probably obtain good grades even if they reduced the amount of time they spend typing. It is not necessarily true that the amount of time spent in typing *causes* good grades. It is much more likely that students who spend more time typing are also the ones who are more highly motivated, who have a past history of good performance in school, and the like, and that these other factors cause good grades.

A common misuse of a high correlation coefficient is to automatically assume that since two things are highly correlated, one causes the other. Be careful that you do not make that mistake when you interpret the results of research studies.

SELF-TEST FOR CHAPTER SEVEN

This Self-Test is designed to show you whether you have mastered the key concepts and skills in Chapter Seven. Answer each question to the best of your ability. Correct answers and review instructions are given at the end of the test.

When working with these problems, use the tear-out sheet in Appendix E for any formulas you need.

1. The director of admissions at a local college has developed a special aptitude test which he thinks will predict freshman grades at his college. He has conducted a pilot test and has obtained the following scores. What is the rank-order correlation between the aptitude test scores and the freshman GPA of his sample of students?

Student	Aptitude Test Score	GPA
1	80	1.5
2	85	3.0
3	90	1.0
4	110	3.5
5	105	1.7
6	115	1.8
7	120	3.0
8	95	4.0
9	100	2.5

2. Let's practice assigning ranks to tied scores to make sure you can do that step accurately. What is the rank of the height of each of the six people given below?

Height	Rank
6'3''	
6'1''	
6'1''	
5'10''	
5'9''	
6'1''	

3. What is the correlation between height and shoe size between the following seven subjects who have lined up by height and then again by shoe size to determine the ranks which are given below? (Men and women are

fitted for shoes on a different scale. Women need to subtract the number 2 from their shoe size in order for them to be on the same scale as the men; thus, in a group of men and women, a woman who wears a size 9 women's shoe should count her shoe size as 7. The women's shoe size has already been adjusted in these ranks.)

Subjects	Rank of Height	Rank of Shoe Size
Teresa N.	6	5.5
Marcia T.	3	3.5
Tim A.	1 (tallest)	1 (largest)
Kit B.	2	2
Dee P.	4.5	3.5
Ann R.	4.5	7
Laurie M.	7	5.5

4. Write up a summary of the results of problem 3, and include a sentence which describes what the correlation means.

5. Suppose you are interested in studying the stability of college students' personality as perceived by their roommates. You decide to concentrate on how "cooperative" these students are rated by their roommates over a two-year period. You find a sample of eight seniors and ask both their sophomore roommate and their junior roommate (who should be different roommates) to rate them on how cooperative they were on a 9-point scale, where a score of 1 would mean "very uncooperative" and a score of 9 would mean "very cooperative." You obtain the following hypothetical data:

Seniors	Roommate's rating (sophomore year)	Roommate's rating (junior year)
Brad A.	8	7
Jim H.	9	9
Tom Q.	3	2
Harry R.	4	5
Sam T.	6	6
Tim A.	7	5
Paul D.	3	3
Doug W.	4	5

What is the rank-order correlation between these two ratings of cooperativeness?

6. Suppose you are interested in determining the relationship between two standardized tests for a group of ninth-grade students: a verbal reasoning

test and a mathematical reasoning test. You have obtained a set of test scores for the following five students. What is the rank-order correlation between their verbal reasoning scores and their mathematical reasoning scores?

Student	Verbal Reasoning Score	Mathematical Reasoning Score
Sally W.	52	63
Tami R.	48	60
Paul O.	65	59
Sam A.	55	60
Tina B.	49	55

7. Write up a summary of the results of problem 6, and include a sentence which describes what the correlation means.

Answers to Self-Test for Chapter Seven

Compare your answers to the questions on the Self-Test with the answers given below. If all of your answers are correct, you are ready to go on to Chapter Eight. If you missed any questions, review the frames indicated in parentheses following the answer. If you miss several questions, you should probably carefully reread the entire chapter.

1.

Student	Aptitude Test Score	GPA	Rank of Aptitude Test Score	Rank of GPA	d	d^2
1	80	1.5	9	8	1	1.0
2	85	3.0	8	3.5	4.5	20.25
3	90	1.0	7	9	-2	4.0
4	110	3.5	3	2	1	1.0
5	105	1.7	4	7	-3	9.0
6	115	1.8	2	6	-4	16.0
7	120	3.0	1	3.5	-2.5	6.25
8	95	4.0	6	1	5	25.0
9	100	2.5	5	5	0	0

$\Sigma d^2 = 82.5$

$$\text{rho} = 1 - \frac{6\Sigma d^2}{N(N^2 - 1)}$$

$$= 1 - \frac{6(82.5)}{9(9^2 - 1)}$$

$$= 1 - \frac{495}{720}$$

$$= 1 - 0.69$$

$$\text{rho} = 0.31 \qquad \text{(frame 1)}$$

2.

Height	Rank
6'3''	1
6'1''	3
6'1''	3
5'10''	5
5'9''	6
6'1''	3

The tallest person is 6'3'' tall, and so that person receives a rank of 1. Three people are tied at the second-tallest height of 6'1'', and so *each* of these people receives the average of the ranks they would have been assigned had they not been tied ($\frac{2 + 3 + 4}{3} = \frac{9}{3} = 3$). We have used up the ranks of 1, 2, 3, and 4; the next-tallest person (5'10'') receives a rank of 5. The smallest person (5'9'') receives a rank of 6.   (frame 1)

3.

Subjects	Rank of Height	Rank of Shoe Size	d	d^2
Teresa N.	6	5.5	0.5	0.25
Marcia T.	3	3.5	−0.5	0.25
Tim A.	1	1	0	0
Kit B.	2	2	0	0
Dee P.	4.5	3.5	1.0	1.0
Ann R.	4.5	7	−2.5	6.25
Laurie M.	7	5.5	1.5	2.25

$$\Sigma d^2 = 10.0$$

$$\text{rho} = 1 - \frac{6\Sigma d^2}{N(N^2 - 1)}$$

$$= 1 - \frac{6(10)}{7(7^2 - 1)}$$

$$= 1 - \frac{60}{7(48)}$$

$$= 1 - \frac{60}{336}$$

$$= 1 - 0.18$$

rho $= 0.82$ (frame 1)

4. The correlation between height and shoe size was .82. Thus, there was a high positive relationship between height and shoe size such that the taller subjects tended to have the larger shoe sizes, while the shorter subjects tended to have the smaller shoe sizes.   (frame 17)

5.

Seniors	Roommate's Rating (sophomore year)	Roommate's Rating (junior year)	Rank of Sophomore Rating	Rank of Junior Rating	d	d^2
Brad A.	8	7	2	2	0	0
Jim H.	9	9	1	1	0	0
Tom Q.	3	2	7.5	8	−0.5	0.25
Harry R.	4	5	5.5	5	0.5	0.25
Sam T.	6	6	4	3	1.0	1.0
Tim A.	7	5	3	5	−2.0	4.0
Paul D.	3	3	7.5	7	0.5	0.25
Doug W.	4	5	5.5	5	0.5	0.25

$\Sigma d^2 = 6.0$

$$\text{rho} = 1 - \frac{6\Sigma d^2}{N(N^2 - 1)}$$

$$= 1 - \frac{6(6)}{8(8^2 - 1)}$$

$$= 1 - \frac{36}{8(63)}$$

$$= 1 - \frac{36}{504}$$

$$= 1 - 0.07$$

rho $= 0.93$ (frame 1)

6.

Student	Verbal Reasoning Score	Mathematical Reasoning Score	Rank of Verbal Reasoning Score	Rank of Math Reasoning Score	d	d^2
Sally W.	52	63	3	1	2.0	4.0
Tami R.	48	60	5	2.5	2.5	6.25
Paul O.	65	59	1	4	–3.0	9.0
Sam A.	55	60	2	2.5	–0.5	0.25
Tina B.	49	55	4	5	–1.0	1.0

$\Sigma d^2 = 20.5$

$$\text{rho} = 1 - \frac{6\Sigma d^2}{N(N^2 - 1)}$$

$$= 1 - \frac{6(20.5)}{5(5^2 - 1)}$$

$$= 1 - \frac{123}{120}$$

$$= 1 - 1.03$$

$$\text{rho} = -.03 \qquad \text{(frame 1)}$$

7. The correlation between the verbal reasoning test and the mathematical reasoning test was –.03. This near-zero correlation means that there was no relationship between the ranks on these two tests for this group of subjects.   (frame 17)

PART FOUR

How to Do a Research Study

This part of the book gives some general guidelines on how to conduct research studies. While the entire book has contained suggestions for conducting research, this final chapter aims to give you an overview of the process, including additional suggestions.

Objectives

After completing Part IV, you will be able to:

- apply the steps involved in planning and conducting a research study.
- identify common pitfalls in the research process and how to avoid them.

CHAPTER EIGHT

Guidelines on How to Do a Research Study

Let's begin with an overview of the research process. Figure 8.1 contains a chart of the nine steps in a research study. You should study this figure carefully when you conduct your own research studies. Let's discuss each of these steps carefully.

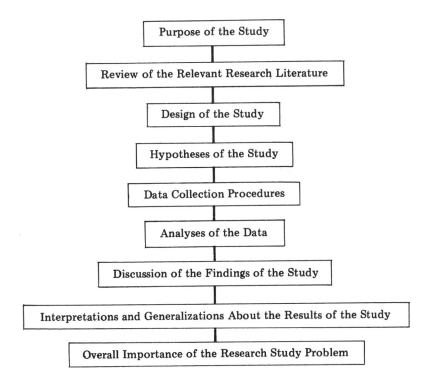

Figure 8.1. *Nine Steps Involved in the Research Process.*

Step 1.   *Purpose of the study.* It is absolutely essential that you have clearly in mind *why* you are doing your research study. If you don't know exactly why you are doing all of the hard work that accompanies a research project, you will have a very difficult time trying to explain the purpose of the study to others.

At the early stages of a research study, it is very tempting to dive right into the many administrative details of the research study so that you can collect your data quickly and proceed to analyze it. Such a procedure is a great mistake, however. The time you spend at the beginning of a research project thinking carefully about the purpose of the study is likely to prevent you from making a mistake later on during the design, data-collection, or data-analysis phase of the study.

Step 2.   *Review of the relevant research literature.* It is essential that you do a thorough library search into the general topic area of your research study before you collect any of the data from the subjects in your study. This library search has two major purposes: (1) to determine what is already known from psychological research so that you do not waste your time plowing over old ground (unless you consciously choose to do so by attempting to replicate some previous findings in the research literature), and (2) to allow you to gain some ideas from published studies that will help you to improve your research study; you will frequently find a research design or a questionnaire in the published literature which will give you some insights into how you can design your own study more effectively. The authors of published journal articles have given their research work a lot of thought, and you can frequently benefit from their thinking when doing a library search.

Published research studies always contain a section early in the article which describes the results of previous research studies on the topic under study in the article. You will need to include such a summary of previous studies when you write a report of your own research project. When summarizing a research study, be sure that your summary contains a clear statement of the results of that study—especially any significant differences obtained in the study. (Note that the proper time to do a library search is *before* you collect any data. Some students collect their data first and then run to the library to find out what previous studies have shown; this is putting the cart before the horse, and it is a very serious mistake in the conduct of a research study.)

In locating published journal articles, you will need to know how to use the *Psychological Abstracts* and the *Social Sciences Index.* Both of these sources are essential tools for a psychological researcher. If you do not know how to use these two references, ask your librarian to explain this process to you. These two references will save you a great deal of time in your library research.

Step 3.   *Design of the study.* After you have decided on the purpose of your research study and have completed a thorough library search of topics closely related to your purpose, you are ready to think seriously about the design of your study. If the purpose of your study is stated clearly, it should help you to formulate the specific design of the study.

The design of a research study should not be done according to some sophisticated, abstract procedure but instead should follow directly from the purpose of the study. The purpose of the study can always be formulated into questions which the design of the research study should enable you to answer. For example, in Chapter One we discussed a research study which was designed to answer this question: If a person is described as "very warm," will that person be perceived differently from someone who is described as "rather cold"? The design of that research study followed nicely from that question: one experimental group in which a person was described as "very warm," and another experimental group in which that person was described as "rather cold."

Some questions you can ask yourself when trying to decide on the design of your research study would be the following:

(1)   How many experimental groups will I have?
(2)   Will I use a control group? If so, what is its purpose?
(3)   What exactly will each experimental group *experience* in this research study? (In other words, what will the subjects do while participating in the study?)
(4)   How will the experimental groups be different from one another?
(5)   What will the control group do?
(6)   How will I measure the responses of the subjects in the experiment?

Step 4.   *Hypotheses of the study.* The hypotheses of the study are the predictions you are willing to make about how you expect the study to turn out; in other words, the hypotheses are your estimates of what the results of the study will be.

If the research area you are studying has already produced many published research studies, there may already be a substantial body of knowledge in the area of your research topic. If this is the case, then you may have a specific prediction about the *direction* of the outcome: Group 1 will score *higher* (or lower) on the test than Group 2. If you ever state your hypotheses in such a way that they do predict the direction of the difference between two groups of subjects, you need to be alert to this special rule:

Rule: When the direction of the difference between two groups is stated in a hypothesis, you can no longer use 3.84 as the cutoff point for a significant difference at the .05 level for the chi-square test, nor can you use the values for t in Appendix D of this book associated with $n_1 + n_2 - 2$ for the cutoff point at the .05 level.

When the direction of the difference between two groups is stated in your hypothesis, you would need a smaller value than 3.84 for chi-square and a smaller value for t than those given in Appendix D in order to obtain a significant difference between two groups at the .05 level. For the chi-square test, for example, you would only need a chi-square value greater than 2.71 in order for there to be a significant difference at the .05 level; when using the t-test, you would only need a value for t greater than 1.70 for $n_1 + n_2 - 2 = 30$ (instead of the value of 2.04 given in Appendix D). The mathematical reasoning behind these revised cutoff points is beyond the scope of this book.* Since these revised cutoff values are smaller than the ones used throughout this book, they are easier to obtain; and since they are easier to obtain, it is easier for you to claim that you have a significant difference.

The rub in all of this, however, is that you are on dangerous ground whenever you use these smaller cutoff scores for chi-square and the t-test. This is because you need to be *very confident* of *which* direction the difference between your two groups will go. And there are few research areas in psychology where we are that confident.

By using these smaller cutoff values, you also take the risk that you will obtain what you call a significant difference, but the results are in *exactly the opposite direction of your prediction.* Since the cutoff values are smaller, this will happen more often than it would if you used the cutoff values we are using throughout this book. And when the results of a study turn out exactly the opposite of the predictions, this is always a little embarrassing (to put it mildly!).

A much safer way out of this dilemma is to avoid altogether making specific predictions about the direction of the difference between two groups, and we recommend that you do just that. Our recommendation is that you always formulate your

---

*Technically speaking, when you predict the direction of the difference between two groups in your hypothesis, you are making a *directional hypothesis*; when you allow the direction of the difference between two groups to go either way by stating the hypothesis in the form of a question, you are making a *nondirectional hypothesis.* If you would like to know more about the mathematical reasoning behind these two types of hypotheses, see Wright (1976, pp. 355-358).

hypotheses in the form of questions (for example, will there be a significant difference between Group 1 and Group 2 on the achievement test?) and that you use the higher cutoff values for chi-square and the t-test that we have used throughout this book. When you formulate your hypotheses in the form of questions, the results can turn out in either one of two ways when there is a significant difference between the two groups at the .05 level:

(1) Group 1 scored significantly higher than Group 2
(2) Group 2 scored significantly higher than Group 1

When either of these results is different from the ones obtained from your review of published research studies (Step 2 as discussed in this chapter), you will then face the interesting challenge of trying to explain *why* your results are different from the present state of knowledge in psychology. Facing that challenge is always an interesting assignment.

Step 5. *Data-collection procedures.* You are now ready to collect the data for your research study. This step includes selecting the sample of subjects for your experiment, randomly assigning each subject to an experimental or control group (see Appendix A for a description of this procedure), preparing the questionnaires or rating forms, presenting a standard invitation to each potential subject in an attempt to recruit him or her for your experiment, and the like. Once you have selected your sample of subjects and obtained their cooperation, you can ask them to fill out the questionnaire or rating form or to do whatever it is the treatment in their particular experimental condition requires them to do. Be sure that you can match the responses of each subject with his or her experimental condition, or you will not be able to analyze your data properly.

If you have promised your subjects anonymity, you must be careful to take the necessary steps to follow through on that promise. Whether or not you are trying to keep the responses of your subjects anonymous, you should always keep your data confidential. Whenever people agree to participate in one of your research studies, they are doing you a favor, and common courtesy (not to mention research ethics) requires that you do not abuse the trust they have placed in you by embarrassing them in any way or by doing anything which would violate the sense of trust which should exist between experimenter and subject in a psychological experiment. The American Psychological Association binds its members to a code of ethics which we have summarized in our comments above, and whenever you are conducting a psychological experiment, that code of ethics applies to you as well.

Step 6.   *Analyses of the data.* Once you have collected your data, you are ready for the next exciting step: the analyses of the data to determine the results of the study. You can ask yourself many helpful questions at this stage of your research study. Some of the more important ones include:

(1)   Will I use a total score or should I analyze the data separately for each item in the questionnaire or rating scale?

(2)   Which is the more appropriate test to use with these data—the chi-square test or the *t*-test?

(3)   Should I compute some rank-order correlations? If so, which pairs of variables will I correlate?

(4)   Do I know enough already to analyze these data, or should I seek the help of someone who has taken several courses in statistics?

Once you have answered these questions to your satisfaction, you can compute the necessary statistics to determine *if* there were any significant differences between the experimental groups under study and what the relationships were between the variables that you want to correlate with one another.

Step 7.   *Discussion of the findings of the study.* After you have completed your data analyses, you are ready to write up the results of your study. These results should be related to the hypotheses of your study so that the person who reads your summary of the results will understand the answers to the questions posed by your hypotheses.

If you found any significant differences, be sure to state them clearly in terms of the direction of the difference so that the reader can understand these significant differences. If some of the results did not produce significant differences, state that clearly as well so that the reader can understand that aspect of your results.

Be sure to report the exact value of any correlations (for example, –.42) as well as your label of these correlations (for example, "high positive" or "moderate negative"), so that the reader knows the exact numerical correlation between the two variables being compared.

Step 8.   *Interpretations and generalizations about the results of the study.* This next step requires that you go beyond Step 7 and interpret the results of your study within the broader context of the results of previous studies in psychology (Step 2). Were the results of your study similar or dissimilar to the results of previous studies? If your results were different, *why* were they different? Did you use an unusual sample of subjects? Was your sample of subjects sufficiently large? Did any special factors bias the results of your study?

The question of *generalization* of the results of your study is important here: Do you think your results are true for people in general? for people like your subjects? Why?

Step 9.   *Overall importance of the research study problem.* This final step allows you to step back from your research study to state the value of the research study to the field of psychology. How has your research study improved the state of knowledge in psychology? How could your study be improved if you were to do it over again? What were the weaknesses in your research study, and how can they be corrected in future studies?

If you have completed these nine steps successfully, you will have accomplished a successful research study. But we want to make one more important suggestion which we have saved until now so that you could perceive its importance more clearly. This suggestion is so important that we want to state it as the final rule in this book:

Rule: Whenever you do a research study, always do a complete pilot study before you collect the final data for your research study.

A *pilot study* is a miniature replica of a research study. It should be identical to the research study you have planned except that it includes only a small sample of subjects. The purpose of a pilot study is to provide a "dry run" of a larger experiment so that you can redesign the larger study as necessary from what you learn from the pilot study.

And you will *always* learn something valuable from a pilot study. The pilot study should be an exact reproduction of your research study. You should follow the same procedures that you plan to follow in your larger study for selecting the sample, asking potential subjects to participate, collecting your data, analyzing your data, and interpreting your results.

A pilot study can help you to learn if and how you need to redesign some aspect of your research study—for example, your standard invitation to potential subjects may be ineffective, the questionnaire ambiguous, or your data analyses procedures improper.

It is especially important that you analyze the data from the pilot study exactly as you plan to analyze it later in your actual study, even though you have only a small sample of subjects in your pilot study. Since only a few subjects are in each experimental or control-group condition in a pilot study, to collect the data and to analyze it will take you relatively little time. The author of this book has been called upon on numerous occasions (sometimes even by people who have already collected the data for their doctoral thesis) to "bail out" someone who has gone to all of the trouble of collecting the final data for a research study but who does not have the foggiest notion of how to analyze that data. This situation is always a sad one; sometimes the study can be salvaged, and sometimes the data need to be thrown away because they are worthless.

You will probably be amazed, especially for the first few research studies which you do on your own, by how much you will learn from a pilot test. The little extra time it takes to complete a pilot test will be well spent.

It is always difficult to do a good research study. Each small step of the study from beginning to end is important, and a mistake at any step of the way can reduce the value of the study, sometimes to the point where the study itself is practically worthless. Many times during any research study you can stumble into a pitfall which could seriously jeopardize the value of your study. A list of some of the more common pitfalls met by the author's students are summarized in Table 8.1. These pitfalls, "The Infamous 13," represent 13 mistakes which you do not want to make when you do a research study.

Table 8.1. The Infamous 13: The Most Common Pitfalls of Research Teams

Pitfall Number	Description	Comment
1	Failing to tell the subjects in the study which course (or company or organization) the research is for.	You should tell the subjects your name(s) and the course (or group) that this research project is for.
2	Failing to keep the subjects' response anonymous.	One research team told the subjects not to put their names on the questionnaire because the data were to be anonymous, and then decided to save the cost of envelopes by writing the names of the subjects on the back of the questionnaire, which was then sent through inter-office mail!
3	Asking subjects to provide data that the research team does not plan to use in testing their hypotheses.	If you don't have a use for the data (for example, the sex of the subject), don't waste the subjects' time (and your own) by asking them to provide you with this data.
4	Poor review of the literature.	Don't forget to look up articles under *related* topics as well as the one topic you think your study is most related to.
5	Poor summary of the research literature.	Don't forget to give a *clear* summary of the studies you cite, including the significant differences in these studies.
6	Creating hypotheses out of thin air based on personal biases.	You should try to create hypotheses that *build upon* the results of published studies which are related to your research topic.
7	Neglecting to do a *complete* pilot test.	You should always do a complete pilot test of your procedures, data analyses, and interpretation of data. And, you should use what you learn from the pilot test to *revise and improve* your research study before you carry out your study with a larger group of subjects.

Pitfall Number	Description	Comment
8	Neglecting to do any correlations or statistical tests with the data collected.	You should do either some correlations between important variables or some statistical tests (or both) with your data. Comments such as: "We could tell by looking at the data that our hypothesis was supported," and "We could tell by looking at the data that there weren't any significant differences" (the eyeball test) are unacceptable.
9	Failing to state the numerical value of rho.	Comments such as "There was a moderate correlation between high school GPA and college GPA" are unacceptable. What *was* the actual correlation? What does it mean?
10	Forgetting to adjust the ranks of tied scores on *both* variables when computing rho.	One research team in ranking the subjects' GPAs gave all subjects with an "A" average a "rank" of 1, all subjects with a B+ average a "rank" of 2, etc.; this procedure is improper.
11	Misinterpreting rho.	One research team had the hypothesis that those subjects who would be opposed to the open-door policy (the policy requires that the door to the dorm room be left open whenever a student is entertaining someone of the opposite sex) would be the ones who dated a lot. Then they asked the subjects two questions: (1) On a scale from 1 to 10, when 1 represents strongly agree and 10 is strongly disagree, rate your opinion of the open-door policy (a score of 10 was given a rank of 1), and (2) On a scale from 1 to 10, when 1 represents very frequently and 10 is very infrequently, how would you rate yourself on the amount of times you go out on dates in an average month (a score of 10 was given a rank of 1)? This research team then mistakenly interpreted a rho of +.40 to mean that students who disagreed with the open-door policy were the ones who dated a lot, whereas, in fact, exactly the opposite was true; those subjects who disagreed with the open-door policy were the ones who did *not* date often; in other words, their results were exactly the *opposite* of their hypothesis!

Pitfall Number	Description	Comment
12	Inflated N in chi-square.	There have been three flagrant examples of this mistake:

Inflated N in chi-square.

	Below average	Above average
High school GPA		
College GPA		

	Total no. of "rarely" or "never" responses	Total no. of "sometimes" or "often" responses
Freshmen		
Seniors		

Rule: You should never end up with more responses in a chi-square table than the number of subjects whom you are comparing at that time!

There have been three flagrant examples of this mistake:

(a) One research team had a sample of 24 college athletes, found their average GPA in high school and in college, split these GPAs into "below average" and "above average" and then tried to compare high school GPA and college GPA. The result was that they ended up with 48 subjects, i.e., they *created* 24 more subjects out of thin air!

(b) Another research team asked each of 60 subjects ten different questions and then compared freshmen to seniors in the total number of times each subject answered *either* "rarely" or "never" *or* "sometimes" or "often" across these ten questions. This means that they suddenly had a total of 600 responses in their chi-square table!

(c) Another research team asked each subject four questions about his academic work in terms of which of his parents influenced him the most in terms of each question, and then took the total number of times each subject said his mother influenced him the most and the total number of times each subject said his father influenced him the most; this created four times as many responses in the chi-square table as there were subjects in the study!

Pitfall Number	Description	Comment
13	Failure to state what they would do differently if they were to do their research study over again.	Don't forget to share with others what you *learned* to do a different way the next time if you were to repeat your study.

A representative sample of the research topics which have been done by students in the author's classes in introductory psychology, educational psychology, and social psychology is given on page 245. Perhaps this list will give you some ideas of research studies which you would like to do. We hope that you will have the opportunity to do a research study—either on your own or with a team of students. There is no better way to learn how to do psychological research than by conducting research studies. While you can learn many useful concepts about psychological research by reading, you will not really master these concepts until you have put them into practice by conducting research studies.

EXAMPLES OF RESEARCH STUDIES COMPLETED BY STUDENTS

Effect of Living Arrangements on the Attitudes of College Students
Sex Differences in the Study Behavior of College Students
Relationship between Student-Initiated Comments during Class and Students'
  GPA
Relationship between Student Activities and GPA
Comparison of Academic Performance of College Athletes and Nonathletes
Relationship between Self-Concept, GPA, and Year in College
Differences in Learning Produced by Three Different Types of Instruction
Relationship of Student Attitude toward Courses and Course Grades
Effect of Immediate and Delayed Review on Retention
Relationship between Memorization Ability and GPA
Effect of Different Types of Activities on Short-Term Memory
Development of Extroversion during College Life
Sex Differences in Dating Preferences
Relationship between High School GPA, SAT-V, SAT-M scores, and College
  GPA
Relationship between Birth-Order and College Academic Performance
Sex Differences in Attitude toward Various Types of Nonverbal Behavior
Relationship between Types of Memorization and Degree of Recall
Relationship between Birth-Order and Leadership Style
Effect of Parent-Child Relationships on Children's Behavior
Effect of Classroom Environment on Learning
Sex Differences in Achievement Motivation
Effect of Eye Contact and Social Distance on Conversational Effectiveness
GPA Comparisons of Athletes during Quarters When Participating or Not
  Participating in a Varsity Sport
Sex Differences in Reactions to Invasion of Personal Space

The conduct of a research study is a messy business. It frequently requires on-the-spot decisions and adjustments which are not apparent when
you read a published research article. Without this first-hand experience of
doing research studies, you are likely to underestimate the complexity and
difficulties inherent in conducting a research study. Editors of psychological
journal articles are likely to emphasize conciseness of experiments in their
dealings with the authors, and this emphasis on brevity can lead you to seriously misjudge the "messiness" of the process of conducting a research
study in psychology from start to finish. This book can only give you a
glimpse into that process, but if it sparks your interest in psychological research or spurs you to try a research study of your own, then it will have
accomplished its major purpose.

Final Examination

The following questions are designed to test your overall understanding of the material presented in this book. Answers and review instructions are given following the test.

Some of the problems on this final exam are based on real data and some on hypothetical data. Whenever an article is cited in a problem, you will be working with the actual data of that published article. Whenever an article is not cited in a problem, we have created some hypothetical data to allow you to practice the skills you have learned.

When working with these problems, use the tear-out sheet in Appendix E for any formulas you need.

1.   Berger *et al.* (1969) placed menus on selected seats in a train and recorded the number of passeners who made a purchase in the train's diner. The following results were produced:

	Used diner	Did not use diner
Menu on seat	14	14
No menu	5	20

If the chi-square value is 5.17, what were the results of this study?

A.   Significantly more subjects used the diner when there was a menu on their seat than when there was not a menu on their seat.

B.   Significantly more subjects used the diner when there was not a menu on their seat than when there was a menu on their seat.

C.   There was no significant difference in the use of the diner whether or not there was a menu on the seat.

2.   Let's suppose that you wanted to find out whether swimming a lap of a swimming pool immediately before taking an exam would improve your performance on that examination. You get together an experimental group of students who swim a lap before an exam and a control group of students who do not swim a lap. Both groups take the same exam. The experimental group of 30 students have a mean of 15.2 and a standard deviation of 5.0 on the exam, while the control group of 30 students has a mean of 24.0 and a standard deviation of 6.3 on the exam.

The t-test produces a value of t equal to 6.20. What are the results of this study?

A. Significantly more subjects who swam a lap scored higher on the exam than subjects who did not swim a lap.
B. Significantly more subjects who did not swim a lap scored higher on the exam than subjects who swam a lap.
C. There was no significant difference between the two groups on their exam scores.

3. Suppose that you wanted to determine if significantly more men than women in one of your classes were above average in height. Suppose, further, that you measured the height of all of the students in that class, and obtained the following table and value of chi-square:

	Above-average height	Below-average height
Men	3	9
Women	8	3

chi-square = 5.24

What were the results of your study?

A. Significantly more men were above average in height than women.
B. Significantly more women were above average in height than men.
C. There was no significant difference between the heights of the men and women.

4. Suppose that you showed one group of subjects a photograph of an automobile (the A group), while you showed another group of subjects a photo of the same automobile but with an attractive male model in the foreground of the photograph (A-M group), and that the following table and value for chi-square resulted:

	Above-average appeal	Below-average appeal
Automobile only (A group)	18	6
Automobile plus male model (A-M group)	8	15

chi-square = 7.69

What were the results of this study?

A. Significantly more subjects who were shown a photograph of the automobile rated that automobile as above average in appeal than subjects who were shown a photograph of an automobile with an attractive male model in the foreground.
B. Significantly more subjects who were shown a photograph of an automobile with an attractive male model in the foreground rated

that automobile as above average in appeal than subjects who were shown a photograph of an automobile.

C. There were no significant differences between the two experimental groups in their rating of the automobile's appeal.

5. Schachter wrote a book called *The Psychology of Affiliation* (1959). That book included a study in which subjects were told either that the electric shocks that they were about to receive would be severe (high-fear condition) or that the electric shocks they were about to receive would be very mild (low-fear condition). He then gave the subjects a choice of where they would like to wait until the experiment began: (1) together with other subjects who were also waiting for the experiment to begin, (2) alone, or (3) no preference for being alone or with other subjects. The following data resulted:

	Together	Alone *or* don't care
High fear	20	12
Low fear	10	20

Use the chi-square formula to set up this problem, but *do not compute the value of chi-square.*

6. Suppose that you gave a reading test to a group of 50 third-grade students in the fall of 1977, and then you gave that same reading test to these same students in the spring of 1978. Suppose, further, that you put the 100 resulting test scores in rank-order and found the average test score. For the fall reading scores, 15 students were above average, while 35 students were below average. For the spring reading scores, 35 students were above average, while 15 students were below average. Is it appropriate to set up this problem by using the chi-square formula? If so, do. (Do not compute the value for chi-square.)

7. Suppose that a guest speaker was described as "very warm" to one group of subjects and as "rather cold" to another group of subjects. Both groups rated the speaker, and the following table and value for chi-square resulted:

	Good-natured	Irritable *or* no opinion
Very warm	19	5
Rather cold	4	19

chi-square = 17.94

Write a one-sentence summary of the results of this study.

8. McClelland has done research on "need for achievement" (nAch) for over 25 years. He collected data on college sophomores in 1947 to determine their need for achievement scores and gathered occupational information

on these people in 1961. He categorized their jobs as either entrepreneurial or nonentrepreneurial in nature, and obtained the following results:

	Above-average nAch scores	Below-average nAch scores
Business entrepreneurs	10	2
Business nonentrepreneurs	3	11

chi-square = 9.90

Write a one-sentence summary of the results of this study.

9. Suppose that one group of subjects is taught how to read by a computer-assisted instruction program (CAI), while another group is taught to read in the regular class by a teacher (R). At the end of the year, the 12 subjects in the CAI group had a mean score of 15.2 and a standard deviation of 5.0 on a reading achievement test, while the 13 subjects in the R group had a mean of 24.0 and a standard deviation of 6.3 on the same reading test. The t-value for these data was 3.70. What were the results of this study?

   A. Subjects taught to read in the CAI group scored significantly higher on the reading test than subjects in the R group.
   B. Subjects taught to read in the R group scored significantly higher on the reading test than subjects in the CAI group.
   C. There were no significant differences in reading achievement scores between the subjects in the CAI group and the R group.

10. Suppose that you have been hired as a research assistant by a political science professor who is interested in studying the effect of a film about Africa on the attitude change of a group of students. You have designed a questionnaire in which the most important question asks the students to indicate their attitude toward Africa on an 11-point scale ranging from –5 to +5. You hand out the questionnaire a week before the film, and the students answer it during class. You then show the film and ask the students to complete the questionnaire again. Your analysis of the data shows that the 35 students had a mean score of 1.2 and a standard deviation of 0.62 on the original questionnaire, and a mean score of 2.3 and a standard deviation of 0.85 on the later questionnaire. Is it appropriate to set up this problem using the formula for the t-test? If so, do. (Do not compute the value for t.)

11. The final exam from one class (Class 1) of 16 introductory psychology students had a mean of 107 and a standard deviation of 10, while another class (Class 2) of 14 students had a mean of 112 and a standard deviation of 8. The t-value for these data was –1.47. Write a one-sentence summary of the results of this study.

12. Greenspoon (1955) studied the effect of an experimenter's saying "mmm-hmm" on the number of plural nouns which a subject would state aloud during a 25-minute test period. A control group of subjects did not receive any type of reinforcement sound during their 25-minute test period. He kept a record of the number of plural nouns stated by the subjects during the test period, and analyzed the data for *each* 5-minute interval of the 25-minute test period. The data for the third 5-minute period showed that the experimental group ($N = 14$) had a mean of 22.4 plural responses and a standard deviation of 16.9 plural responses during this interval. The control group ($N = 15$) had a mean of 11.0 plural responses and a standard deviation of 6.83 plural responses during this same period. The resulting value of t was 2.31. Write a one-sentence summary of the results of this study.

13. Suppose that you have been hired as a research assistant by a professor who is teaching educational psychology. He has handed out a set of directions to students in his class, has given a lecture on a topic, and has turned the results of a quiz on the topic over to you. You found that the seven subjects in the experimental group (those subjects instructed to act like "A" students during the lecture) had a mean score of 6.3 and a standard deviation of 0.95 on the quiz. The seven subjects in the control group (those subjects who were not instructed to act like "A" students during the lecture) had a mean score of 5.0 and a standard deviation of 1.05. Set up this problem, using the formula for the *t*-test, but *do not compute* the value for *t*.

14. If the rank-order correlation between the number of hours spent in typing practice and the number of typing errors on an examination is –.75, this means that:

   A. As typing practice time increases, error rate is reduced 75 percent.
   B. This correlation is meaningless since it is negative.
   C. It is likely that as the amount of time spent practicing typing is increased, the number of typing errors will decrease.
   D. For 25 percent of the students who took typing, there was no relationship between practice time and error rate.

15. Which of the following rank-order correlations represents the highest degree of relationship?

   A. .45
   B. .30
   C. .00
   D. –.55
   E. –.65

16. Mr. World's Greatest Basketball Coach is concerned that his screening test for selecting his players might not be the best possible predictor of their success as basketball players. In the past, he has used a judge's score during a game situation as the *criterion* against which he has

selected his players. He had been using a 30-second shooting exhibition (by which each player tried to make as many baskets as possible when shooting outside of the foul line) as the *predictor* for selecting his players.

Our great coach has decided to see if he can find a better predictor of the judge's score than the 30-second shooting score, and, in desperation, he has settled on the number of push-ups per minute.

Given the scores for the seven players trying out for the team,

(a) What is the correlation between the 30-second shooting exhibition and the judge's score?

(b) What is the correlation between the push-ups per minute test and the judge's score?

(c) Which of these two predictors is the better predictor of the judge's rating score?

Player	Push-ups Per Minute	30-Second Shooting Score	Judge's Rating Score
1	16	11	10
2	14	5	2
3	13	4	9
4	12	3	3
5	12	1	8
6	11	2	4
7	11	1	7

17. Dyson (1967) studied the relationship between self-concept and the type of ability grouping experienced by seventh-graders. He administered the *Index of Adjustment and Values* (IAV) to measure the pupils' acceptance of self in terms of how each pupil felt about himself or herself as a person and split the pupils into "above average" and "below average" groups in terms of their self-acceptance. The pupils attended either a school that used homogeneous ability grouping (pupils of similar ability were placed in the same class) or a school that used heterogeneous ability grouping (pupils of a wide range of ability were placed in the same class). How were ability grouping and self-concept related?

	Above-average self-acceptance	Below-average self-acceptance
Homogeneous ability grouping	137	108
Heterogeneous ability grouping	159	164

18. Suppose you have been hired as a research assistant for a computer-assisted instruction (CAI) program which is attempting to improve the mathematical ability of first-grade students by using the computer as an instructional tool. Suppose the students have been randomly assigned to an experimental group (CAI) and a control group (regular classroom

instruction) and that at the end of eight months you obtain the following results for their mathematics scores:

Experimental Group (CAI)	Control Group (Regular Classroom Instruction)
7	6
8	5
6	4
5	2
7	6
8	4
5	3
7	4
7	5
	6

Use the *t*-test to determine the results of this hypothetical study, and then write up the results of the experiment.

Answers to Final Exam

Compare your answers with those that follow. If you miss any and wish to go back for review, use the chapter and frame references which follow each answer.

1. A (Chapter 1, frame 8)

2. B (Chapter Four, frames 11–12)

3. B (Chapter One, frame 8)

4. A (Chapter One, frame 8)

5. chi-square $= \dfrac{62 \, (400 - 120)^2}{(32) \, (30) \, (30) \, (32)}$ (Chapter One, frames 5–8)

6. It is not legal to use the chi-square test on these data since the two groups of subjects are not independent, and you would have an inflated N. (Chapter One, frames 14–15)

7. Significantly more subjects who were told that a guest speaker was "very warm" rated that speaker as good-natured than subjects who were told the speaker was "rather cold." (Chapter One, frame 8)

8. Significantly more subjects who became business entrepreneurs had above average nAch scores than subjects who became business nonentrepreneurs. (Chapter One, frame 8)

9. B   (Chapter Four, frame 12)

10. You cannot use the *t*-test for independent samples on these data because the two groups of subjects are not independent; the same subjects are tested at two different points in time.   (Chapter Four, frame 1)

11. There was no significant difference in the final exam scores between these two classes of introductory psychology students. (Chapter Four, frame 14)

12. Subjects who were told "mmm-hmm" stated significantly more plural nouns in the third 5-minute period than subjects who did not receive any reinforcement sound.   (Chapter Four, frame 14)

13. $$t = \frac{6.3 - 5.0}{\sqrt{\dfrac{7(0.95)^2 + 7(1.05)^2}{7 + 7 - 2}\left(\dfrac{1}{7} + \dfrac{1}{7}\right)}}$$ (Chapter Four, frames 10–11)

14. C   (Chapter Seven, frame 17)

15. E   (Chapter Seven, frame 17)

16. (a)

Rank of 30-Second Shooting Score	Rank of Judge's Rating Score	d	d^2
1	1	0	0
2	7	−5	25
3	2	1	1
4	6	−2	4
6.5	3	3.5	12.25
5	5	0	0
6.5	4	2.5	6.25
		sum =	48.50

$$\text{rho} = 1 - \frac{6\Sigma d^2}{N(N^2 - 1)}$$

$$= 1 - \frac{6(48.50)}{7(49 - 1)}$$

$$= 1 - \frac{291}{336}$$

$$= 1 - 0.87$$

$$\text{rho} = .13$$

(b)

Rank of Push-ups	Rank of Judge's Rating Score	d	d^2
1	1	0	0
2	7	−5	25
3	2	1	1
4.5	6	−1.5	2.25
4.5	3	1.5	2.25
6.5	5	1.5	2.25
6.5	4	2.5	6.25

$$\text{sum} = 39.0$$

$$\text{rho} = 1 - \frac{6\Sigma d^2}{N(N^2 - 1)}$$

$$= 1 - \frac{6(39)}{7(49 - 1)}$$

$$= 1 - \frac{234}{336}$$

$$= 1 - 0.70$$

$$\text{rho} = .30$$

(c)   Since .30 is greater than .13, push-ups per minute is a better predictor of the judge's rating score than the 30-second shooting score. (Chapter Seven, frame 17)

17.

$$\text{chi-square} = \frac{N(AD - BC)^2}{(A + B)(C + D)(A + C)(B + D)}$$

$$= \frac{568(22,468 - 17,172)^2}{(245)(323)(296)(272)}$$

$$= \frac{568(5,296)(5,296)}{(245)(323)(296)(272)}$$

$$= \frac{568(28,047,616)}{(79,135)(80,512)}$$

$$\text{chi-square} = 2.50$$

Since this value for chi-square is less than 3.84, there was no significant relationship between the pupils' self-acceptance and the type of ability grouping used in their school.   (Chapter One, frames 5–8)

18. The mean of the experimental group is:

$$\frac{7 + 8 + 6 + 5 + 7 + 8 + 5 + 7 + 7}{9} = \frac{60}{9} = 6.67$$

The mean of the control group is:

$$\frac{6 + 5 + 4 + 2 + 6 + 4 + 3 + 4 + 5 + 6}{10} = \frac{45}{10} = 4.50$$

The standard deviation of the experimental group is:

$$\text{s.d.} = \sqrt{\frac{\Sigma X^2}{N} - \bar{X}^2}$$

$$= \sqrt{\frac{410}{9} - 6.67^2}$$

$$= \sqrt{45.56 - 44.49}$$

$$= \sqrt{1.07}$$

$$\text{s.d.} = 1.03$$

The standard deviation of the control group is:

$$\text{s.d.} = \sqrt{\frac{\Sigma X^2}{N} - \bar{X}^2}$$

$$= \sqrt{\frac{219}{10} - 4.5^2}$$

$$= \sqrt{21.90 - 20.25}$$

$$= \sqrt{1.65}$$

$$\text{s.d.} = 1.28$$

The value for t is:

$$t = \frac{\bar{X}_1 - \bar{X}_2}{\sqrt{\dfrac{(n_1)\,(\text{s.d.}_1)^2 + (n_2)\,(\text{s.d.}_2)^2}{n_1 + n_2 - 2}\left(\dfrac{1}{n_1} + \dfrac{1}{n_2}\right)}}$$

$$= \frac{6.67 - 4.50}{\sqrt{\dfrac{9\,(1.03)^2 + 10\,(1.28)^2}{9 + 10 - 2}\left(\dfrac{1}{9} + \dfrac{1}{10}\right)}}$$

$$= \frac{2.17}{\sqrt{\dfrac{9.54 + 16.4}{17}\,(0.21)}}$$

$$= \frac{2.17}{\sqrt{\dfrac{25.94}{17}\,(0.21)}}$$

$$= \frac{2.17}{\sqrt{(1.53)\,(0.21)}}$$

$$= \frac{2.17}{\sqrt{0.32}}$$

$$= \frac{2.17}{0.57}$$

$$t = 3.81$$

Since $n_1 + n_2 - 2$ equals $9 + 10 - 2 = 17$, we note from Appendix D that the obtained value for t must be greater than 2.11 in order for there to be a significant difference between the two groups. Since 3.81 is greater than 2.11, there was a significant difference between the two groups.

Since the experimental group (CAI) had a mean score of 6.67, while the control group (regular classroom instruction) had a mean score of 4.50, the students who were tutored by the computer scored significantly higher on the mathematics test than the students who were taught by the regular classroom teachers.
(Chapter Five, frames 4–8)

APPENDIX A

How to Use a Table
of Random Numbers

1.   This appendix has two purposes: (1) to teach you how to assign subjects to different experimental conditions in an objective, impersonal way, and (2) to teach you how to select a sample of subjects from a larger group of people. A true experiment requires both the control of aspects of the research study which could influence the result of the study, and a random method of assigning subjects to the two groups being compared so that each subject has an equal chance of being in one of the two groups. The purpose of randomization of subjects to the two groups is to increase the likelihood that only chance differences exist between the two groups. Random assignment to experimental conditions is essential if we are to make causal inferences based on the results of experiments.

You might say: "But why should I learn to use a table of random numbers when I could just flip a coin or roll a pair of dice to decide to which group each subject should be assigned?" The main problem with flipping a coin or rolling a pair of dice is that you can easily end up with a different number of subjects in each group. If you have 24 subjects in your sample, for example, and you want to assign them to an experimental and control group, you could end up with 13 subjects in one group and 11 in the other, or 14 subjects in one group and 10 in the other if you used a coin or a pair of dice.

The statistical tests which we have used in this book work more effectively when there is an *equal* number of subjects in each group. Using a table of random numbers guarantees that you will have an equal number of subjects in each of the two groups whenever there is an even number of subjects in your sample, and only one more subject in one of the two groups whenever you are assigning an odd number of subjects to these groups (for example, if you have 23 subjects in your sample, this would split into 12 subjects in one group and 11 in the other).

We will need to agree on some terminology in order to use the random number table presented on pages 272-275. Each of the four pages of the random number table consists of five "blocks" of numbers; each block of numbers contains 10 columns of single-digit numbers (which are organized into five pairs of two digits each). Each block of numbers starts at the top of the page and goes to the bottom of the page.

For example, let Ⓐ be the symbol designating the first block of numbers on page 272. The numbers at the top of block Ⓐ are:

31 75 15 72 60

The numbers at the bottom of block Ⓐ are:

41 39 68 05 04

The numbers in the first two single-digit columns of block Ⓐ are:

31
88
30
22
.
.
.
94
41
50
41

Note that you can start to read at the top of block Ⓐ and read down this block in a variety of ways depending on how many single-digit columns you read at a time:

(1) as a group of single-digit columns. For example, the first column of single-digit numbers is:

3
8
3
2
.
.
.
9
4
5
4

(2) as a group of two-digit columns. For example, the last column of two-digit numbers on the right is:

60
82
44
.
.
.
60
13
04

(3)   as a group of three-digit columns. For example, using the first three single-digit columns gives you these numbers:

317
884
309
.
.
.
416
502
413

(4)   as any group of n-digit numbers where n can vary from 1 to 10. For example, if $n = 10$, the first 10-digit number at the top of block Ⓐ is:

31 75 15 72 60

Your first step is to write one letter at the top of each block so that you can locate each block easily. Starting on page 272 and proceeding through all four pages of the random number table, write Ⓐ at the top of the first block of numbers, Ⓑ at the top of the second block, Ⓒ at the top of the third block, and so forth until you have written a circled letter at the top of each of the blocks. When you finish, the last block on the right on page 275 should have the letter Ⓣ written above it. Do that now before you read any further in this appendix.

2.   Let's see if we have agreed on this procedure. What letter is at the top of the third block on the second page of random numbers?

— — — — — — — — — — — — — — — —

Ⓗ

3.   What numbers are at the top of block Ⓗ ?

— — — — — — — — — — — — — — — —

72 68 20 73 85

4.   What are the middle two digits at the top of block Ⓜ ?

— — — — — — — — — — — — — — — —

95

5.   What letter did you write at the top of the last block on the right of the fourth page of random numbers (page 275)?

— — — — — — — — — — — — — — — —

Ⓣ

6.   What numbers are at the top of block Ⓣ ?

————————————————

32 62 46 86 91

7.   The table of random numbers helps you to assign the subjects to the experimental (or control) conditions in your study in an unbiased manner. Let's do a simple example first so that you can get the general idea of how you can use a table of random numbers.

Suppose that you had four subjects and that you wanted to assign two of them to an experimental group and two of them to a control group. If we put one of the numbers 1-4 beside each subject's name (to make it easier to identify the subject), then the experimental group could have any one of the following six combinations of subjects in it:

    1, 2
    1, 3
    1, 4
    2, 3
    2, 4
    3, 4

Whichever one of these combinations we select for the experimental group, the other two numbers which we did not select should be assigned to the control group. But which of these six combinations of subject pairs should we assign to the experimental group?

One way to answer this question is to use the table of random numbers to make this decision. Since *all* of the numbers in this table are in a random order, each subject pair would have an equal chance of being selected. To keep the procedure simple, let's use the *first column* of single digit numbers in block Ⓐ

What are the first three numbers if you start to read at the top of this block and read down the page?

————————————————

    3
    8
    3

8.   What are the last three numbers at the bottom of this column?

————————————————

    4
    5
    4

9.   Let's use this column to determine which two subjects we should assign to the experimental group. We want to find the first two numbers from the set of numbers 1, 2, 3, 4 (these numbers correspond to the four subjects in our sample). Since we are looking only for the numbers 1-4, we should ignore any number which is larger than 4 (that is, 5, 6, 7, 8, 9) as these numbers lie outside of the range of numbers we are looking for.

Starting at the top of block Ⓐ , what is the first number from 1 to 4 that you find as you read down that column of numbers using the first single-digit column on the left?

———————————————————

3

10.   We assign subject 3 to the experimental group; then only one more subject needs to be assigned to the experimental group from the remaining subjects.

Continuing to read down this same column, what is the second number from the remaining numbers 1, 2, 4 that you find?

———————————————————

2. Notice that before you came to this number 2, you read the number 3 immediately above it; but since you have already assigned subject 3 to the experimental group, you should skip this number whenever you come across it again.

11.   We now know that the two subjects we would assign to the experimental group would be subjects 3 and 2. This means that subjects 1 and 4 would automatically be assigned to the control group, since the experimental and control groups were each supposed to have two subjects assigned to them.

Are you getting the idea of how you can use a table of random numbers? If you have not understood frames 1-11 sufficiently, reread these frames now. If you do have a good grasp of the discussion so far, continue reading.

12.   The process which we just described can be summarized by the following six steps which you should use whenever you are using a table of random numbers:

Step 1.   Create a list containing the names of the subjects in your research study. These names can be written on this list in any order.

Step 2.   Assign the first name on the list the identification number (I.D.) of 1, the second name the I.D. number of 2, the third name an I.D. number of 3, and so forth until all of the subjects have been assigned a unique I.D. number.

Step 3.   Let N be the I.D. number assigned to the last person on your list. The number N is an "upper limit" to the numbers you want to select from the table of random numbers; in using the table of random numbers, whenever you come across a number which is larger than N, ignore that number (since it does not match the I.D. number of any subject in your sample) and continue searching the table until you find a number which is less than or equal to N. For example, if there are a total of 30 subjects in your experiment, N is 30.

Step 4.   Count the number of digits in the number N. This tells you the number of single-digit *columns* of the random number table which you will need to use. If N has one digit (that is, there are nine or less subjects on your list), you need to use only one column of single-digit numbers in your search of the random number table. If N has two digits (that is, the number of subjects ranges between 10 and 99), you will need to use two adjacent columns of single-digit numbers in the random number table, and so forth.

Step 5.   Decide on a procedure to use to search the random number table for numbers matching your I.D. numbers. (For example: "I will start at the top of block Ⓚ and use the first two columns of single-digit numbers in this block to choose my sample. If I do not finish selecting my sample by the time that I reach the bottom of this block of numbers, I will continue to search starting at the top of block Ⓛ and using the first two columns of this block, and so forth, until I have completed the selection of subjects.")

Step 6.   Make a list of your I.D. numbers on a separate sheet of paper. Whenever you select one of these numbers from the table of random numbers, cross off the corresponding I.D. number on this separate sheet of paper so that you do not select the same I.D. number more than once. The I.D. number of each subject should appear once and only once in your final list of I.D. numbers which are arranged in a random order.

When using a table of random numbers, the most important thing to remember is that you can enter the table in any way you like as long as you decide on a starting place without looking at any of the numbers in the table. (Otherwise you may start to select your sample in a way which is biased in favor of some of the subjects.) For example, you could decide to start at the top of the third block of the second page of the random number table. And once you have entered the random number table, you can proceed through it in any direction (left-to-right, right-to-left, top-to-bottom, bottom-to-top, along a diagonal, and so forth) as long as you have predetermined the procedure you are using.

Let's apply these steps to another problem. Suppose that you have two experimental groups in your research study: Group 1 and Group 2. You have a total sample of 12 subjects and you want to assign 6 subjects to each of these experimental groups. Since there are 12 subjects, you should assign the numbers from 1-12 (in whatever way you prefer) so that each subject has a unique I.D. number.

You could then use any arbitrary procedure to enter and proceed through the table of random numbers. For example, a selection procedure like the following would be quite satisfactory:

I will start at the top of block Ⓗ on the second page of the table of random numbers and use the last two columns on the right within that block to assign the subjects to the two experimental conditions. If all of the subjects have not been assigned by the time that I reach the bottom of these two columns, I will use the last two columns on the right starting at the top of block Ⓘ on this same page, and so on, until all 12 subjects have been assigned to one or the other experimental groups.

Let's try that procedure together. What number appears at the top of the last two columns on the right in block Ⓗ of the second page of the table of random numbers?

— — — — — — — — — — — — — — — — —

85

13. Our sample contains only 12 subjects, so we are interested only in numbers 01-12. Since the number 85 is larger than 12, we skip it.

We should also skip any number which we have already selected so that we don't choose it twice.

What is the first number from 01-12 which appears in the last two columns of block Ⓗ when we start at the top of the table and work downwards?

— — — — — — — — — — — — — — — — —

08. Therefore, the subject who has an I.D. number of 8 would be the first subject chosen randomly.

14. The easiest way to assign subjects to one of two experimental groups is to choose all of the subjects for one of the groups first, and then automatically assign the remaining subjects to the other experimental group.

Let's suppose that we have decided to assign the first 6 subjects chosen to Group 1, and the remaining subjects to Group 2. Thus, the first subject chosen for Group 1 would have an I.D. of 8. What is the I.D. number of the second subject in Group 1 if we continue to follow our selection procedure?

— — — — — — — — — — — — — — — — —

01. If you understand everything we have discussed so far in this appendix, continue reading. If you are not sure that you are following exactly what we are talking about, please go back and reread frames 12-14 of this appendix before you read any further.

15. Let's review what we have accomplished so far. We are trying to assign 12 subjects to experimental groups so that 6 subjects are assigned to Group 1 and 6 subjects are assigned to Group 2. We decided to select the 6 subjects for Group 1 by using a table of random numbers. So far we have selected two of these 6 subjects: 8 and 1. Now what I.D. numbers would be the remaining four subjects in Group 1 if we continue to follow the same selection procedure?

———————————————————

09
05
03
02

16. Now that you have done that successfully, fill in the table below to show which I.D. numbers would be assigned to each group. Note that once you know the I.D. numbers of the six subjects that should be assigned to Group 1, you can stop using the random number table since the remaining six subjects in your list of subjects will *automatically* be assigned to Group 2 since each group was supposed to have only six subjects in it. If you keep a list of the 12 I.D. numbers on a separate sheet of paper and cross numbers off this list as you locate the I.D. numbers of the 6 subjects in Group 1, then the 6 numbers *not crossed off your list* will be the I.D. numbers of the 6 subjects in Group 2. These I.D. numbers of the subjects in Group 2 can be written in any order.

I.D. Numbers

Group 1	Group 2
———	———
———	———
———	———
———	———
———	———
———	———

———————————————————

I.D. Numbers

Group 1	Group 2
8	4
1	6
9	7
5	10
3	11
2	12

As it turned out, we were able to select the 6 subjects in Group 1 by using only the last two columns of block Ⓗ and we did not need to use block Ⓘ.

17. Now let's try a final example which you can do on your own.

A Career Education Survey of the Senior Class

Imagine that you are working at a public high school as director of guidance services. The guidance staff of your school wants to survey the current senior class to determine their perception of the effectiveness of your school's career education program and to obtain suggestions from these students as to how this program could be improved.

You are enthusiastic about this project, and you have agreed to conduct this survey. Your current senior class contains 128 students, and you have decided to interview a random sample of 10 percent of these students (that is, 13 students) and to use the results of these interviews to develop a questionnaire survey which will be sent to the remaining seniors.

Your immediate problem is to select this sample of students for the interviews. You have in front of you an alphabetical list of the seniors in your high school, and each student has been given a number from 1 to 128. You plan to use the table of random numbers in this appendix to select the 13 students who will be interviewed. (Remember that you wanted to select a 10 percent sample of the 128 seniors; 10 percent of 128 = 12.8 which you would need to round off to 13 seniors.)

You should now choose a random sample of 13 students using the following restrictions:

(1) Use only the first three digits of each block (for example, the first three digits at the top of block Ⓐ on the first page of random numbers are 317).

(2) Read the table from top to bottom using one block at a time, and beginning with the first number at the top of that block.

(3) Start with the first three digits of block Ⓐ on the first page of random numbers. Read down these first three columns until you reach the bottom of the page. Then go to the top of block Ⓑ on

this same page and read down the first three digits of this block. Repeat this procedure using blocks Ⓒ , Ⓓ , and so on until all 13 subjects have been selected.

(4)   Given these constraints, write the I.D. numbers of the 13 students you would randomly select to be interviewed in the spaces below.

_____

_____

_____

_____

_____

_____

_____

_____

_____

_____

_____

_____

_____

— — — — — — — — — — — — — — — — — —

110
045
052
113
123
091
083
074
053
081
003
073
058

Thus, from your alphabetical list you would select the 13 seniors who have the following I.D. numbers: 110, 45, 52, 113, 123, 91, 83, 74, 53, 81, 3, 73, 58.

You will need to use a table of random numbers in two different ways when you do your research studies: (1) to randomly select a sample of subjects from a larger group of people, and (2) to randomly assign your sample of subjects to experimental conditions. We have practiced both of these procedures in the examples used in this appendix, and so you should now feel confident that you can use a table of random numbers correctly.

18. Throughout this book you are given several opportunities to practice the use of the table of random numbers. We have presented below the six situations in this book that involve the use of the random number table so that you will have additional opportunities to use this table to randomly assign subjects to experimental conditions. As you come to each situation in the book, see if you can use the random number table correctly by checking your solution against the correct ones given below.

Situation 1 (Chapter 1, frame 23). Suppose that you want to assign 23 subjects to the experimental conditions so that there are 12 subjects in the experimental group and 11 subjects in the control group. Start at the top of block Ⓒ and use the first two digits and read down this block; if you need to continue beyond the first two digits of block Ⓒ, start at the top of block Ⓓ and repeat this procedure.

Which 12 subjects would you assign to the experimental group (that is, what are the first twelve I.D. numbers that you find in the table using this procedure)?

_____

_____

_____

_____

_____

_____

_____

_____

_____

_____

_____

_____

— — — — — — — — — — — — — — — — —

15
20
16
 5
14
19
 8

4
13
12
11
1

Note that the I.D. numbers of the 11 subjects *not in the above list* would automatically be assigned to the control group.

19. *Situation 2* (pages 97–98). Let's keep this example simple. Suppose that you wanted to use a total of nine subjects in this research study and that you wanted to assign five subjects to the A-M group and four subjects to the A-F group. If you started at the top of block Ⓘ and used the last single-digit column on the right, what I.D. numbers would be assigned to each of these experimental conditions?

A-M group	A-F group
_____	_____
_____	_____
_____	_____
_____	_____
_____	

— — — — — — — — — — — — — —

A-M group	A-F group
6	1
9	2
3	5
8	7
4	

20. *Situation 3* (Chapter Four, frame 20). Suppose that you want to use a total of 23 subjects in your experiment and assign 12 subjects to Group 1 and 11 subjects to Group 2. Start at the top of block Ⓚ and use the first two digits on the left of this block.

Group 1	Group 2
_____	_____
_____	_____
_____	_____
_____	_____

——	——
——	——
——	——
——	——
——	——
——	——
——	——
——	——
——	

Group 1	Group 2
21	1
15	2
12	4
3	6
17	8
19	10
11	14
5	16
13	18
9	20
23	22
7	

21. *Situation 4* (Chapter Five, frame 2). Suppose that you want to use 15 subjects in this research study and that you want to assign 8 subjects to the experimental group and 7 subjects to the control group. Start at the top of block Ⓓ and use the last two digits. What I.D. numbers would be assigned to each group?

Experimental group	Control group
——	——
——	——
——	——
——	——
——	——
——	——
——	

Experimental group	Control group
13	4
5	7
14	9
1	10
8	11
2	12
6	15
3	

22. *Situation 5* (Chapter Five, frame 16). Suppose that you want to use 11 subjects in this research study and that you want to assign 5 subjects to the I-E group and 6 subjects to the E-I group. Start at the top of block Ⓜ and use the first two digits; if you need to continue beyond these first two digits of block Ⓜ, continue to search starting at the top of block Ⓝ using the first two digits of that block. What I.D. numbers would be assigned to each group?

I-E group	E-I group
_____	_____
_____	_____
_____	_____
_____	_____
_____	_____
	_____

I-E group	E-I group
1	2
8	3
5	4
11	6
10	7
	9

23. *Situation 6* (page 183). Suppose that you want to use 13 subjects in this research study and that you want to assign 7 subjects to the MVP group and 6 subjects to the DR group. Start at the top of block Ⓒ and use the middle two digits; then use the middle two digits of block Ⓓ (starting at the top of this block) if you need to continue your search beyond the middle two digits of block Ⓒ. What I.D. numbers would be assigned to each group?

	MVP	DR
	_____	_____
	_____	_____
	_____	_____
	_____	_____
	_____	_____
	_____	_____
	_____	

MVP	DR
4	1
6	3
12	5
8	7
9	10
2	13
11	

Random Digits*

31	75	15	72	60	68	98	00	53	39	15	47	04	83	55	88	65	12	25	96	03	15	21	91	21
88	49	29	93	82	14	45	40	45	04	20	09	49	89	77	74	84	39	34	13	22	10	97	85	,08
30	93	44	77	44	07	48	18	38	28	73	78	80	65	33	28	59	72	04	05	94	20	52	03	80
22	88	84	88	93	27	49	99	87	48	60	53	04	51	28	74	02	28	46	17	82	03	71	02	68
78	21	21	69	93	35	90	29	13	86	44	37	21	54	86	65	74	11	40	14	87	48	13	72	20
41	84	98	45	47	46	85	05	23	26	34	67	75	83	00	74	91	06	43	45	19	32	58	15	49
46	35	23	30	49	69	24	89	34	60	45	30	50	75	21	61	31	83	18	55	14	41	37	09	51
11	08	79	62	94	14	01	33	17	92	59	74	76	72	77	76	50	33	45	13	39	66	37	75	44
52	70	10	83	37	56	30	38	73	15	16	52	06	96	76	11	65	49	98	93	02	18	16	81	61
57	27	53	68	98	81	30	44	85	85	68	65	22	73	76	92	85	25	58	66	88	44	80	35	84
20	85	77	31	56	70	28	42	43	26	79	37	59	52	20	01	15	96	32	67	10	62	24	83	91
15	63	38	49	24	90	41	59	36	14	33	52	12	66	65	55	82	34	76	41	86	22	53	17	04
92	69	44	82	97	39	90	40	21	15	59	58	94	90	67	66	82	14	15	75	49	76	70	40	37
77	61	31	90	19	88	15	20	00	80	20	55	49	14	09	96	27	74	82	57	50	81	69	76	16
38	68	83	24	86	45	13	46	35	45	59	40	47	20	59	43	94	75	16	80	43	85	25	96	93
25	16	30	18	89	70	01	41	50	21	41	29	06	73	12	71	85	71	59	57	68	97	11	14	03
65	25	10	76	29	37	23	93	32	95	05	87	00	11	19	92	78	42	63	40	18	47	76	56	22
36	81	54	36	25	18	63	73	75	09	82	44	49	90	05	04	92	17	37	01	14	70	79	39	97
64	39	71	16	92	05	32	78	21	62	20	24	78	17	59	45	19	72	53	32	83	74	52	25	67
04	51	52	56	24	95	09	66	79	46	48	46	08	55	58	15	19	11	87	82	16	93	03	33	61
15	88	09	22	61	17	29	28	81	90	61	78	14	88	98	92	52	52	12	83	88	58	16	00	98
71	92	60	08	19	59	14	40	02	24	30	57	09	01	94	18	32	90	69	99	26	85	71	92	38
64	42	52	81	08	16	55	41	60	16	00	04	28	32	29	10	33	33	61	68	65	61	79	48	34
79	78	22	39	24	49	44	03	04	32	81	07	73	15	43	95	21	66	48	65	13	65	85	10	81
36	33	77	45	38	44	55	36	46	72	90	96	04	18	49	93	86	54	46	08	93	17	63	48	51
05	24	92	93	29	19	71	59	40	82	14	73	88	66	67	43	70	86	63	54	93	69	22	55	27
56	46	39	93	80	38	79	38	57	74	19	05	61	39	39	46	06	22	76	47	66	14	66	32	10
96	29	63	31	21	54	19	63	41	08	75	81	48	59	86	71	17	11	51	02	28	99	26	31	65
98	38	03	62	69	60	01	40	72	01	62	44	84	63	85	42	17	58	83	50	46	18	24	91	26
52	56	76	43	50	16	31	55	39	69	80	39	58	11	14	54	35	86	45	78	47	26	91	57	47
78	49	89	08	30	25	95	59	92	36	43	28	69	10	64	99	96	99	51	44	64	42	47	73	77
49	55	32	42	41	08	15	08	95	35	08	70	39	10	41	77	32	38	10	79	45	12	79	36	86
32	15	10	70	75	83	15	51	02	52	73	10	08	86	18	23	89	18	74	18	45	41	72	02	68
11	31	45	03	63	26	86	02	77	99	49	41	68	35	34	19	18	70	80	59	76	67	70	21	10
12	36	47	12	10	87	05	25	02	41	90	78	59	78	89	81	39	95	81	30	64	43	90	56	14
09	18	82	00	97	32	82	53	95	27	04	22	08	63	04	83	38	98	73	74	64	27	85	80	44
90	04	58	54	97	51	98	15	06	54	94	93	88	19	97	91	87	07	61	50	68	47	66	46	59
73	18	95	02	07	47	67	72	62	69	62	29	06	44	64	27	12	46	70	18	41	36	18	27	60
75	76	87	64	90	20	97	18	17	49	90	42	91	22	72	95	37	50	58	71	93	82	34	31	78
54	01	64	40	56	66	28	13	10	03	00	68	22	73	98	20	71	45	32	95	07	70	61	78	13
08	35	86	99	10	78	54	24	27	85	13	66	15	88	73	04	61	89	75	53	31	22	30	84	20
28	30	60	32	64	81	33	31	05	91	40	51	00	78	93	32	60	46	04	75	94	11	90	18	40
53	84	08	62	33	81	59	41	36	28	51	21	59	02	90	28	46	66	87	95	77	76	22	07	91
91	75	75	37	41	61	61	36	22	69	50	26	39	02	12	55	78	17	65	14	83	48	34	70	55
89	41	59	26	94	00	39	75	83	91	12	60	71	76	46	48	94	97	23	06	94	54	13	74	08
77	51	30	38	20	86	83	42	99	01	68	41	48	27	74	51	90	81	39	80	72	89	35	55	07
19	50	23	71	74	69	97	92	02	88	55	21	02	97	73	74	28	77	52	51	65	34	46	74	15
21	81	85	93	13	93	27	88	17	57	05	68	67	31	56	07	08	28	50	46	31	85	33	84	52
51	47	46	64	99	68	10	72	36	21	94	04	99	13	45	42	83	60	91	91	08	00	74	54	49
99	55	96	83	31	62	53	52	41	70	69	77	71	28	30	74	81	97	81	42	43	86	07	28	34
60	31	14	28	24	37	30	14	26	78	45	99	04	32	42	17	37	45	20	03	70	70	77	02	14
49	73	97	14	84	92	00	39	80	86	76	66	87	32	09	59	20	21	19	73	02	90	23	32	50
78	62	65	15	94	16	45	39	46	14	39	01	49	70	66	83	01	20	98	32	25	57	17	76	28
66	69	21	39	86	99	83	70	05	82	81	23	24	49	87	09	50	49	64	12	90	19	37	95	68
44	07	12	80	91	07	36	29	77	03	76	44	74	25	37	98	52	49	78	31	65	70	40	95	14
41	46	88	51	49	49	55	41	79	94	14	92	43	96	50	95	29	40	05	56	70	48	10	69	05
94	55	93	75	59	49	67	85	31	19	70	31	20	56	82	66	98	63	40	99	74	47	42	07	40
41	61	57	03	60	64	11	45	86	60	90	85	06	46	18	80	62	05	17	90	11	43	63	80	72
50	27	39	31	13	41	79	48	68	61	24	78	18	96	83	55	41	18	56	67	77	53	59	98	92
41	39	68	05	04	90	67	00	82	89	40	90	20	50	69	95	08	30	67	83	28	10	25	78	16

*Source: P. G. Hoel, *Elementary Statistics,* 4th edition (New York: John Wiley & Sons, Inc., 1976), pp. 343–346. By permission.

Random Digits (continued)

```
25 80 72 42 60   71 52 97 89 20   72 68 20 73 85   90 72 65 71 66   98 88 40 85 83
06 17 09 79 65   88 30 29 80 41   21 44 34 18 08   68 98 48 36 20   89 74 79 88 82
60 80 85 44 44   74 41 28 11 05   01 17 62 88 38   36 42 11 64 89   18 05 95 10 61
80 94 04 48 93   10 40 83 62 22   80 58 27 19 44   92 63 84 03 33   67 05 41 60 67
19 51 69 01 20   46 75 97 16 43   13 17 75 52 92   21 03 68 28 08   77 50 19 74 27

49 38 65 44 80   23 60 42 35 54   21 78 54 11 01   91 17 81 01 74   29 42 09 04 38
06 31 28 89 40   15 99 56 93 21   47 45 86 48 09   98 18 98 18 51   29 65 18 42 15
60 94 20 03 07   11 89 79 26 74   40 40 56 80 32   96 71 75 42 44   10 70 14 13 93
92 32 99 89 32   78 28 44 63 47   71 20 99 20 61   39 44 89 31 36   25 72 20 85 64
77 93 66 35 74   31 38 45 19 24   85 56 12 96 71   58 13 71 78 20   22 75 13 65 18

91 30 70 69 91   19 07 22 42 10   36 69 95 37 28   28 82 53 57 93   28 97 66 62 52
68 43 49 46 88   84 47 31 36 22   62 12 69 84 08   12 84 38 25 90   09 81 59 31 46
48 90 81 58 77   54 74 52 45 91   35 70 00 47 54   83 82 45 26 92   54 13 05 51 60
06 91 34 51 97   42 67 27 86 01   11 88 30 95 28   63 01 19 89 01   14 97 44 03 44
10 45 51 60 19   14 21 03 37 12   91 34 23 78 21   88 32 58 08 51   43 66 77 08 83

12 88 39 73 43   65 02 76 11 84   04 28 50 13 92   17 97 41 50 77   90 71 22 67 69
21 77 83 09 76   38 80 73 69 61   31 64 94 20 96   63 28 10 20 23   08 81 64 74 49
19 52 35 95 15   65 12 25 96 59   86 28 36 82 58   69 57 21 37 98   16 43 59 15 29
67 24 55 26 70   35 58 31 65 63   79 24 68 66 86   76 46 33 42 22   26 65 59 08 02
60 58 44 73 77   07 50 03 79 92   45 13 42 65 29   26 76 08 36 37   41 32 64 43 44

53 85 34 13 77   36 06 69 48 50   58 83 87 38 59   49 36 47 33 31   96 24 04 36 42
24 63 73 87 36   74 38 48 93 42   52 62 30 79 92   12 36 91 86 01   03 74 28 38 73
83 08 01 24 51   38 99 22 28 15   07 75 95 17 77   97 37 72 75 85   51 97 23 78 67
16 44 42 43 34   36 15 19 90 73   27 49 37 09 39   85 13 03 25 52   54 84 65 47 59
60 79 01 81 57   57 17 86 57 62   11 16 17 85 76   45 81 95 29 79   65 13 00 48 60

94 01 54 68 74   32 44 44 82 77   59 82 09 61 63   64 65 42 58 43   41 14 54 28 20
74 10 88 82 22   88 57 07 40 15   25 70 49 10 35   01 75 51 47 50   48 96 83 86 03
62 88 08 78 73   95 16 05 92 21   22 30 49 03 14   72 87 71 73 34   39 28 30 41 49
11 74 81 21 02   80 58 04 18 67   17 71 05 96 21   06 55 40 78 50   73 95 07 95 52
17 94 40 56 00   60 47 80 33 43   25 85 25 89 05   57 21 63 96 18   49 85 69 93 26

66 06 74 27 92   95 04 35 26 80   46 78 05 64 87   09 97 15 94 81   37 00 62 21 86
54 24 49 10 30   45 54 77 08 18   59 84 99 61 69   61 45 92 16 47   87 41 71 71 98
30 94 55 75 89   31 73 25 72 60   47 67 00 76 54   46 37 62 53 66   94 74 64 95 80
69 17 03 74 03   86 99 59 03 07   94 30 47 18 03   26 82 50 55 11   12 45 99 13 14
08 34 58 89 75   35 84 18 57 71   08 10 55 99 87   87 11 22 14 76   14 71 37 11 81

27 76 74 35 84   85 30 18 89 77   29 49 06 97 14   73 03 54 12 07   74 69 90 93 10
13 02 51 43 38   54 06 61 52 43   47 72 46 67 33   47 43 14 39 05   31 04 85 66 99
80 21 73 62 92   98 52 52 43 35   24 43 22 48 96   43 27 75 88 74   11 46 61 60 82
10 87 56 20 04   90 39 16 11 05   57 41 10 63 68   53 85 63 07 43   08 67 08 47 41
54 12 75 73 26   26 62 91 90 87   24 47 28 87 79   30 54 02 78 86   61 73 27 54 54

33 71 34 80 07   93 58 47 28 69   51 92 66 47 21   58 30 32 98 22   93 17 49 39 72
85 27 48 68 93   11 30 32 92 70   28 83 43 41 37   73 51 59 04 00   71 14 84 36 43
84 13 38 96 40   44 03 55 21 66   73 85 27 00 91   61 22 26 05 61   62 32 71 84 23
56 73 21 62 34   17 39 59 61 31   10 12 39 16 22   85 49 65 75 60   81 60 41 88 80
65 13 85 68 06   87 64 88 52 61   34 31 36 58 61   45 87 52 10 69   85 64 44 72 77

38 00 10 21 76   81 71 91 17 11   71 60 29 29 37   74 21 96 40 49   65 58 44 96 98
37 40 29 63 97   01 30 47 75 86   56 27 11 00 86   47 32 46 26 05   40 03 03 74 38
97 12 54 03 48   87 08 33 14 17   21 81 53 92 50   75 23 76 20 47   15 50 12 95 78
21 82 64 11 34   47 14 33 40 72   64 63 88 59 02   49 13 90 64 41   03 85 65 45 52
73 13 54 27 42   95 71 90 90 35   85 79 47 42 96   08 78 98 81 56   64 69 11 92 02

07 63 87 79 29   03 06 11 80 72   96 20 74 41 56   23 82 19 95 38   04 71 36 69 94
60 52 88 34 41   07 95 41 98 14   59 17 52 06 95   05 53 35 21 39   61 21 20 64 55
83 59 63 56 55   06 95 89 29 83   05 12 80 97 19   77 43 35 37 83   92 30 15 04 98
10 85 06 27 46   99 59 91 05 07   13 49 90 63 19   53 07 57 18 39   06 41 01 93 62
39 82 09 89 52   43 62 26 31 47   64 42 18 08 14   43 80 00 93 51   31 02 47 31 67

59 58 00 64 78   75 56 97 88 00   88 83 55 44 86   23 76 80 61 56   04 11 10 84 08
38 50 80 73 41   23 79 34 87 63   90 82 29 70 22   17 71 90 42 07   95 95 44 99 53
30 69 27 06 68   94 68 81 61 27   56 19 68 00 91   82 06 76 34 00   05 46 26 92 00
65 44 39 56 59   18 28 82 74 37   49 63 22 40 41   08 33 76 56 76   96 29 99 08 36
27 26 75 02 64   13 19 27 22 94   07 47 74 46 06   17 98 54 89 11   97 34 13 03 58
```

Random Digits (continued)

```
38 10 17 77 56   11 65 71 38 97   95 88 95 70 67   47 64 81 38 85   70 66 99 34 06
39 64 16 94 57   91 33 92 25 02   92 61 38 97 19   11 94 75 62 03   19 32 42 05 04
84 05 44 04 55   99 39 66 36 80   67 66 76 06 31   69 18 19 68 45   38 52 51 16 00
47 46 80 35 77   57 64 96 32 66   24 70 07 15 94   14 00 42 31 53   69 24 90 57 47
43 32 13 13 70   28 97 72 38 96   76 47 96 85 62   62 34 20 75 89   08 89 90 59 85

64 28 16 18 26   18 55 56 49 37   13 17 33 33 65   78 85 11 64 99   87 06 41 30 75
66 84 77 04 95   32 35 00 29 85   86 71 63 87 46   26 31 37 74 63   55 38 77 26 81
72 46 13 32 30   21 52 95 34 24   92 58 10 22 62   78 43 86 62 76   18 39 67 35 38
21 03 29 10 50   13 05 81 62 18   12 47 05 65 00   15 29 27 61 39   59 52 65 21 13
95 36 26 70 11   06 65 11 61 36   01 01 60 08 57   55 01 85 63 74   35 82 47 17 08

40 71 29 73 80   10 40 45 54 52   34 03 06 07 26   75 21 11 02 71   36 63 36 84 24
58 27 56 17 64   97 58 65 47 16   50 25 94 63 45   87 19 54 60 92   26 78 76 09 39
89 51 41 17 88   68 22 42 34 17   73 95 97 61 45   30 34 24 02 77   11 04 97 20 49
15 47 25 06 69   48 13 93 67 32   46 87 43 70 88   73 46 50 98 19   58 86 93 52 20
12 12 08 61 24   51 24 74 43 02   60 88 35 21 09   21 43 73 67 86   49 22 67 78 37

03 99 11 04 61   93 71 61 68 94   66 08 32 46 53   84 60 95 82 32   88 61 81 91 61
38 55 59 55 54   32 88 65 97 80   08 35 56 08 60   29 73 54 77 62   71 29 92 38 53
17 54 67 37 04   92 05 24 62 15   55 12 12 92 81   59 07 60 79 36   27 95 45 89 09
32 64 35 28 61   95 81 90 68 31   00 91 19 89 36   76 35 59 37 79   80 86 30 05 14
69 57 26 87 77   39 51 03 59 05   14 06 04 06 19   29 54 96 96 16   33 56 46 07 80

24 12 26 65 91   27 69 90 64 94   14 84 54 66 72   61 95 87 71 00   90 89 97 57 54
61 19 63 02 31   92 96 26 17 73   41 83 95 53 82   17 26 77 09 43   78 03 87 02 67
30 53 22 17 04   10 27 41 22 02   39 68 52 33 09   10 06 16 88 29   55 98 66 64 85
03 78 89 75 99   75 86 72 07 17   74 41 65 31 66   35 20 83 33 74   87 53 90 88 23
48 22 86 33 79   85 78 34 76 19   53 15 26 74 33   35 66 35 29 72   16 81 86 03 11

60 36 59 46 53   35 07 53 39 49   42 61 42 92 97   01 91 82 83 16   98 95 37 32 31
83 79 94 24 02   56 62 33 44 42   34 99 44 13 74   70 07 11 47 36   09 95 81 80 65
32 96 00 74 05   36 40 98 32 32   99 38 54 16 00   11 13 30 75 86   15 91 70 62 53
19 32 25 38 45   57 62 05 26 06   66 49 76 86 46   78 13 86 65 59   19 64 09 94 13
11 22 09 47 47   07 39 93 74 08   48 50 92 39 29   27 48 24 54 76   85 24 43 51 59

21 44 58 27 93   24 83 19 32 41   14 19 97 62 68   70 88 36 80 02   03 82 91 74 43
72 51 37 64 00   52 22 59 23 48   62 30 89 84 81   29 74 43 31 65   33 14 16 10 20
71 47 94 50 27   76 16 05 74 11   13 78 01 36 32   52 30 87 77 62   88 87 43 36 97
83 21 05 14 66   09 08 85 03 95   26 74 30 53 06   21 70 67 00 01   99 43 98 07 67
68 74 99 51 48   94 89 77 86 36   96 75 00 90 24   94 53 89 11 43   96 69 36 18 86

05 18 47 57 63   47 07 58 81 58   05 31 35 34 39   14 90 80 88 30   60 09 62 15 51
13 65 16 25 46   96 89 22 52 40   47 51 15 84 83   87 34 27 88 18   07 85 53 92 69
00 56 62 12 20   00 29 22 40 69   25 07 22 95 19   52 54 85 40 91   21 28 22 12 96
50 95 81 76 95   58 07 26 89 90   60 32 99 59 55   71 58 66 34 17   35 94 76 78 07
57 62 16 45 47   46 85 03 79 81   38 52 70 90 37   64 75 60 33 24   04 98 68 36 66

09 28 22 58 44   79 13 97 84 35   35 42 84 35 61   69 79 96 33 14   12 99 19 35 16
23 39 49 42 06   93 43 23 78 36   94 91 92 68 46   02 55 57 44 10   94 91 54 81 99
05 28 03 74 70   93 62 20 43 45   15 09 21 95 10   18 09 41 66 13   78 23 45 00 01
95 49 19 79 76   38 30 63 21 92   82 63 95 46 24   72 43 49 26 06   23 19 17 46 93
78 52 10 01 04   18 24 87 55 83   90 32 65 07 85   54 03 46 62 51   35 77 41 46 92

96 34 54 45 79   85 93 24 40 53   75 70 42 08 40   86 58 38 39 44   52 45 67 37 66
77 96 33 11 51   32 36 49 16 91   47 35 74 03 38   23 43 52 40 65   08 45 89 53 66
07 52 01 12 94   23 23 80 17 48   41 69 06 73 28   54 81 43 77 77   10 05 74 23 32
38 42 30 23 09   70 70 38 57 36   46 14 81 42 58   29 23 61 21 52   05 08 86 58 25
02 46 36 55 33   21 19 96 05 55   33 92 80 18 17   07 39 68 92 15   30 72 22 21 02

83 76 16 08 73   43 25 38 41 45   60 83 32 59 83   01 29 14 13 49   20 36 80 71 26
14 38 70 63 45   80 85 40 92 79   43 52 90 63 18   38 38 47 47 61   41 19 63 74 80
51 32 19 22 46   80 08 87 70 74   88 72 25 67 36   66 16 44 94 31   66 91 93 16 78
72 47 20 00 08   80 89 01 80 02   94 81 33 19 00   54 15 58 34 36   35 35 25 41 31
05 46 65 53 06   93 12 81 84 64   74 45 79 05 61   72 84 81 18 34   79 98 26 84 16

39 52 87 24 84   82 47 42 55 93   48 54 53 52 47   18 61 91 36 74   18 61 11 92 41
81 61 61 87 11   53 34 24 42 76   75 12 21 17 24   74 62 77 37 07   58 31 91 59 97
07 58 61 61 20   82 64 12 28 20   92 90 41 31 41   32 39 21 97 63   61 19 96 79 40
90 76 70 42 35   13 57 41 72 00   69 90 26 37 42   78 46 42 25 01   18 62 79 08 72
40 18 82 81 93   29 59 38 86 27   94 97 21 15 98   62 09 53 67 87   00 44 15 89 97
```

Random Digits (continued)

34	41	48	21	57	86	88	75	50	87	19	15	20	00	23	12	30	28	07	83	32	62	46	86	91
63	43	97	53	63	44	98	91	68	22	36	02	40	08	67	76	37	84	16	05	65	96	17	34	88
67	04	90	90	70	93	39	94	55	47	94	45	87	42	84	05	04	14	98	07	20	28	83	40	60
79	49	50	41	46	52	16	29	02	86	54	15	83	42	43	46	97	83	54	82	59	36	29	59	38
91	70	43	05	52	04	73	72	10	31	75	05	19	30	29	47	66	56	43	82	99	78	29	34	78
19	61	27	84	30	11	66	19	47	70	77	60	36	56	69	86	86	81	26	65	30	01	27	59	89
39	14	17	74	00	28	00	06	42	38	73	25	87	17	94	31	34	02	62	56	66	45	33	70	16
64	75	68	04	57	08	74	71	28	36	03	46	95	06	78	03	27	44	34	23	66	67	78	25	56
92	90	15	18	78	56	44	12	29	98	29	71	83	84	47	06	45	32	53	11	07	56	55	37	71
03	55	19	00	70	09	48	39	40	50	45	93	81	81	35	36	90	84	33	21	11	07	35	18	03
98	88	46	62	09	06	83	05	36	56	14	66	35	63	46	71	43	00	49	09	19	81	80	57	07
27	36	98	68	82	53	47	30	76	41	53	63	37	08	63	03	74	81	28	22	19	36	04	90	88
59	06	67	59	74	63	33	52	04	83	43	51	43	74	81	58	27	82	69	67	49	43	54	39	51
91	64	79	37	83	64	16	94	90	22	98	58	80	94	95	49	82	95	90	68	38	83	10	48	38
83	60	59	24	19	39	54	20	77	72	71	56	87	56	73	35	18	58	97	59	44	90	17	42	91
24	89	58	85	30	70	77	43	54	39	46	75	87	04	72	70	20	79	26	75	91	62	36	12	75
35	72	02	65	56	95	59	62	00	94	73	75	08	57	88	34	26	40	17	03	46	83	36	52	48
14	14	15	34	10	38	64	90	63	43	57	25	66	13	42	72	70	97	53	18	90	37	93	75	62
27	41	67	56	70	92	17	67	25	35	93	11	95	60	77	06	88	61	82	44	92	34	43	13	74
82	07	10	74	29	81	00	74	77	49	40	74	45	69	74	23	33	68	88	21	53	84	11	05	36

Finding the Square Root
of a Number*

Tables B.1 and B.2 may be used to find the square root of any two-digit number. For any value find the first two digits in the colum labeled n. Two columns are provided. Consult Table B.1 to decide which column to use and by what to multiply the value in the table.

Example 1

Find the square root of 8.3.

8.3 is between 1.0 and 9.9, therefore from Table B.1 we find $\sqrt{n}$ and multiply by 1.0. From Table B.2 we obtain 2.8810.

n	$\sqrt{n}$
8.3	2.8810

Example 2

Find the square root of 760.

This is between 100 and 990. Table B.1 refers you to Column $\sqrt{n}$; multiply by 10. From Table B.2 we find:

n	$\sqrt{n}$
7.6	2.7568

Therefore

$$\sqrt{760} = 10(2.7568) = 27.568.$$

*Source: N. R. Ullman, *Statistics: An Applied Approach* (New York: John Wiley & Sons, Inc., 1972), pp. 544–546. By permission.

Example 3

Find the square root of 0.37.

    This is between 0.10 and 0.99. From Table B.1 we find that we should use the column labeled $\sqrt{10n}$ and multiply by 0.1. From Table B.2 we find:

n	$\sqrt{10n}$
3.7	6.083

Therefore

$$\sqrt{0.37} = 0.1(6.083) = 0.6083.$$

Table B.1.

For numbers between	To find square roots	
	Use column labeled	Multiply by this value
1 and 9.9	$\sqrt{n}$	1
10 and 99	$\sqrt{10n}$	1
100 and 990	$\sqrt{n}$	10
1,000 and 9,900	$\sqrt{10n}$	10
10,000 and 99,000	$\sqrt{n}$	100
0.10 and 0.99	$\sqrt{10n}$	0.1
0.010 and 0.099	$\sqrt{n}$	0.1
0.0010 and 0.0099	$\sqrt{10n}$	0.01

Table B.2. Square Roots.

n	$\sqrt{n}$	$\sqrt{10n}$	n	$\sqrt{n}$	$\sqrt{10n}$
1.0	1.0000	3.162	2.1	1.4491	4.583
			2.2	1.4832	4.690
1.1	1.0488	3.317	2.3	1.5166	4.796
1.2	1.0954	3.464	2.4	1.5492	4.899
1.3	1.1402	3.606	2.5	1.5811	5.000
1.4	1.1832	3.742			
1.5	1.2247	3.873	2.6	1.6125	5.099
			2.7	1.6432	5.196
1.6	1.2649	4.000	2.8	1.6733	5.292
1.7	1.3038	4.123	2.9	1.7029	5.385
1.8	1.3416	4.243	3.0	1.7321	5.477
1.9	1.3784	4.359			
2.0	1.4142	4.472			

Table B.2. Square Roots (continued)

n	$\sqrt{n}$	$\sqrt{10n}$	n	$\sqrt{n}$	$\sqrt{10n}$
3.1	1.7607	5.568	6.6	2.5690	8.124
3.2	1.7889	5.657	6.7	2.5884	8.185
3.3	1.8166	5.745	6.8	2.6077	8.246
3.4	1.8439	5.831	6.9	2.6268	8.307
3.5	1.8708	5.916	7.0	2.6458	8.367
3.6	1.8974	6.000	7.1	2.6646	8.426
3.7	1.9235	6.083	7.2	2.6833	8.485
3.8	1.9494	6.164	7.3	2.7019	8.544
3.9	1.9748	6.245	7.4	2.7203	8.602
4.0	2.0000	6.325	7.5	2.7386	8.660
4.1	2.0248	6.043	7.6	2.7568	8.718
4.2	2.0494	6.481	7.7	2.7749	8.775
4.3	2.0736	6.557	7.8	2.7928	8.832
4.4	2.0976	6.633	7.9	2.8107	8.888
4.5	2.1213	6.708	8.0	2.8284	8.944
4.6	2.1448	6.782	8.1	2.8460	9.000
4.7	2.1679	6.856	8.2	2.8636	9.055
4.8	2.1909	6.928	8.3	2.8810	9.110
4.9	2.2136	7.000	8.4	2.8983	9.165
5.0	2.2361	7.071	8.5	2.9155	9.220
5.1	2.2583	7.141	8.6	2.9326	9.274
5.2	2.2804	7.211	8.7	2.9496	9.327
5.3	2.3022	7.280	8.8	2.9665	9.381
5.4	2.3238	7.348	8.9	2.9833	9.434
5.5	2.3452	7.416	9.0	3.0000	9.487
5.6	2.3664	7.483	9.1	3.0166	9.539
5.7	2.3875	7.550	9.2	3.0332	9.592
5.8	2.4083	7.616	9.3	3.0496	9.644
5.9	2.4290	7.681	9.4	3.0659	9.695
6.0	2.4495	7.746	9.5	3.0822	9.747
6.1	2.4698	7.810	9.6	3.0984	9.798
6.2	2.4900	7.874	9.7	3.1145	9.849
6.3	2.5100	7.937	9.8	3.1305	9.899
6.4	2.5298	8.000	9.9	3.1464	9.950
6.5	2.5495	8.062	10.0	3.1623	10.000

A Procedure
for a Research Team Project

The purpose of this appendix is to describe a procedure which has been used to teach undergraduates (who are not psychology majors) the process of psychological research. It is based on a paper given by Quirk (1976) at the annual meeting of the American Psychological Association. To date, this procedure has been used with a total of almost 400 students who were randomly assigned to over 60 research teams during the past three years as part of courses dealing with introductory psychology, educational psychology, and social psychology at Principia College.

The performance of the students on the projects counted either 15 percent or 20 percent toward each student's final grade in the course. All students on each research team received the identical grade for the team project, except in those cases in which a student was dropped from a team because of insufficient contribution to the team effort.

Early in each course the students were taught to do three statistical procedures: (1) a rank-order correlation coefficient, (2) a chi-square test based on a fourfold table (the students were taught not to inflate N in chi-square and not to use percentages in the cells of the fourfold tables when computing a value for chi-square), and (3) a t-test for independent samples. These procedures gave the students three of the skills which are necessary to do a good research project.

Each team was required to submit to the instructor a one-page abstract of the research project which they planned to do (signed by all the members of the research team) at least 10 days before their scheduled class presentation, so that the instructor could approve the project. This quality-control procedure insured that: (1) proper ethical issues had been considered by the research team (for example, one research team wanted to drop a wallet in the student center and then record the number of students who returned it to its owner; the abstract enabled the instructor to question the interpretation which the members of the research team would make of the actions of a student who did not immediately return it, and the research team decided to abandon this project because they were concerned about labeling students as "honest" or "dishonest" in their own thoughts), and (2) that the research project was substantive enough to be worth the effort involved in carrying it out.

A class hour was set aside for each research team's presentation. Each team was required to make a verbal presentation of its study to the class (no written report was required) for the first 20-30 minutes of the class and to respond to questions and comments from the members of the class for the next 10-20 minutes.

The instructor has found that this discussion period works best as a learning experience for the class and for the research team if the instructor withholds his comments and questions until after the students in the class have had an opportunity to comment and to question the research team. This provides the students with an opportunity to interact with and to learn from one another, and to test their own understanding of the process and procedures for doing psychological research. Further, after the class has had the opportunity to comment, the instructor has tried to restrict his questions and comments to two types: (1) those directed at an incorrect *statistical treatment* of the data, and (2) those directed at an incorrect *interpretation* of the results of the research study.

Form 1 contains the rating scale items that correspond to Figure 8.1; these items were filled out by the instructor immediately after each research team's presentation, and they represented his opinion of the quality of the research project. As soon as each research team had finished its presentation, all members of the class were asked to respond anonymously and to rate the quality of the research project using the rating scale items given in Form 1. Also each member of the research team was asked to rate anonymously his or her perception of the quality of the presentation of the research team, using the rating-scale items given in Form 2. Finally, each team member was asked to rate anonymously the performance of each other member of the research team, using the rating scale items given in Form 3.

The use of Form 3 requires that each team member know the "Team Member Number" of the other members of the team so that he or she can write this number in the space provided at the top of this form. The easiest way to accomplish this is to have the instructor write the names of the team members on the board, and then write a different I.D. number beside each member's name. For example, if there are five members of the team, one of the numbers 1-5 can be arbitrarily written beside each team member's name so that each team member is assigned a unique I.D. number.

A Fortran program was written* and a computer was used to summarize each research team's performance. Tables C.1, C.2, and C.3 contain a sample of the printouts given to each research team member for one of the actual research projects.

Table C.1 summarizes the instructor(s) rating (INSTR MEAN), the mean rating of the team's performance given by the members of the class (TEAM

---

*I wish to acknowledge the contribution of John Ernisse who wrote this computer program.

MEAN), and the weighted mean of the team means for the class (CLASS MEAN) for the results of the rating-scale items contained in Form 1.

Table C.2 presents a sample printout of the team's average perception of the quality of its performance (TEAM MEAN) and the weighted mean of the team means for the class (CLASS MEAN) for Form 2.

Table C.3 summarizes the average perception of this particular team member by the other members of his or her research team (INDIV MEAN), the weighted average perception of the team members for one another (TEAM MEAN), and the weighted average perception of the members of all the teams for the other members of their research team (CLASS MEAN) for Form 3. Each page of the three-page computer printout also contained the raw score frequency data for the rating-scale items.

The research team projects are really an opportunity for students to engage in a cooperative experiment within a *task-oriented* framework. The research teams were not competing against one another in terms of the grade assigned their research project; each team was assigned a grade for its project on the same day as its presentation to the class without the instructor's knowledge of the computer printout results. All of the students in a class received their grade for their project during class on the day following the last research team's presentation.

Each team had to agree on the research study they would do, review the research literature relevant to their topic, plan their study, collect their data, analyze their data, and interpret the results of their study to the class. Since no written report was required, each research team had to decide among its members how to distribute the tasks involved in carrying out their study and in reporting their research results to the class.

The research teams have had four to nine students on them, but the optimal size has been five to seven students per team. As many as 70 students have been in one class that has used this research training procedure, but that class was split into two sections during the week of the research team's presentations in order to reduce the number of class days that had to be set aside for these presentations.

The research team projects provide students with a first-hand experience in the process of psychological research. Students who do not have a first-hand experience in carrying out psychological research projects are likely to underestimate the complexity and difficulties inherent in conducting a research study if their knowledge of psychological research is based solely on articles that they have read in psychological journals. Journal editors are likely to emphasize conciseness of experiments in their dealings with the authors of journal articles, and this brevity can lead a student who is a novice, in terms of his participation in the description and conduct of psychological research studies, to seriously misjudge the "messiness" of the process of conducting a research study in psychology from start to finish.

The procedures described in this appendix provide a first-hand opportunity for students to experience an exercise in cooperation within a task-oriented requirement of the design, conduct, analysis, and interpretation of data connected with a research study planned by a group of students. This procedure has proven to be a useful and effective teaching technique.

Research Team Number _____   Form 1

Class Perception of the Research Team's Presentation

1. Was the purpose of this research study clear?

1	2	3	4	5	6	7	8	9

   Not very clear   Clear

2. Did the research team present a good review of the relevant research literature?

1	2	3	4	5	6	7	8	9

   Very poor review   Very good review

3. How would you rate the design of the research study?

1	2	3	4	5	6	7	8	9

   Very poor design   Very good design

4. Was the hypothesis of the study clear?

1	2	3	4	5	6	7	8	9

   Not very clear   Clear

5. How would you rate the data collection procedures?

1	2	3	4	5	6	7	8	9

   Not very adequate   Adequate

6. How would you rate the analysis of the data?

1	2	3	4	5	6	7	8	9

   Very poor analysis   Very good analysis

7. How well were the findings of the study discussed?

1	2	3	4	5	6	7	8	9

   Very poor discussion   Very good discussion

8. How would you rate the interpretations and generalizations about the results of the study?

1	2	3	4	5	6	7	8	9

   Very poor   Very good

9. How would you rate the overall importance of the research study problem?

1	2	3	4	5	6	7	8	9

   Trivial research question   Significant research question

Research Team Number _____   Form 2

Research Team's Perception of Its Own Performance

1. How well did your group work together as a team?

    1   2   3   4   5   6   7   8   9
    Not very well   Very well

2. How would you rate the overall quality of your group's presentation?

    1   2   3   4   5   6   7   8   9
    Very poor   Very good

3. How would you rate the overall value of this research project for yourself as a learn-
    ing experience?

    1   2   3   4   5   6   7   8   9
    Very poor   Very good

4. How would you rate your overall contribution to this group's research project?

    1   2   3   4   5   6   7   8   9
    Very poor   Very good

5. How would you rate this research project in terms of its value to you as an oppor-
    tunity for interpersonal growth and development?

    1   2   3   4   5   6   7   8   9
    Not very valuable   Very valuable

6. How well did the research group achieve the objectives it had set for itself for its
    presentation to the class?

    1   2   3   4   5   6   7   8   9
    Not very well   Very well

7. How much did you enjoy the experience of this research project?

    1   2   3   4   5   6   7   8   9
    Not very much   Very much

Form 3

Research Team Number _____   Team Member Number _____

Team Member's Perception of Other Members of the Research Team

1. How serious was this person's attitude toward this research project?

   1   2   3   4   5   6   7   8   9

   Not very serious   Very serious

2. How cooperative was this group member?

   1   2   3   4   5   6   7   8   9

   Not very cooperative   Very cooperative

3. How would you rate this person's leadership in the research project?

   1   2   3   4   5   6   7   8   9

   Low   High

4. Was this person helpful and encouraging to the other members of the group?

   1   2   3   4   5   6   7   8   9

   Not very helpful   Very helpful

5. How would you rate this person's attendance at the group planning sessions?

   1   2   3   4   5   6   7   8   9

   Very poor   Very good

6. How would you rate the quality of this person's ideas in terms of the development and presentation of this research project?

   1   2   3   4   5   6   7   8   9

   Very poor   Very good

7. How hard did this person work in order to help the group prepare a high-quality presentation?

   1   2   3   4   5   6   7   8   9

   Not very hard   Very hard

8. How enthusiastic was this person in contributing to the group's development of its presentation?

   1   2   3   4   5   6   7   8   9

   Not very enthusiastic   Very enthusiastic

Table C.1. Sample Computer Printout for Form 1

CLASS PERCEPTION OF THE RESEARCH TEAM'S PRESENTATION

ITEM	CLASS MEAN	TEAM MEAN	INSTR MEAN	FREQUENCY TABLE									
				0	1	2	3	4	5	6	7	8	9
1	7.4	7.6	7.0	0	0	0	0	0	2	1	5	5	6
2	6.9	8.0	8.0	0	0	0	0	0	1	1	3	6	8
3	6.8	7.1	8.0	0	0	0	0	0	2	3	8	3	3
4	7.2	6.7	7.0	0	0	0	0	2	2	3	6	4	2
5	6.9	6.9	7.0	0	0	0	0	0	2	6	3	8	0
6	6.6	7.5	9.0	0	0	0	0	0	1	4	2	8	4
7	7.0	7.4	8.0	0	0	0	0	1	1	2	4	7	4
8	6.8	7.4	7.0	0	0	0	0	0	1	4	4	7	3
9	7.0	7.1	7.0	0	0	0	0	2	1	2	5	7	2

Table C.2. Sample Computer Printout for Form 2

PAGE 2

TEAM 4
MEMBER 1

RESEARCH TEAM'S PERCEPTION OF THEIR OWN PERFORMANCE

ITEM	CLASS MEAN	TEAM MEAN	FREQUENCY TABLE									
			0	1	2	3	4	5	6	7	8	9
1	7.6	8.6	0	0	0	0	0	0	0	1	1	5
2	7.1	7.4	0	0	0	0	0	0	1	3	2	1
3	7.5	7.7	0	0	0	0	0	0	2	1	1	3
4	7.3	8.0	0	0	0	0	0	0	0	2	3	2
5	7.5	8.0	0	0	0	0	0	0	1	1	2	3
6	7.4	8.1	0	0	0	0	0	0	0	1	4	2
7	7.3	8.7	0	0	0	0	0	0	0	1	0	6

Table C.3. Sample Computer Printout for Form 3

TEAM MEMBER'S PERCEPTION OF OTHER MEMBERS
OF THE RESEARCH TEAM

ITEM	CLASS MEAN	TEAM MEAN	INDIV MEAN	FREQUENCY TABLE									
				0	1	2	3	4	5	6	7	8	9
1	7.2	7.8	5.2	0	0	1	2	0	0	1	0	1	1
2	7.3	7.4	3.3	0	1	1	1	2	0	1	0	0	0
3	6.5	6.6	2.3	0	2	2	0	2	0	0	0	0	0
4	6.7	7.2	3.3	0	1	2	0	0	3	0	0	0	0
5	7.2	7.2	1.2	0	5	1	0	0	0	0	0	0	0
6	6.9	7.4	4.0	0	0	1	1	2	1	1	0	0	0
7	7.1	7.3	3.8	0	0	1	3	0	1	0	1	0	0
8	7.1	7.5	4.8	0	0	0	1	3	0	0	2	0	0

APPENDIX D

Values of t
for the .05 Level of Significance*

$n_1 + n_2 - 2$	t	$n_1 + n_2 - 2$	t
6	2.45	21	2.08
7	2.37	22	2.07
8	2.31	23	2.07
9	2.26	24	2.06
10	2.23	25	2.06
11	2.20	26	2.06
12	2.18	27	2.05
13	2.16	28	2.05
14	2.15	29	2.05
15	2.13	30	2.04
16	2.12	40	2.02
17	2.11	60	2.00
18	2.10	120	1.98
19	2.09	infinity	1.96
20	2.09		

Decision Rule: If the value you obtained for t is *greater* than the value associated with t for $n_1 + n_2 - 2$ in this table, then there is a significant difference between the two groups of subjects ($p < .05$). If the value you obtained for t is *less* than the value associated with t for $n_1 + n_2 - 2$ in this table, then there is no significant difference between the two groups of subjects.

*Source: Appendix D is taken from Table III of Fisher and Yates, *Statistical Tables for Biological, Agricultural and Medical Research*, published by Longman Group, Ltd., London (previously published by Oliver and Boyd, Edinburgh), and by permission of the authors and publishers.

Formulas for the Chi-Square Test, the *t*-Test, and the Rank-Order Correlation

Chi-square test

A	B
C	D

$$\text{chi-square} = \frac{N (AD - BC)^2}{(A + B) (C + D) (A + C) (B + D)}$$

where

A = the number of subjects in cell A

B = the number of subjects in cell B

C = the number of subjects in cell C

D = the number of subjects in cell D

N = the total number of subjects being compared
$(A + B + C + D)$

Rule: If the value for chi-square is greater than 3.84, then there is a significant difference between the two characteristics being compared ($p < .05$).

t-Test for Independent Samples

(1) Formula for the mean ($\overline{X}$) = the sum of the scores for this group of subjects divided by the number of subjects in this group.

(2)　Formula for the standard deviation

$$\text{s.d.} = \sqrt{\frac{\Sigma X^2}{N} - \bar{X}^2}$$

where

ΣX^2 = the sum of the squares of the scores of this group of subjects

N = the number of subjects in this group

$\bar{X}^2$ = the square of the mean score of this group of subjects

(3)　Formula for the t-test

$$t = \frac{\bar{X}_1 - \bar{X}_2}{\sqrt{\frac{(n_1)\,(\text{s.d.}_1)^2 + (n_2)\,(\text{s.d.}_2)^2}{n_1 + n_2 - 2} \left(\frac{1}{n_1} + \frac{1}{n_2}\right)}}$$

where

n_1 = the number of subjects in Group 1

n_2 = the number of subjects in Group 2

s.d._1 = the standard deviation of Group 1

s.d._2 = the standard deviation of Group 2

$\bar{X}_1$ = the mean for Group 1

$\bar{X}_2$ = the mean for Group 2

Rule:　If the value obtained for t is greater than the value for t associated with $n_1 + n_2 - 2$ in Appendix D, then there is a significant difference between the scores of the two groups of subjects being compared ($p < .05$).

Rank-Order Correlation

$$\text{rho} = 1 - \frac{6\Sigma d^2}{N\,(N^2 - 1)}$$

where

N = the number of subjects for whom you have scores on both of the variables being correlated

d = the difference between the ranks of a subject on the two variables being compared

Σd^2 = the sum of the square of d for each subject for whom you have scores on both of the variables being correlated

References

This list of references contains the complete reference for all of the articles cited in this book. If you are especially interested in some of the articles cited in this book, you might enjoy finding those articles in a library and reading them in their entirety.

The format of the journal references may be different from what you are used to reading. Here is an example of one of the references:

Quirk, T., B. Witten, and S. Weinberg. Review of Studies of the Concurrent and Predictive Validity of the National Teacher Examinations. *Review of Educational Research*, 1973, *43*, 89-113.

The meaning of this format is as follows:

Authors: T. Quirk, B. Witten, and S. Weinberg

Title of Article: Review of Studies of the Concurrent and Predictive Validity of the National Teacher Examinations

Journal: *Review of Educational Research*

Year of Publication: 1973

Volume: *43*

Pages: 89-113

Thus, each of the articles in this list of references contains the name of the author(s), the title of the article, the journal in which the article was published, the year of publication, the volume number, and the pages on which the article appears.

Aronson, E., and D. Linder. Gain and Loss of Esteem as Determinants of Interpersonal Attractiveness. *Journal of Experimental Social Psychology*, 1965, *1*, 156-170.

Asch, S. E. Forming Impressions of Personality. *Journal of Abnormal and Social Psychology*, 1946, *41*, 258-290.

Bem, S., and D. Bem. Does Sex-biased Job Advertising "Aid and Abet" Sex Discrimination? *Journal of Applied Social Psychology*, 1973, *3*, 6-18.

Berger, P., G. Fraley, and L. Tarpey. The Effect of Advertising on the Use of a Train's Diner. *Journal of Advertising Research*, 1969, *9*, 25-29.

Bernstein, A. *A Handbook of Statistics Solutions for the Behavioral Sciences.* New York: Holt, Rinehart & Winston, Inc., 1964.

Campbell, D., and J. Stanley. Experimental and Quasi-experimental Designs for Research on Teaching. In *Handbook of Research on Teaching*, edited by N. L. Gage. Chicago: Rand McNally, 1963, pp. 171-246.

Cox, D. R. *Planning of Experiments.* New York: John Wiley & Sons, Inc., 1958.

Cullen, J. Social Identity and Motivation. *Psychological Reports*, 1973, *33*, 338.

Dember, W. Birth Order and Need Affiliation. *Journal of Abnormal and Social Psychology*, 1964, *68*, 555-557.

Duggan, T., and C. Dean. Common Misinterpretations of Significance Levels in Sociological Journals. *The American Sociologist*, 1968, *3*, 45-46.

Dyson, E. A Study of Ability Grouping and the Self-Concept. *The Journal of Educational Research*, 1967, *60*, 403-405.

Feather, N. T., and J. G. Simon. Reactions to Male and Female Success and Failure in Sex-Linked Occupations: Impressions of Personality, Causal Attributions, and Perceived Likelihood of Different Consequences. *Journal of Personality and Social Psychology*, 1975, *31*, 20-31.

Fleming, M. Why Women Should Study Accounting. *Educational Horizons*, Winter 1975-76, 90-93.

Freund, J. *Statistics: A First Course*, Second Edition. Englewood Cliffs, N.J.: Prentice-Hall, Inc., 1976.

Gewirtz, J., and D. Baer. Deprivation and Satiation of Social Reinforcers as Drive Conditions. *Journal of Abnormal and Social Psychology*, 1958, *57*, 165-172.

Glenn, N. American Sociologists' Evaluations of Sixty-three Journals. *The American Sociologist*, 1971, *6*, 298-303.

Gold, D. Statistical Tests and Substantive Significance. *The American Sociologist*, 1969, *4*, 42-46.

Goldberg, P. Misogyny and the College Girl. Paper presented at the meetings of the Eastern Psychological Association, Boston, April 1967. In M. P. Golden (ed.), *The Research Experience.* Itasca, IL: Peacock Publishers, Inc., 1976, pp. 147-153.

Grant, W., and C. Lind. *Digest of Educational Statistics: 1973 Edition.* Washington, D.C.: U.S. Department of Health, Education, & Welfare, 1974.

Greenspoon, J. The Reinforcing Effect of Two Spoken Sounds on the Frequency of Two Responses. *American Journal of Psychology*, 1955, *50*, 409-416.

Hamm, B., M. Perry, and H. Wynn. The Effect of a Free Sample on Image and Attitude. *Journal of Advertising Research*, 1969, *9*, 35-37.

Harshbarger, T. *Introductory Statistics: A Decision Map*, Second Edition. New York: Macmillan Publishing Co., Inc., 1977.

Helson, H., R. Blake, and J. Mouton. Petition-signing as Adjustment to Situational and Personal Factors. *Journal of Social Psychology*, 1958, *48*, 3-10.

Herman, W. Teaching Attitude as Related to Academic Grades and Athletic Ability of Prospective Physical Education Teachers. *The Journal of Educational Research*, 1967, *61*, 40-42.

Hornstein, H., E. Fisch, and M. Holmes. Influence of a Model's Feeling About His Behavior and His Relevance As a Comparison Other on Observers' Helping Behavior. *Journal of Personality and Social Psychology*, 1968, *10*, 222-226.

Kelley, Harold. The Warm–Cold Variable in First Impressions of Persons. *Journal of Personality*, 1950, *18*, 431-439.

Koosis, Donald J. *Statistics.* Second Edition. New York: John Wiley & Sons, Inc., 1977.

Labovitz, S. Criteria for Selecting a Significance Level: a Note on the Sacredness of .05. *The American Sociologist*, 1968, *3*, 200-222.

Latane, B., and J. Darley. Group Inhibition of Bystander Intervention in Emergencies. *Journal of Personality and Social Psychology*, 1968, *10*, 215-221.

Levin, J. *Elementary Statistics in Social Research*, Second Edition. New York: Harper & Row, Publishers, 1977.

Luchins, Abraham S. Primacy-Recency in Impression Formation. In Hovland, Carl J. (ed.), *The Order of Presentation in Persuasion.* New Haven, Conn.: Yale University Press, 1957, pp. 33-61.

McClelland, David. Achievement and Entrepreneurship: A Longitudinal Study. *Journal of Personality and Social Psychology*, 1965, *1*, 389-391.

McNemar, Q. *Psychological Statistics*, Fourth Edition. New York: John Wiley & Sons, Inc., 1969.

Marco, G., R. Murphy, and Thomas Quirk. A Classification Scheme for Methods of Using Student Data to Assess School Effectiveness. *Journal of Educational Measurement*, 1976, *13*, 243-252.

Mischel, Harriet. Sex Bias in the Evaluation of Professional Achievements. *Journal of Educational Psychology*, 1974, *66*, 157-166.

Morrison, D., and R. Henkel. Significance Tests Reconsidered. *The American Sociologist*, 1969, *4*, 131-140.

Morrison, D., and R. Henkel. Significance Tests in Behavioral Research: Skeptical Conclusions and Beyond. In *The Significance Test Controversy: A Reader*, edited by D. Morrison and R. Henkel. Chicago: Aldine Publishing Co., 1970, pp. 305-311.

Noether, G. *Introduction to Statistics: A Nonparametric Approach*, Second Edition. Boston: Houghton Mifflin Co., 1976.

Occupational Outlook for College Graduates: 1974-75 Edition (Bulletin 1786). Washington, D.C.: U.S. Department of Labor, 1974.

Piliavin, I., J. Rodin, and J. Piliavin. Good Samaritanism: an underground phenomenon? *Journal of Personality and Social Psychology*, 1969, *13*, 289-299.

Pollinger, K. Teaching Statistics in Sociology, In D. C. Miller, *Handbook of Research Design and Sociological Measurement*, Third Edition. New York: David McKay Co., Inc., 1977, pp. 152-155.

Quirk, Thomas. Performance Tests for Beginning Teachers: Why All the Fuss? *Educational Technology*, 1973, *13*, 14-16.

Quirk, Thomas. Teaching Undergraduates the Process of Psychological Research. Paper presented at the Annual Meeting of the American Psychological Association in Washington, D.C., on September 3, 1976.

Quirk, Thomas, B. Witten, and S. Weinberg. Review of Studies of the Concurrent and Predictive Validity of the National Teacher Examinations. *Review of Educational Research*, 1973, *43*, 89-113.

Samuels, S. Attentional Process in Reading: The Effect of Pictures on the Acquisition of Reading Responses. *Journal of Educational Psychology*, 1967, *58*, 337-342.

Scandura, J., and J. Wells. Advance Organizers in Learning Abstract Mathematics. *American Educational Research Journal*, 1967, *4*, 295-301.

Schachter, Stanley. *The Psychology of Affiliation*. Stanford: Stanford University Press, 1959.

Siegel, S. *Nonparametric Statistics for the Behavioral Sciences*. New York: McGraw-Hill, 1956.

Siegel, A., and S. Siegel. Reference Groups, Membership Groups, and Attitude Change. *Journal of Abnormal and Social Psychology*, 1957, *55*, 360-364.

Skipper, J., Jr., A. Guenther, and G. Nass. The Sacredness of .05: A Note Concerning the Uses of Statistical Levels of Significance in Social Science. *The American Sociologist*, 1967, *2*, 16-18.

Smith, G., and R. Engel. Influence of a Female Model on Perceived Characteristics of an Automobile. Paper presented at the annual meeting of the American Psychological Association, 1968.

Touhey, J. Effects of Additional Women Professionals on Ratings of Occupational Prestige and Desirability. *Journal of Personality and Social Psychology*, 1974, *29*, 86-89.

Ullman, N. R. *Statistics: An Applied Approach*. Lexington, MA: Xerox College Publishing, 1972.

Wright, R. L. *Understanding Statistics: An Informal Introduction for the Behavioral Sciences*. New York: Harcourt Brace Jovanovich, Inc., 1976.

Index

NOTES

NOTES

NOTES

NOTES

NOTES

NOTES

NOTES

NOTES